THE CLIMAX OF CAPITALISM

Also available from Longman by Tom Kemp:

Historical Patterns of Industrialization (1978)
Industrialization in Nineteenth-Century Europe (second edition 1985)
Industrialization in the Non-Western World (second edition 1989)

The Climax of Capitalism: The US Economy in the Twentieth Century

Tom Kemp

Longman
London and New York

Longman Group UK Limited,
Longman House, Burnt Mill, Harlow,
Essex CM20 2JE, England
and Associated Companies throughout the world.

Published in the United States of America by Longman Inc., New York

First published 1990

British Library Cataloguing in Publication Data
Kemp, Tom
The climax of capitalism: the U.S. economy in the twentieth century.
1. United States. Capitalism
I. Title
330.1220973

ISBN 0-582-06616-6 CSD
ISBN 0-582-49423-0 PPR

Library of Congress Cataloging-in-Publication Data
Kemp, Tom.
The climax of capitalism: the US economy in the twentieth century /Tom Kemp.
p. cm.
Includes bibliographical references.
ISBN 0–582–06616–6. — ISBN 0–582–49423–0 (pbk.)
1. United States—Economic conditions—1945– 2. United States––Economic conditions—1918–1945. 3. United States—Economic policy. 4. Capitalism—United States—History—20th century. I. Title.
HC106.5.K415 1990
330.973′09—dc20 89-13783
CIP

Set in Linotron 202 10/12 Bembo Roman
Produced by Longman Singapore Publishers (Pte) Ltd.
Printed in Singapore

Contents

List of Tables

Preface

We are reminded every day of the way in which developments in the United States and its role as a superpower in a troubled world affect our lives. Day and night American bombers based in Britain are ready to deliver a deadly nuclear cargo on Eastern Europe or the Soviet Union. The military and strategic power of the American colossus is a tangible thing to people throughout the world. But the influence of America is not only visible in its military form. Throughout the world, television viewers are served a daily diet of American programmes. In the supermarkets of Frankfurt, Tokyo or South Africa it is difficult to shop without buying American brands of cereals, soaps and canned foods. What street or town in the 'civilized' world does not have its McDonalds, Dunking Do'nuts or Kentucky Fried Chicken, or an indigenous imitation? Lifestyles, consumer tastes and ways of thought are moulded more than we realize by the American model. While there is much talk of American 'decline', the Americanization of the world continues its irresistible march even into the society of the Cold War adversary.

The upsurge of American power in the twentieth century coincided with the decline of Europe, speeded as it was by two internecine wars. American military intervention in these wars tipped the scale, making the United States first a world power and then, after 1945, a (or perhaps the only) superpower, economic, political and military, with an incredible nuclear weapon stockpile as well as massive conventional naval and land weaponry. Economic strength was demonstrated in the First, and even more in the Second, World War, especially in the weight and variety of military equipment. 'Quel matériel!' was the general comment as the liberating armies marched into Europe in 1945.

After 1918 the Americans had over-hastily withdrawn from Europe, leaving chaos behind and a successful, anti-capitalist revolutionary regime in power in Russia, formerly a bedrock of the status quo. Policy-makers in Washington considered that they had learned the lesson: Europeans could not be left to their own devices, the European market was too valuable and the threat from the supposedly expansionist drive of the Soviet Union too potent to permit it. There began the quasi-permanent military presence of the United States in Europe, which first of all had to be put back on its feet economically. There came the Truman Doctrine and the Marshall Plan, without which capitalism might not have survived in Western Europe. Likewise, on the other side of the Pacific, the occupation of Japan, intended at first to make it incapable of again waging an aggressive war, served to re-build the economy and thus, unintentionally, to begin the process which made Japan a formidable economic power. As it happened, the obsession with the threat from the Soviets resulted in the rapid reconstruction and recovery of West Germany and Japan which, by the 1960s, were to become America's principal economic competitors. The dollar, once the hard currency *par excellence*, is at the mercy of speculators in Tokyo or Frankfurt.

The weaknesses and vulnerability of the American economy have also been amply demonstrated in the twentieth century. Even to this day, the traumatic experience of the 1930s' Depression has left its impression (in the same way that German fear of inflation goes back to the monetary collapse of 1923), recalled whenever Wall Street experiences an abnormal fall, as happened in October 1987. Everyone at once made the comparison with 1929 and feared, or assumed, that the fall-out would be similar. Although through the 1950s and 1960s it seemed that the trade cycle had been tamed, and graduate students in economics were advised to find more urgent subjects for research, in 1974–5 and in 1980–2 it came back with a vengeance. While not comparable with the early 1930s, these severe recessions (or mild depressions) reproduced some of the same features: lines of unemployed, depressed areas, bankrupt farmers and small businessmen, increased poverty. The assurances that it could not happen again seemed to have less conviction, and monetary authorities in the United States and outside over-reacted to the crash of 1987 as a result.

If, to understand the present-day world, it is necessary to understand the roots of American economic power, then it is to history that we must look both for an explanation of that overreaching power as well as its limitations, now so apparent that it is widely assumed that the

United States is in decline. There is renewed interest in the reasons for Britain's loss of world leadership, as well as a plethora of writing about America's lost hegemony. Meanwhile, not only is no part of the world immune from the influence of the United States, but the worldwide operations of the giant multi-nationals bring back into the United States the problems of other countries. In these days of 'globalization', isolation is impossible. The United States is interested also in opening up, or keeping open, the doors to the markets and investment fields of the entire world. The drive for the global open door, though couched in the vocabulary of liberalism and free trade, is palpably in the interests of the United States' corporations, with their worldwide interests, though it may harm other sections of the economy. There are periodic signs of a protectionist backlash when America's trading partners (notably Japan, but at times the European Community), are seen not to be playing the game.

While there is a library of specialist works on all aspects of the economy, books on economic history (chiefly written with the American undergraduate in mind), and topical books on the issues of the day, a manageable account of the rise of the American economy and its recent history seems to be lacking. This book seeks to fill a gap by providing an overall view of developments in the twentieth century. The emphasis will be mainly on the period from the 1920s until the present day, the post-Reagan period which, under the Republican George Bush, can be expected to continue at least part of the Reagan legacy into the future. It should enable the student, or anyone interested in America's economic role in the world, to grasp the main trends in development. The aim has been not to be overly factual or to be too theoretical, but to attempt to combine theory and facts into a comprehensive and coherent explanation. This cannot be done without expressing one's own views. There is no pretence that this book has said the last word, or that it is free from bias. The reader will, we hope, find this book a helpful guide to understanding the dynamism of American capitalism as well as its failures, and a useful basis for a more thorough study both of its rise and its possible 'decline'.

The writing of this book has been spread over several years and carried on in various places; begun at the University of Hull until my retirement in 1986, it was continued at the University of North Carolina at Chapel Hill where I was a guest in 1987–8 and concluded after my return to Britain. I must thank Sandy Darity of the Department of Economics at UNC for reading a number of chapters and making useful and incisive comments; he is in no way responsible for the contents of the book.

Perhaps most of all I should thank my publishers, Longman, for their encouragement and the readers and copy editor they appointed to put the material into some kind of order and to oblige me to hunt down facts, figures, names and personalities to make it easier for the reader to assimilate. I hope that their efforts have not been in vain and that readers will find this book a useful introduction to a huge, fascinating and important subject. In any case, like many another enthusiastic (and critical) visitor to the United States, I will have succeeded in writing a book about it.

I almost forgot to thank my ever-patient and loving wife.

Gravesend, November, 1989.

CHAPTER 1

Setting the stage

During the first half of the twentieth century, the United States became the dominant world power, assuming a role analogous to that played by Great Britain in the previous century. This predominance rested upon a mighty industrial base built up in a country of immense size and bountiful natural resources. At the time of its foundation as an independent country, the United States had consisted of a collection of European colonies stretched out along the eastern seaboard of an as yet unexplored continent, dependent upon agriculture for its existence. In little more than a century it had been transformed into an industrial giant, soon to enjoy a world leadership in practically every field.

The process of colonization and settlement going back to the seventeenth century had created a society of a unique kind. It was the largest and most successful of those countries classified as of recent European settlement, a transplant of European institutions, techniques, customs and practices to a virtual wilderness. Here, in a new physical and increasingly different social environment, a characteristically 'American' society came into existence.

Territory and resources were appropriated by the newcomers as though by a God-given right, regardless of the claims of the existing inhabitants, many of whom were to be killed or humiliated as settlement proceeded. In this environment of virgin land, untramelled by feudal vestiges or inhibiting traditions, the newcomers and their descendants could establish a more purely capitalist society than the one left behind in the Old World, still shaped by its feudal past. Institutional forms and legal codes could be shaped in accordance with the imperatives of individual acquisition and accumulation, guaranteeing property rights and offering greater scope for the operation of market forces. People were free to practise the religion of their choice or none at all.

Beginning at Independence (the Declaration of Independence and Adam Smith's *Wealth of Nations* – fountain-head of the doctrine of the free market which has been so important in American history, both date from 1776) as a country of small farmers, largely self-sufficient, with a wealthier stratum of merchants and plantation slave-owners, its transformation over the next century or so into a mighty industrial giant was one of the most remarkable, and fateful, that history has to offer.

In the decades following the Civil War (1861–5), a modest primary-producing and exporting country became the leading industrial power, out-stripping the European powers and assuming world leadership after the First World War. The intervention of the United States in the two World Wars, decisively turning the scales in both of them, was both cause and consequence of the rise to world dominance. At that point it was easy to assume that the American century had come, and Europeans were warned to take up 'the American Challenge' by the French political figure Jean-Jacques Servan-Schreiber (Eng. trans. 1968) if they did not want to be overwhelmed by the transatlantic giant. Almost before the message of this one-time best-selling and now heavily dated book could sink in, American hegemony itself appeared to be under challenge, not from America's main rival and adversary, the Soviet Union, but from changes in the world economy which had undermined it, notably the resurgence of the war-scarred capitalist countries and the rise of 'newly industrializing countries'. By the 1980s the so-called 'decline' of the United States was at the centre of fashionable debate.

This book will attempt to indicate what were the forces which made the United States the world's leading economic power, and what factors, domestic or foreign, eventually undermined that position. After examining the long-term factors in America's ascent, subsequent chapters will look back at recent economic history, from the 1920s onwards, seeking the historical roots of both the strengths and weaknesses of the American economy today.

The rise of America's economic power rested upon the ability of its entrepreneurs to develop the most advanced technology and to organize large-scale production in a scientific way. Through most of the twentieth century achievements in production and in raising the productivity of labour outstripped those of any other country. American techniques of production, business organization and management became models for even the most advanced industrial countries, and continued to be such for some time after the Second World War, when American influence on business practice internationally reached its highest point.

To understand why this was so, it is necessary to cast a backward glance at the specific conditions under which American industrialization took place. Europeans who colonized the continent of North America came from that part of the world which had already developed the most advanced techniques and forms of organization, as their arrival, invasion and successful settlement of the colonies suggests. There was little or no basis, in the colonial environment, for the transplanting from Europe of feudal forms of land tenure or pre-capitalist institutions. The high ratio of land to labour in colonial times, which made it possible for almost all free men to acquire some property, made it difficult for anything like a landed nobility to establish itself and impose serfdom. The nearest form, for white people, indentured labour, lasted for only a fixed term of years, after which the servant might be granted a plot of land and become independent of wage-labour. The general scarcity of labour, indicated by the importation of indentured servants, was overcome by the large landowners, in the regions of plantation agriculture, by the importation of black slaves, mere chattels, whose labour made it possible to produce the great export staples like tobacco, indigo, sugar and later, above all, cotton, upon which the wealth of early America was based. For decades, the 'peculiar institution' of the South co-existed with free labour in the North; a contradiction between two divergent societies resulted, only to be resolved in bloody civil war which cost perhaps 600,000 lives.

Material improvement – a higher standard of living in their lifetime – was a compelling motive of the early settlers, their descendants and successors. It remained the major driving force in American society. Conditions were extremely favourable for the eventual realization of such hopes, not easily, but through hardship and hard work. The gospel of hard work as the means to material success had its religious counterpart in the assumption that success so achieved had divine approval. In the new land most families made their living by tilling the soil. The virtues of the family farm became part of American mythology, and its praises are still sung, though it has all but disappeared as a viable economic unit. Even by the early nineteenth century the goal of most farmers was not self-sufficiency but the production of a surplus to sell in the market. Many saw their land as a speculation, and were ready to sell-up and move on to where new lands at low price beckoned. Pre-industrial America was a land of small commodity producers, with the ubiquitous merchant playing a linking role. It was already quite different from Europe in its social relations, mainly because of the pervasive forces of the market, and the emphasis on material advancement and success. The geographical mobility of many Americans contrasted with the close ties to their place of birth of European peasants.

COLONIZATION AND GROWTH

During the late seventeenth and the eighteenth centuries, the American colonies became staple producers and exporters geared to the markets of industrializing Britain and other parts of Europe. Long after Independence, this 'colonial' relationship persisted. The United States exported primary products and imported manufactured goods. It continued to draw upon Europe for supplies of labour and it borrowed heavily, mainly in the London capital market.

The ability to produce a surplus for export depended upon the high ratio of resources to population and the response of producers to pecuniary incentives. As long as slavery endured, a large surplus could be exacted from the labour of the slaves. Part of the latter found its way into the conspicuous consumption for which the slave-owners were notorious. Even so, part of that surplus, together with that generated by Northern agriculture, found its way into productive investment, directly or indirectly. Farmers, who commercialized as much as possible of their output, appeared in the market as purchasers, both of agricultural inputs (such as tools or seeds) and of consumer goods; local and regional markets sprang up. While the more sophisticated manufactured goods might still be imported, the expansion of the domestic market offered opportunities for local production of household articles and agricultural implements by specialized craftsmen and artisans. In time the market grew sufficiently large to encourage the setting up of larger units of production.

Since most sections of the population enjoyed a relatively high per capita income by contemporary European standards, and numbers grew at a steady rate, the market expanded and, with it, the division of labour. A country of vast distances, the internal market at this stage was bound to be fragmented, owing to the high costs of transport. Transport improvements, which lowered the cost of hauling freight, became a key to growth, making possible greater regional specialization. By the late eighteenth and early nineteenth century, industry was concentrating in the north-east; farmers were moving westward, opening up new lands for cereal production both for the domestic market and for export. With the invention of Eli Whitney's cotton gin (1798) making it possible to separate the cotton fibre from the seed with a considerable economy of labour-time, a plantation slave-economy producing cotton for export was riveted upon the South.

At this stage, the main form of capital was employed in buying and selling goods, in holding stocks and goods in process. Capital took a mainly mercantile form; industry employed little fixed capital and was still mainly in the hands of small artisans and craftsmen. Larger plants only appeared as entrepreneurs began to set up factories, mainly in the spinning and weaving of textiles, on the pattern of those which were leading the way in the industrialization of Britain. When that country was at war with France (1793–1815) and was no longer able to export manufactures to the United States on the same scale as before, enterprising New England capitalists pursued a policy of 'import-substitution', setting up factories of their own using the abundant water-power of the region and the daughters of farmers as their main source of labour supply. Other forms of production, such as flour-milling and saw-milling, also became more concentrated as the market widened, but they did not require a technological breakthrough or need new sources of power; fast-running streams or rivers would suffice. The metal industries continued to operate on a small scale with traditional methods, using charcoal.

Until the mid-nineteenth century the transplant of new technologies, especially in textiles, then in the metal-producing and using industries, took place steadily, though unevenly, but without a spectacular breakthrough. However, American conditions were particularly hospitable to techniques which promised to economise on the relatively scarce factor, labour, and give greater economic value to the abundant factors, land and natural resources. New resources were revealed by the westward movement, especially anthracite coal and petroleum. Borrowers at first, American innovators began to adapt and improve imported technology and then develop their own in the light of the relative scarcity of labour and capital and the abundance of land and natural resources in America and the nature of demand. Thus wood-working machines were labour-saving but appeared to use wood wastefully, but it was cheap and plentiful. There was a growing market for cheap, strong, serviceable and standardized articles of everyday use in the household or on the farm (and most families still cultivated the land). At the same time, there was no mass movement off the land. Hard labouring jobs might be filled by new immigrants and, as mentioned, the early New England mills looked to farm families for their labour supply. Labour, especially for more skilled work, tended to be relatively scarce. Many Americans possessed industrial skills, were better educated than their European counterparts and accustomed to turning their hand to whatever task came their way. But they might be more interested in working for themselves than for a boss and would expect a relatively high wage. The labour market was different from that in Europe and encouraged a search for labour-saving methods.

At this time (from the 1830s) new industries grew out of handicraft production, by splitting up complicated processes into their component parts, reducing each one, as far as possible, to a repetitive operation which could be performed by an unskilled worker or a machine. Production on a larger scale, with a more complex division of labour or the use of machinery, required a bigger capital investment. Large outlays of this kind would not be undertaken unless the entrepreneur expected to be able to sell a larger volume of commodities. It was the growth of the internal market for cheap, standardized goods which encouraged entrepreneurs to take the risk of investing in new techniques and producing on a larger scale. The heavier fixed costs could be spread over a larger volume of output, thus realizing economies of scale.

Confronted with particularly favourable market conditions, American innovators grasped the logic of the machineprocess, taking it even further than the British inventors, whose work they at first emulated. An important step was the development of tools which could work metals, as well as wood, to higher degrees of accuracy and which could be used to make machines, in turn able to produce the finished consumer goods. While the handicraftsman had turned out an individual product, using a hand-guided tool, counting on the co-ordination of eye and muscle attained with practice, the machine-tool was able to produce standardized parts which were interchangeable. The machine-made product was not a distinct and individual creation but one of a series of identical articles, reproduceable to order. The interchangeability of machine-turned parts had the great advantage that it was possible to replace from stock any part which proved defective or wore out. Each complete article, whether a gun or a plough, would also be one of a series made up of these interchangeable parts. The power-driven machine tool thus made possible standardization and interchangeability of the parts, the basis of modern large-scale production.

Conditions in the United States, notably the existence of a large, uniform market for articles of everyday use, led to the adoption of these methods earlier than in Europe. Already, in 1851, at the Great Exhibition held at the Crystal Palace in London, American exhibits attracted the attention of foreign, especially British, observers. The British government sent a commission to the United States to study on the spot what became known as 'the American System of Manufactures'. It was not always clear that what was specifically new in American production methods arose from particular conditions. In any case, from about this time American technology began to break new ground and move into the vanguard, a harbinger of the rapid industrialization of the last quarter of the nineteenth century which was to transform the United States into an industrial giant. Interchangeability and standardization of parts began with handguns (one of the key contributors to this development being Eli Whitney, inventor of the cotton gin). They rapidly spread to other branches of industry, such as watches and clocks, agricultural machinery, wherever moving parts were involved. Use of these methods undoubtedly assisted American industry to occupy a leading position in new types of manufacture such as the sewing machine, the typewriter and later the automobile.

However impressive such industrial advances were, they took place, at first, in what was still a small sector of an economy dominated by primary production. In 1840 manufacturing accounted for only ten per cent of Gross National Product, reaching a modest seventeen per cent on the eve of the Civil War. But it was the most dynamic sector and already the dominant one in some areas, particularly in the North East.

Meanwhile, improvements in transport were knitting together the older settled regions into a single, more integrated market and pushing settlement further west across the continent. Exports continued to be dominated by the products of the Southern plantation system and the cereal-growing West. On the eve of the Civil War, the United States could be characterized as a prosperous country of commercial agriculture and merchant capitalism; industry was still largely organized on the older handicraft lines, but there was a significant, and growing, part of industry which was highly capitalized, technologically advanced and poised to take the lead in the world market. As a primary producer and a debtor country the United States was still dependent upon Europe. The inflow of capital, like that of labour, was vital for continued expansion, leaving locally generated capital free to exploit the possibilities of what was becoming a continental economy.

THE CIVIL WAR AND ITS AFTERMATH

That the United States was already a rich country, producing a large surplus over subsistence needs, was established lugubriously by the mass destruction and slaughter of the Civil War. A 'modern' large-scale war, though fought mainly between infantrymen, it required an enormous mobilization of manpower and resources on both sides. It proved to be an inordinately costly method of preserving the Union and abolishing slavery, its only positive results.

Thanks to the intensive use of labour in the gang system and the buoyant market for cotton (largely from Britain), the slave economy remained highly profitable in the *ante-bellum* period. Slavery was not collapsing under the weight of its own contradictions, nor were the slave-owners in any mood to be bought off by some kind of compensated emancipation. Force was perhaps the only way in which 'the peculiar institution' could have been ended. On the other hand, growing opposition to slavery could have been expected from both workers and employers in the North; nor should the possibility of slave strikes or revolts on a growing scale be ruled out.

The Civil War resulted in the loss of over 600,000 lives, mostly young men in their most productive years, and it diverted to destructive purposes resources which might otherwise have been used productively, to raise incomes and promote growth. It left scars which proved difficult to heal. It held back the Southern economy for decades; although it freed the black masses from slavery, it left them landless, poor, segregated and exploited. Most freed slaves continued to till the land and grow cotton, unable to extricate themselves from unequal contracts and crop liens, which effectively tied them to the land with little hope of improvement.

The outcome of the Civil War meant that the future policy of the United States would be determined by the interests of Northern business. This was reflected in subsequent policies concerning the disposal of public lands, tariff protection, railways, banking and the currency. The destruction of property and wealth in the South, as well as the break-up of the planter economy, meant stagnation in that region for decades to come. After the war, the industrializing economy of the North showed great recuperative powers. While the war had slowed economic growth, especially in cotton textiles, some industries had been stimulated by it. The view that the war acted as a forcing house for more rapid industrialization, however, has not stood up to statistical verification. Military needs did not place the same demands on heavy industry or encourage advances in technology as has been the case with the wars of the twentieth century. Nevertheless, the Civil War may have assisted the accumulation and concentration of capital, enabling Northern business to stride forward more confidently now that some major policy issues had been decided in its favour.

The decades after the Civil War saw an acceleration of innovative change and structural transformation which laid the basis for the establishment of American industrial power. This was industrialization on a massive scale, opening up and exploiting the resources of a continent and turning them into capitalist private property, making the United States the richest country in the world. While agriculture continued to grow absolutely, as colonization and settlement of new lands took place, made possible by improvements in transport, its place in the national economy went into decline. Agriculture continued to provide cheap food and fibre for the export trade as well as itself constituting a market for manufactured goods. The labour force grew both by natural increase (though at a slower rate than in the early nineteenth century) and by mass immigration, increasingly from Southern and Eastern Europe. The main thrust for growth, however, came from new capital formation, embodying more productive technology as resources were shifted into manufacturing and mining (Tables 1.1 and 1.2).

The historical experience of American businessmen had been that labour was a relatively scarce factor and that labour costs would continue to rise. Hence investment continued to flow into labour-saving methods of production, thus promoting further mechanization, the substitution of capital for labour. The high ratio of capital to labour characteristic of American industry meant the building up of a powerful capital goods industry – iron and steel, coal-mining, heavy engineering – all concentrated in the North East. Industry required both a supply of skilled and qualified workers in the machine-making and other

Table 1.1: US economic growth: the Civil War to the 1920s

	Population 000s	*GNP* (in 1958 prices) $bn	*GNP per capita*
1860	31,513		
1869		23.1	$531
1880	50,262		
1890		52.7	$836
1900	76,094	76.9	$1011
1910		120.1	$1299
1920	106,466	140.0	$1315

Table 1.2: Growth of American heavy industry, 1870–1920:

(a) output of bituminous coal and steel

	Bituminous coal (tons)	*Steel (tons)*
1870	20,471,000	77,000
1880	50,757,000	1,397,000
1890	111,302,000	4,779,000
1900	212,316,000	11,227,000
1910	417,111,000	28,330,000
1920	568,607,000	46,183,000

(coal supplied as much as 90% of fuel for industry)

(b) comparative output of the two leading European economies in 1913

UK	292,000,000	7,700,000
Germany	190,000,000	17,500,000

complicated processes, as well as an abundance of cheap, unskilled labour to operate machines and perform the heavy manual tasks in mills, mines and on the construction sites. A large part of this new labour force was recruited from the immigrants who arrived in unprecedented numbers in the decades before the First World War.

With a vast and growing internal market, well integrated thanks to a growing transport network, industry was encouraged to produce on a large scale both existing products and those issuing from new technologies. The nature of this market, and relative factor prices (reflecting the cost of land, capital and labour), gave further emphasis to those features associated with 'the American System of Manufactures' already referred to. Standardized, mass-produced articles such as consumer durables, office and farm machinery, had a larger market in America than anywhere else in the world. In such fields American firms were often the world leaders, and by the early twentieth century were setting up branch plants abroad – Remington in office machinery, Westinghouse in electrical power, Singer sewing machines, Ford cars. The application of labour-saving machine technologies and the systematic organization of the production process made possible important gains in productivity, thus enabling entrepreneurs to reduce the price of the product and extend the market. American industry was forging ahead of the older industrial countries of Europe not only in aggregate output – to be expected in view of the size of the national market – but also in productivity and competitiveness. The new expanding industries, embodying the technologies of the late nineteenth and early twentieth centuries, were highly capitalized, putting more power behind the elbow of the American worker and providing him with more specialized and complex machinery than his European counterpart: in return, his wage was two or three times larger. But the expanding industries also depended upon a supply of cheaper, immigrant labour. Mobile, imposing no costs of upbringing or training, it could be directed into those occupations where it was most in demand, mostly manual and menial jobs. Established American workers often feared and opposed immigration, fearing that their wages and living standards would be undermined by the newcomers. There was hostility to the Irish and other Catholics in the 1850s, to newcomers from Southern and Eastern Europe in the 1880s and especially to the Chinese brought in to work in California. The Chinese Exclusion Act (1882) was followed by attempts to stop Japanese immigration which culminated in the 'Gentleman's Agreement' with Japan (1907), effectively ending direct immigration from the Orient.

The mass of the American population was strongly motivated towards material advancement and monetary gain. That was what had drawn colonists and immigrants to the New World in the first place. Average money incomes were high by European standards, which meant a large and growing market for standardized machine-made goods such as tools, guns, utensils and farm machinery; precisely the type of product in which American manufacturing excelled. This was the basis for the surge of industrialization which precipitated the United States into economic leadership in the early twentieth century.

As industrialization proceeded, so did its usual accompaniments. Population density thickened with the growth of towns in the industrial regions. Some older industrial areas in New England stagnated or were in decline, but new industrial areas came on the scene. New York and other big cities grew as centres of trade and finance, with mostly light industry. Heavy industry was drawn to the coalfields and nodal points in the transport network – Buffalo, Cleveland, Chicago, Detroit, Pittsburg, Philadelphia, Minneapolis and other centres. Rapid urban growth, and especially the rise of big cities, resulted in housing shortage, overcrowding and slums; poverty, insecurity and unemployment were the lot of many urban dwellers. At times workers in the mines and factories revolted against the harshness of their conditions or their low wages. In such cases, labour struggles could be fought out with bitterness and violence. Class solidarity was often slow in forming where masses of people of varied ethnic origin and social background were thrown together in a struggle for existence. Many sought a solution for themselves and their families by striving to move upwards in the social scale. Those who achieved some modest success could look down upon more recent immigrants and, of course, blacks, the poorest paid and the most vulnerable to unemployment and poverty.

The growing prevalence of patterns of urban living offered new opportunities for the mass production and marketing of consumer goods. Basic products in the food and drink line were processed into convenient form, put into packets with brand labels and advertised in the press and on bill-boards until they became household names. Large firms were established in fields in which they had never existed before such as processed and packaged foods and beverages. Their share of the market, a measure of their success, was inconsistent with perfect competition. Indeed, branding and advertising aimed to make a product so distinctive that there was no substitute for it, at least in the mind of the purchaser. Entry into some fields became more difficult because of the high initial costs as in iron and steel and engineering or industries like branded food products, which now included those necessary for nationwide distribution and advertising. Access to capital and credit was necessary to increase sales of an existing product or launch a new one.

THE RISE OF CORPORATE BUSINESS

By the end of the nineteenth century, in the main industries, business was taking on its modern, corporate form; the dynamic individual capitalist entrepreneur was giving way to the salaried executive. This trait had been apparent for some time in the case of railway companies. It was perhaps obscured by the continued prominence of a few noted entrepreneurs, of whom Andrew Carnegie was the archetype: self-made, ruthless, authoritarian and fabulously wealthy. It was in the United States that the potentialities of the company enjoying limited liability for its shares into which its capital was divided (common stock in American parlance) were most fully realized.

The corporation became a legal personality, separate both from its owners and managers. It could sue or be sued in the courts; it had to be pronounced dead by lawyers, not by doctors; as long as it remained solvent, it achieved a kind of immortality. Corporate businesses could raise additional capital through the Stock Exchange by selling stock or by borrowing at a fixed rate of interest. As a means for raising capital the corporation has not been surpassed, and it is impossible to conceive of modern capitalism without it. It was a necessary complement to those technical changes which were greatly increasing the need for fixed capital in manufacturing industry. A whole new strategy of business was devised on the basis of the corporation and stock dealing, which became a model for the capitalist world. In Britain industry was slower to adopt the corporate form while in continental Europe at this time the banks played an important promotional role. New organizational structures and innovative forms of management carried the logic of capital accumulation to its highest point in twentieth-century America.

The rise and consolidation of the business corporation was at first a response to the depression of the 1870s and 1880s. Pressure on prices and profits intensified competition, and when this became self-destructive there was a turn towards mergers and combinations to keep it in check. There was a tendency for a small number of firms to survive in each field, bolstered by their greater financial viability and support from the banks as well as superior access to markets or raw materials. This tendency was most pronounced in large-scale industry needing large amounts of fixed capital embodying advanced technology. The great firms built up in the closing years of the nineteenth century, some the product of the merger movement, proved to have real staying power; they made up the core of industrial America and were the forerunners of the multinational corporations of the following century.

The success of the corporation, based as it frequently was on market power, enabled it to accumulate financial reserves or to call upon fresh capital from the stock market and the banks as required. The large standardized market was essential for its operations, while what might seem to have been the handicap of high labour costs was an invitation to introduce more and more labour-saving machinery. This led to heavy outlays on fixed capital as well as distributive and marketing costs which therefore had to be spread over the largest possible volume of output. There was a constant striving to reduce costs by improving existing methods, installing new machines and raising labour productivity through more efficient organization of the labour process. There was, however, a limit to what could be done in any one product market, which could easily become saturated. To keep up the rate of profit it was necessary to deploy capital, labour, management skills, technology and manufacturing facilities in the development of new processes and, especially, new products.

Diversification by the giant manufacturing companies became one of the outstanding features of twentieth-century American capitalism. A manufacturing firm which began with one product, say a vacuum cleaner, might move into the production of other domestic appliances. Later, the big car firms in the 1920s went into tractors, accessories, diesel motors and aviation. Continuous research and development by the big corporations became a condition for survival, both to improve existing products and to develop new ones.

The major impulse behind these changes in business strategy was to keep up profit rates. Costs had to be kept down and new outlets found for accumulated capital. Big business developed an aggressive armoury not available to the old-style entrepreneur. Large-scale organization, backed by huge financial resources, made possible, and necessary, specialization in all directions. As the scale of business and the complexity of its operations grew, it became impossible for one man, however skilful, or even a board of directors, to keep track of many different and geographically dispersed operations. While overall decision-making on strategic questions remained with head office, decentralization took place both on the product and the plant level. Many decisions, of a day-to-day type, had to be delegated to lower rungs of management.

Consequently, business built up an hierarchical command structure, a veritable bureaucracy, located in office buildings, often away from the plants, and subject to their own laws of growth. On the vertical plane a similar specialization of management structures took place to deal with such questions as production control, labour relations, research, marketing and so on. These, in turn, could be split up still further if the size and complexity of the corporation warranted it.

The different operations of management could therefore be systematically examined, analysed, theorized and made into a set of rules. Management became professionalized; these theories and rules could be passed on as a body of knowledge, revised and added to in the light of experience, through business schools and managerial courses. While business ideology was a dominant influence in the universities, financed as they were largely by donations from businessmen, they also established special schools of business management. The first was the Wharton School of Finance at the University of Pennsylvania (1881). The prestigious graduate School of Business at Harvard was founded in 1908. In the 1920s there was a rapid increase in business courses and in colleges specializing in business studies. By 1928 there were eighty nine business schools with 67,000 students in addition to courses offered by other colleges. This professionalization of management, the business 'revolution' of the twentieth century, was first embarked upon and developed in the United States. In time it was disseminated to other countries, adapted to other conditions and improved upon; in time, pupils might become masters.

Besides displacing the rule-of-thumb methods of the individual entrepreneur of the old type, management 'science' provided an avenue of advancement for young men from the middle class who had little prospect of going into business on their own account, as a result of the dominant role played by the corporation in many areas of business. The old middle class, based upon property ownership, was being superseded by a 'new' middle class of salaried managers and professionals, educated in the universities and the business schools.

Corresponding changes were taking place in the labour process at the plant level. At least in the larger and more modern plants, the assembly line and continuous flow methods were being adopted. Besides speeding up the tempo of work, the object was to make the most out of capital investment by using all the plant to the maximum. There was a growing tendency for the movements of the workers to be scientifically observed and synchronized with those of the machinery. The main innovator was the engineer Frederick W. Taylor, who introduced time-and-motion study. The object of what became known as 'Taylorism' was to remove all initiative from the workers and to place it firmly in the hands of management. This could be done by studying each job and then comprehensively specifying the movements which the human operator should perform in the course of doing it, eliminating those not indispensable for achieving maximum output.

'Taylorism', though not as revolutionary as its inventor claimed, nor applied over the whole of American industry, went well beyond the older forms of factory discipline. It pushed the detailed division of labour, about which Adam Smith and Karl Marx had written, to its utmost point. As they had seen, the worker then became an ancillary of the machine and was reduced to the endless repetition of a limited number of operations, the very duration of which were determined in advance. Clearly, the main benefits of 'Taylorism' and similar systems accrued to the employer in lower labour costs per unit of output, an increase in labour productivity. The carrot for the worker was that part of the increase in production was promised to him as an incentive to accept the imposition of complete control over his working life. 'Taylorism' met with much hostility and was opposed by trade unionists; even non-union workers resented its interference with old-established working practices. Such methods of production made great demands upon the physical stamina and the nervous system of the workers involved, leading in some cases to high labour turnover, which partly defeated their object. At the same time, it was claimed that consumers gained, in the form of a supply of cheaper, mass-produced goods.

It should be added that, during the first decades of the twentieth century, these changes in the organization of the labour process were mainly confined to some of the large-scale mass production plants concentrated in the north-eastern industrial region. Elsewhere, many varieties of productive enterprises could be found: domestic work in the back streets of big cities, the artisan's workshop in the many small towns which dotted the landscape of rural America, and more traditional factory industry in textiles and other consumer goods. There were still many localized small-scale units of production, just as there was an enormous variety and number of small businesses of every type of trade and industry. These still appeared to offer some hope of success to those pursuing the American dream of becoming an independent businessmen by dint of honest toil, and making a fortune.

AMERICAN INDUSTRY BEFORE THE FIRST WORLD WAR

The overall picture of American industrialization can be summed up in a few statistics. Physical output per man hour rose at an annual rate of 1.6% between 1889 and 1919 (Table 1.3). GNP per capita rose at an annual rate of 1.76% from 1879 to 1919, while aggregate GNP rose by 5.69% per annum. Total population had grown approximately threefold to ninety-one million between 1860 and 1910. By this time the American market was the largest and most homogeneous in the world; and it continued to grow rapidly. By the time that the European great powers had become locked in conflict in 1914, the United States had become the largest industrial nation, leading the world in total output of steel, coal and many other industrial products. It had taken the lead in such new fields as motor vehicles, electricity and petroleum refining. It had the most advanced industrial technology, the highest level of labour productivity and the highest standard of living. Americans tended to take this leadership for granted,

Table 1.3: Manufacturing output per man hour

(1958 = 100)

1890	22.2
1900	22.9
1910	26.6
1920	43.0
1930	52.3
1940	68.7
1945	71.5
1950	81.4
1955	94.9
1960	108.8
1965	131.0
1969	145.7

(*Historical Statistics of the United States,* Bicentennial Edition)

not realizing how recent it was; not until decades later did they awaken to the fact that it was conditional, and could be challenged. Outside the industrial heartlands, however, the United States was still very much a rural society of family farms and small towns, which were more typical than the great metropolitan cities. Until after the First World War more Americans lived in rural than in urban territory. There was still plenty of room in the twentieth century for extensive development, as well as for continued industrialization and urbanization in the South and West (which later made up the 'sun-belt'): California, Florida, Georgia, Texas and the Carolinas, for example.

The most significant feature of American industrialization was its distinctively 'modern' character, taking place, as it did, on the basis of the new industries of the late nineteenth and early twentieth centuries. The most impressive example of this vanguard role was the automotive industry, far in advance in methods of production of any other country, and the first to make the car and the truck an indispensable part of everyday living, while in Europe the car was only slowly ceasing to be a rich man's toy. Henry Ford and his competitors, by going over to assembly-line production (adapting and extending 'the American System of Manufactures'), brought the car within the reach of a much wider section of the population, both as a business tool and a convenience for the family.

Compared with the old countries of Europe, the United States had always been distinguished by the fluidity of its social relations, the absence of a landed aristocracy or a ruling class based upon hereditary privilege. Its reputation was that of a land of opportunity but also of the relentless pursuit of material success and the piling up of money as an end in itself. Europeans marvelled at the sight of self-made men who went on accumulating more wealth, when they might have retired from business and lived a life of luxury. British and French entrepreneurs were often criticized (especially by American historians) for doing just that. The pursuit of wealth, the acquisitive drive and the fascination with accumulation were blended with the Protestant work ethic (that success in this world was a mark of divine favour) and a firm belief in market forces to create a distinctive and pervasive ideological atmosphere. Individualism was its keynote.

At the same time there had always been a distrust of great concentrations of wealth and an idealization of the small property owner and working farmer. The rise of giant corporations and banks bred a critical reaction which took the form of Populism, a movement based mainly on the farmers but with the support of sections of the traditional middle class. The Populist or People's Party was founded in 1892; its campaign against 'the money power' was not successful, but as a political tendency hostile to big business it survived. The movement pressed for legislation to break up the 'trusts'. Originally a method of combining a number of independent firms into a single unit, the term 'trust' was extended to describe any amalgamation or giant firm. Populism also showed itself in the 'muck-raking' themes of part of the press or the perception of successful businessmen not too scrupulous in their methods as 'robber barons'.

Although the state assisted the process of capital accumulation, mainly by providing resources for the creation of an infrastructure and a variety of measures favourable to business, its activities were less prominent than in most countries of continental Europe or even Britain. There was nothing resembling the state system of welfare provision of the kind begun by Bismarck in Germany in the 1880s, and in Britain under the Liberal government, 1906–14. The state in America was expected to play only a limited role and not to enter the social or economic arena except under very special circumstances: protecting industry with tariffs, upholding property rights, or mobilizing resources in time of war. Free enterprise – the individual pursuit of material success with the maximum of freedom – was the American creed and the philosophy of the revered Constitution. By hard work, thrift and personal enterprise, the individual could contribute towards, and participate in, the wealth-creating process.

The prevailing ideology saw the market economy as a competitive struggle in which the fittest survived and individuals were rewarded according to their worth. Those who failed did so through their own fault. Apart from the really deserving – the aged, infirm, chronic sick and orphaned children, appropriate recipients of charity – poverty was seen as a consequence of personal weakness, even of moral turpitude. At the same time it was claimed that employers and workers had a common interest: to increase the size of the pie, each receiving what they had contributed. Orthodox economic theory gave this quasi-scientific expression, up-dating the teaching of Adam Smith and the classics. Market forces, if left to themselves, would ensure an optimum allocation of resources and a fair distribution of goods. These complacent and self-satisfied views were to be rudely shaken by the Depression of the 1930s.

Until the later years of the nineteenth century the United States appeared to be too engrossed in the opening up of a continent to be much concerned with what was happening in the wider world. Equally, European statesmen scarcely bothered with what was happening on the other side of the Atlantic. From the 1890s, however, the United States began to turn outwards and soon found that in the imperialist division of the world then almost completed, it had different interests than those of other powers, and that it needed more substantial armed forces, particularly a navy, in order to uphold them. The most important clash came in the war with Spain in 1898, which resulted in the acquisition of a small colonial empire – Puerto Rico, Cuba, the Philippines and Guam. Hawaii had already been annexed. More significantly, from this time the United States assumed a general right of intervention to protect its growing interests in Latin America and began to look at the Pacific basin as a sphere of influence. The aim was not to acquire territory, but rather to maintain an 'open door' for American trade and investment. The outbreak of the war in Europe in August 1914, soon showed that Washington could not stand aloof from events in other parts of the world which threatened the existing division and, more especially, American interests. In particular, a potentially hostile power could not be permitted to assume a dominant position in the world and close off large areas to American trade and influence. The very growth of American economic power thus imposed an outward-looking, nationalist policy, claiming a right to share in the shaping of world events. Step-by-step, from 1914, the United States was forced into a hegemonic role, first economic, then political and strategic.

CHAPTER 2

Trends in the 1920s

THE UNITED STATES: A WORLD POWER

The First World War abruptly thrust the United States into a position of world economic leadership commensurate with its wealth and resources. A process which might otherwise have been spread over decades was telescoped into years. Nothing had prepared American leaders for such a role, nor was it clearly understood. While the European great powers tore themselves apart in over four years of internecine warfare, the United States prospered as never before.

While in the nineteenth century the United States had been a major debtor, borrowing in Europe to release the productive capacity of a continent, especially to construct an infrastructure of transport links, in the twentieth it was generating a surplus of capital seeking profitable investment in foreign lands. Big corporations were setting up branch plants, while investors were turning to foreign stocks and bonds to complete their portfolios. Until the war the United States had been a net debtor but, by the early years of the twentieth century, receipts from abroad on visible and invisible trade were exceeding payments, so that the net debt fell. Holdings abroad amounted in 1914 to about $2,600 million, but foreign investments in the United States amounted to over $3,700 million. The war drastically reversed the balance. In order to wage war, Britain and France sold off their holdings in the United States and went into debt, first by borrowing on the New York financial market through the medium of the Morgan bank, and then through loans extended by the government. At the end of the war, therefore, foreigners owed the United States government and private investors no less than $7,000 million more than the value of remaining foreign assets held in the United States. The Allied war effort had thus been able to draw upon the huge pool of investible funds available in New York, which remained the main source of funds for foreign borrowers, including the now capital-starved European countries beset with the problems of reconstruction and reconversion. American investment financed a war of unparalleled destructiveness and created no wealth-producing assets from which the debt could be serviced. Washington would not hear of a cancellation of the inter-Allied debts; for example, as the counterpart of the ending of the reparations payments which Britain and France sought to exact from defeated Germany.

The 1920s saw the world drifting into further debt with the United States, which had taken Britain's place as the leading international creditor. Besides financing the Dawes and Young Plans, enabling Germany to borrow to pay reparations, the flow of private capital to Europe became a feature of the period. Many of these loans were of a speculative nature, such as the so-called 'stadium loans' to local government authorities in Germany and other countries. There was also a considerable increase in investment in Canada and Latin American countries, hitherto fiefs of British capital. The war with Spain in 1898 had left the United States with a small territorial empire and a growing interest in the Pacific zone. Washington assumed a general right of supervision over Latin America, intervening militarily, if necessary, to secure friendly governments protective of American trade and investment. What may be called American 'imperialism' was not concerned with the acquisition of colonies but rather with maintaining 'the open door', ensuring that foreign rivals did not block off full and free access to markets and investment fields. It could, therefore, paradoxically assume an 'anti-imperialist' form as far as the colonies of other powers were concerned, and this motive helps to explain American entry into the World War in 1916. The American 'empire' had no frontiers, was not built on conquest, but was defined by the extent of investments and commercial interests abroad which Washington was prepared to uphold, if necessary with armed force. This policy meant that the United States was obliged to play an increasingly active role in world affairs despite apparent isolationism and the clear retreat from Europe after the Treaty of Versailles.

Concentrated financial power, backed by the most dynamic as well as the largest industry, projected the United States into playing a world role after generations which had mainly turned inwards, opening up the continent. Neither politicians nor financiers had a clear idea of what this new role entailed, especially in the way of responsibilities in upholding the world capitalist economy as a whole.

In the 1920s the dollar began to usurp the role of sterling but without the backing of institutions as varied and mature as those of the City of London. Impoverished Europe was obliged to fall back upon American support, which was only granted at a price. A central problem was how America's debtors could pay off the interest and principal of the loans they had contracted during or since the War. A similar problem faced America's other debtors, mainly primary-producing countries. In short, repayment meant the willingness of the United States to accept an increasing flow of imports from these debtor countries as free-trade Britain had done in the nineteenth century. Unlike Britain in that era, the United States had no need to import basic foods or even raw materials; indeed the United States was itself a primary exporting country. Nor did there seem, at that time, to be much room in the home market for an increase in the importation of manufactured goods. To make sure, American producers jealously guarded their huge home market from foreign competitors. The level of tariffs was high enough to keep out many foreign goods or to restrict demand by making them more expensive than domestic products. Agriculture, as well as industry, clung to tariffs as a remedy for problems which did not arise from foreign competition and were probably made worse by protection.

The Fordney-McCumber Tariff Act of 1922 had as one of its aims the protection of new industries which had grown up during the War. Average duties under this measure stood at about thirty-three per cent. Despite the claims of protectionists that it had assisted the prosperity of the 1920s, it probably made little difference. Despite the free-trade proclivities of most economists, a major lowering of tariffs was out of the question for political reasons. When industry or agriculture were in trouble, the tariff was a popular remedy. The ultimate anomaly came when a powerful creditor (receiving interest and repayment from abroad), with the most advanced industry and the most productive agriculture, sought in still higher protection, in the shape of the Hawley-Smoot tariff of 1932, a remedy for depression. So far as it had any effect, it aggravated the plight of America's trading partners by making it difficult for them to sell their goods in the US market to pay their debts without offering any way out for the stricken farmers and depressed industries at home. By further checking imports (with an average tariff of forty per cent) and inviting retaliation, it was an example of the beggar-thy-neighbour policies which further reduced foreign trade. In prosperity as well as depression, mighty America lived in fear of weaker foreign rivals. It was assumed that an increased inflow of foreign products would undermine industry's hold on the home market and undermine wage levels. Although there was no shortage of expert economic opinion to point out the fallacies in the protectionist case, legislators, responding to the clamour of their constituents, trade unionists as well as businessmen, could not afford to listen. The contradiction between America's status as the biggest creditor and a heavily protected home market remained throughout the inter-war period.

Protectionism was only one way in which policy became more nationalist and inward-looking after the First World War. Strict controls on immigration also indicated a more exclusive nationalist policy in tune with growing isolationism. When the gates had been wide open, before 1914, immigrants streamed in, their numbers topping 1.2 million in 1914. The war sharply curtailed the inflow and this total was never to be exceeded. Although the restriction of immigration from China and Japan dates from the end of the nineteenth century, that from Europe was not curtailed until the 1920s. An Emergency Quota Act was passed in 1921 and a still more restrictive Quota Act in 1924. Once these laws took effect, the overall total was fixed at 160,000 per annum, with quotas for each country which discriminated against immigrants from Southern and Eastern Europe. There were still over 2.6 million immigrants in the five years 1921–5, falling to under 1.5 million in the following five years as the quota system began to take effect; during the 1930s immigration was reduced to a trickle. These measures were backed by the labour unions, fearful of the influx of low-wage foreign workers, as well as by a xenophobic public opinion. Fear of foreign influence had been generated by a new factor, the supposed threat of 'Bolshevism', which gave rise to a major 'red scare'. In the 'Palmer raids' of April 1920 (named after Attorney-General Mitchell Palmer), hundreds of suspected 'communists' were rounded up; over five thousand foreign-born people were given expulsion orders. Not only was the United States no longer able (apparently) or willing to absorb Europe's overflow population, but the practice of rounding up and deporting undesirables continued.

THE PROSPERITY DECADE

Industrialization continued at an impressive rate (Table 2.1), continuing and confirming the position of the United States as the leading

Table 2.1: (a) Growth in the 1920s

	GNP (1958 prices)	*GNP per capita (1958 prices)*	*Gross Investment*
1920	$140 bn	$1.315	$12.8 bn
1925	$179.4 bn	$1.549	$16.4 bn
1929	$203.6 bn	$1.671	$16.2 bn

(b) Index of industrial production (*1913 = 100*)

		Unemployment %
1920	124.0	4.0
1921	100.0	11.9
1922	125.9	7.6
1923	144.4	3.2
1924	137.7	5.5
1925	153.0	4.0
1926	163.1	1.9
1927	164.5	4.1
1928	171.8	4.4
1929	188.3	3.2

industrial country and setting the pace for the other advanced countries. The new techniques of the twentieth century, based upon applied physics, chemistry and mechanics, were generally first applied on a large scale in the United States, though they may have been invented elsewhere. The financial resources of the big corporations, the huge size of the internal market and the innovative flair of its entrepreneurs made the American economy the trail-breaker, not only in new technology, but also in organizing the large-scale manufacture and marketing of the product. Favoured with plentiful natural resources, a large and expanding home market and uniquely mobile population aspiring to material success, the American economy never ceased to startle the world with its power and dynamism. It was the prosperity of the 1920s, America's own 'economic miracle', which set new standards and established new models which other economies could only try to emulate.

The strength of American industry lay in its ability to turn out long runs of standardized machine-made products. By lowering unit costs, this brought within the grasp of large numbers of consumers goods embodying the new technologies of the twentieth century, making possible a new style of consumption summed up in the phrase 'the American Way of Life'. A big role in new patterns of consumption came with the mobility offered by the automobile and by the ability of many to buy (usually on mortgage) a one-family house, equipped with an array of electrically-driven appliances. But it also included expenditure on a range of services reflecting a high per capita income, such as restaurants, beauty parlours, movie theatres, dry-cleaning establishments and spectator sports.

The 1920s are usually regarded as a decade of prosperity; especially because of the contrast with the 1930s. As it turned out, the prosperity, though real enough, did not herald a new era and was short-lived. Looked at more closely, economic performance was patchy both by sector and from year to year. There were minor recessions in 1924 and 1927. A number of older industries did not share in the general prosperity. Coal-mining suffered from the competition of other fuels as well as from economies in its use. The cotton industry, especially in the older regions, was not expansive because, as income rose, consumers tended to spend a smaller proportion on textile products. There was also competition from synthetic fibres. Competition for New England mills came from the more modern plants set up in low-wage areas of the South. Ship-building had been artificially stimulated by the War, and now, like the shipping industry as a whole, suffered from over-capacity in a period of sluggish foreign trade. The railways were also entering upon their long decline as competition from road transport took away much of their best paying traffic. After the war-time boom, farmers had to contend with falling prices; agriculture was already facing severe problems before the Depression of the 1930s, as will be seen below, and was calling for government assistance.

There were also a number of regions which hardly shared in 'prosperity'. Poverty and deprivation remained endemic throughout much of the South, in the Appalachians and in the slums and ghettos of the big cities. Poverty fell disproportionately upon the black minority (about one-tenth of the population), still mainly concentrated in the South (some eighty-five per cent in 1920) though northward migration had accelerated during the war and continued.

What typified the decade was the business optimism generated by the spectacular rise of new industries, the evidence of growing wealth in the cities and suburbs, the high returns on capital and the boom on the Stock Exchange. The growth of new, profitable outlets for capital in the expanding industries and service trades overshadowed the mediocre performance and decline of others.

The most striking feature of the 1920s was that for the first time in history, and some thirty years ahead of Europe, a nation took to four wheels. The automobile industry had already grown to adolescence before the First World War; now it became a leading sector, drawing other industries behind it through its manifold backward and forward linkages. Most obvious was the new market it offered for such industries as steel, aluminium, rubber and petroleum. By 1929 total sales of cars reached over 4,455,000 vehicles, with another 881,000 trucks and buses. In that year there were over 26 million vehicles on the road, one for every 4.5 inhabitants of the United States. They consumed over 15,000 million gallons of petrol and needed regular supplies of oil and spare parts. Service stations, garages and wayside eating places sprouted like mushrooms. US production of cars in 1929 was nine times that of Britain and France combined; over half a million were exported. American car-makers, especially Ford and General Motors, had already set up branch plants in Canada and Europe. In the city the horse had been eliminated as a means of transport; it held its own longer as a source of power for the farmer, but the tractor was steadily being adopted.

American production methods, especially the assembly line, made it possible to produce as complicated a piece of machinery as the motor car at low unit cost, using standardized, interchangeable parts. This is what Henry Ford and his rivals found out. It was therefore possible to aim at a mass market and realize economies of scale in the production process. On the side of the car-makers was the relatively high per capita income of American consumers, the need for cheap and flexible means of transport in a country of vast distances, and the very size of the market. It is understandable, therefore, that the motor car should have caught on so much earlier and more completely than in Europe where it was still something of a rich man's toy. With the help of easily available instalment credit, the Ford Model T, its competitors and successors, were brought within the range of a steadily increasing number of families. The car was becoming a necessity of life. Those who could not afford a new model might find a used car within the range of their income.

American firms assumed a dominant position in the petroleum industry, based upon the fact that the United States, unlike the European countries, had its own supplies, thus enabling them to lead the way in drilling technology. The big corporations which dominated the industry built up an advanced marketing structure boosted by growing domestic demand. The huge output of cars and trucks opened up a new market for a variety of other industries. Some, such as rubber, glass or electrical components tended to be concentrated in the hands of a few large firms. At the same time, opportunities arose for a host of smaller businesses in garages and service stations as well as in dealerships, where competition was intense. Public investment was also required in highways, bridges and urban traffic control systems. Unfortunately, accidents also took their toll of dead and injured; by the late 1920s road deaths reached 20,000 per annum.

The car profoundly influenced life-styles, from courting to ways of doing business. The journey to work, taking the children to school, going on a shopping expedition or a family outing, now meant getting out the car. Cars, buses and trucks helped break down rural isolation, connecting farmers with their markets and perhaps revealing the temptations of urban life to members of their families. Truck drivers, organized in the Teamsters' Union, became a new and important part of the labour force. Most of all, the car enhanced still further the personal mobility of the American population. With a car and a tankfull of 'gas', people could take off in any direction they pleased in search of a new job and a new life. Even the ruined farmers of the Depression years loaded their belongings on to an ancient car or truck, not on to a horse and cart. The personal mobility made possible by the motor vehicle influenced social relations in many ways; it might be said that it permeated the whole of American life. It made possible, in time, a geographical re-distribution of the population, opening up areas not accessible by rail and contributing to the urban sprawl and suburbanization of twentieth-century America.

Besides the car, the growing use of electricity in the shape of domestic appliances driven by fractional horse-power electric motors was the most notable and characteristic innovation of the decade. This took place alongside a change less visible to the public at large, which had been taking place since earlier in the century: the adoption of electricity as a prime mover in industry, replacing steam or water power. By 1920 one-third of power for industry came from electrical power stations. Use of the electric motor provided a more versatile and flexible source of energy, easier to combine, for example, with the assembly line and continuous flow systems which were coming into use. The corporate giants who quickly established themselves in the generation of electric power and the manufacture of the heavy equipment required, set out deliberately to develop new uses for electricity, especially domestic appliances, because it was there that a big mass market could be opened up.

Consumption of electricity doubled between 1921 and 1929. In part this reflected the rapid growth of the electrical appliance industry. The urban middle class and better-off workers were able to equip their homes with a variety of household appliances, not only electrical (or gas) cookers, but electrically powered vacuum cleaners, washing machines and refrigerators. This caused something like a revolution in the American kitchen for those able to afford them. The fridge superseded the clumsy ice-box and was a boon in a country of generally hot summers.

Appliances such as the vacuum cleaner, the electric iron and the washing machine cut down the time taken no perform household chores and were an important factor in changing the position of women, few of whom, at this time, continued to work after marriage. The mass production of domestic appliances, bringing them within the reach of a growing number of families, the skilful use of advertising to create a demand and the use of instalment buying acted to put the United States far ahead of Europe in this field (not until after the Second World War did Europe begin to catch up).

Motorized America, as well as the all-electric kitchen with its gleaming appliances, became familiar throughout the world thanks to another innovation in which the United States led the world: the production of motion pictures. The Hollywood movie, with its exaggerations and idealizations, only came fully into its own in the depressed 1930s, but it was already becoming a powerful propaganda medium for 'the American Way of Life' and the ideology of material well-being which went with it. The glossy illusion of the cinema distorted reality, especially by giving the impression that ordinary Americans were better off than they really were; nevertheless it set a goal to which people aspired. The fact that not everyone benefited was underlined by the fact that, in the 1920s, rural electrification had hardly begun. There was no revolution in the farm kitchen. Indeed, at this time, many homes lacked such an amenity as a flush toilet, as was the case for the majority of rural houses.

The new domestic appliances come within the category of 'consumer durables', the name given to those goods which form a kind of household 'capital', yielding their satisfactions over a period of years and not having to be renewed daily or weekly. Products of this kind were not exactly a novelty. Furniture, objects like pianos, or manually operated household appliances like mangles, had existed in the past and took an important part of the income at least of the better-off. There is some debate, therefore, about whether it is correct to speak about a 'consumer goods revolution' in the 1920s, as some have done. Consumption as a whole was on a rising trend and expenditure on the old-style durables also continued to rise. The novelty lay particularly in the widespread method of purchase: instalment credit. To buy cars – new or used – and the more expensive appliances, families were going into debt. The old shibboleths like the virtues of thrift (and living within one's income) were breaking down as what was later to be called 'consumerism' took hold. Future income was pledged in advance to secure instant gratification; spending, not saving was becoming the new virtue. Now, for manufacturers and merchants, the willingness of consumers to go into debt was a condition for successful business. The debt economy, which was to balloon in later decades, was already taking shape.

In order to buy and equip a home, more and more families accepted debt as a fact of life. As long as the economy was booming and jobs and incomes seemed secure there was no problem. When depression and unemployment struck, many families would find that they were unable to meet existing payments, let alone contract new debts. It was characteristic of high-price items like cars and appliances, as well as new houses, that purchases could be postponed. The car would always run for another year; there was no need to replace the refrigerator if the old one was still in working order. At some point the house market would find that there was a drastic fall in the number of people able, or willing, to contract mortgages. Such factors as these intensified the depressive tendencies after 1929 and had begun to show themselves earlier.

Needless to say, not all American families could afford the full panoply of kitchen appliances and other durables. The trend began among those with relatively high and stable incomes, mostly in what can be called the middle class, though that term now embraced a wide swathe of salaried people working for the big corporations or employed in the tertiary sector. No doubt the purchasers also included better paid workers in the urban areas. Even the working poor, on low incomes, needed a gas or electric cooker as a minimum, and perhaps a refrigerator as well. It should not be overlooked that there was a second-hand market for such items, as well as cars, to which those unable to pay the full price of a new item could resort. In the meantime, they also acted as incentive goods; people were ready to work harder or longer in order to be able to afford to buy them, or to change what they had for newer and better products.

The construction industry witnessed a surge of growth in the 1920s. In the major cities there was a threefold increase in new building between 1919 and 1925. Government expenditure on highways became the second largest item in the budget. Property speculation – an old American habit, now boosted by the motor car – was going strongly, especially in prospective vacation areas, notably Florida, where there was a frantic 'land bubble'. Outlays on construction contributed to the boom but the more speculative types were highly volatile. The construction boom peaked in 1927, preceding that in industry and the financial market. The building boom was financed by an increase in debt, the almost inevitable mortgage which purchasers had to obtain. House sales were thus sensitive to changes in interest rates.

THE WORKING CLASS AND THE LABOUR MOVEMENT

Looking back from the years of the Depression, many analysts concluded that America's phenomenal capacity to produce had run ahead of demand. 'Underconsumption', in some form, became the most widespread of the explanations offered for the sudden and complete reversal of trend, from prosperity to depression, after the crash of 1929. In some versions it led to the conclusion that if only income had been higher, or more evenly distributed, the Depression could have been averted. Indeed, some such assumption influenced policy in the 1930s and after. Higher wages, shorter hours or the redistribution of income by raising costs, would have lowered profitability and adversely affected the willingness of capitalists to invest.

In the sense that the capacity of industry and agriculture to produce was not matched by the ability to pay on the part of consumers 'underconsumption' becomes virtually a truism, but it has little explicative value. Such a situation also prevailed during the years of the boom; consumption is always based upon ability to pay, which, in turn, is a function of income. Despite the reputation of the 1920s as the prosperity decade, and the claim of business spokesmen that poverty was on its way out, many Americans were in fact needy. Successive layers of poverty have been discovered or rediscovered over the past sixty years. There were many who could not find work or earn enough to support themselves and their families above the poverty level (however measured).

The benefits of the 'high wage economy' were not enjoyed by all and for some categories the conditions of life were precarious. The bulk of the black population had not shaken off the poverty which was the legacy of slavery, especially in the Deep South where they made up the bulk of the population ('the Black Belt'). But there were also many poor rural whites in the South and in areas like the Appalachians, who had never participated in the benefits of American prosperity. In parts of New England deindustrialization had blighted some communities; there were mining areas whose minerals had been exhausted. In such regions joblessness was endemic. These structural problems were slow to yield to prosperity in the economy as a whole. Poverty was also widespread in the big cities, especially where recent immigrants crowded into slummy quarters where there own ethnic group predominated. Little was done to tackle the problem of urban slums, or to prevent the formation of black ghettoes as the black migration northwards got under way.

The lower layers of the working class faced a hard struggle for existence in the best of times: insecurity, low wages and unemployment were endemic. For the casualties of the market economy there was no national system of relief; they were dealt with by private charity or by some local equivalent of the poor law administered by local government. The absence of a public system of social security was the corollary of the confidence in the free market and the virtues of individualism which prevailed with little challenge in the pre-Depression period. Middle-class Americans generally saw poverty as a result of moral turpitude and this assumption, that everyone could make an honest living if they tried, fared badly in a period of mass unemployment when it was palpably not true. Philanthropy was widely esteemed and practised as a moral conscience-saver. The most advanced country of industrial capitalism thus continued to operate with a mid-Victorian code of social values, which blamed the poor for their own misfortunes and denied any responsibility on the part of the public authorities for dealing with social problems. By this time, of course, most other advanced industrial countries, whatever their political system, had adopted some of the features of what was to be known as the Welfare State. Once again, the United States was something of an anomaly, completely unprepared to deal with the problems thrown up by the Depression.

Although official figures suggest an average unemployment rate of only five per cent during the 1920s, the actual number looking for work (especially in years of recession) was probably higher. There was much part-time or short-time working (e.g. in textiles) and much underemployment in the agrarian sector. A ten per cent average would perhaps be nearer the truth. Besides the millions of recent immigrants, many of whom could not speak much English, who were anxious to get a job of any kind, there was a constant flow into the urban labour market of newcomers from rural areas, including many Blacks. Most of these people (whether 'native' or first generation Americans), like the urban immigrants, had no skills or their skills had no marketable value. A factory job of any kind gave some security and was preferable, in any case, to low-paid labouring or employment in the back-street sweatshops. Employers found that it was not difficult to recruit all the labour they required for unskilled or semi-skilled jobs. The workers they hired were glad of the opportunity to earn a regular wage, seldom had any tradition of union organization, were geographically mobile (especially if recent arrivals), and adaptable to new forms of factory labour. Significantly, too, about a quarter of all miners were foreign-born.

Besides the fact that class solidarity grew slowly among workers of varied ethnic origin, with different cultures and religion, the big corporations adopted a paternalistic approach to inoculate their employees against trade unionism and left-wing politics. Many firms had welfare schemes and departments run by social-work professionals, to deal with the welfare of the workers and their families. 'welfare capitalism' assumed that workers who bought the firm's stock, belonged to its insurance plans for accident, sickness, old age and death would be harder-working and more faithful employees, would identify their own and their families' interests with those of the firm and not risk their stake in its success by asking for higher wages, going on strike, or joining a union.

Attractive as it was to the supporters of free enterprise, this much-vaunted 'welfare capitalism' of the 1920s had definite limits. The very scale and impersonality of the giant corporation made it difficult to give life to even the most comprehensive welfare schemes, bureaucratically administered as they were bound to be. They did bring on to the scene a new breed of social-work professionals, as well as experts in 'industrial relations', but the old personal touch between employer and worker possible in the workshop or even the small factory, could not be brought back to life in great mass production plants where the emphasis was upon exacting maximum production from the work force. Inevitably, the conditions of factory life gave rise to many grievances to which welfare schemes had no answer. In practice they were not proof against 'labour unrest'. In times of recession management would be obliged to sack redundant workers or lower wages. In the main, such benefits as did flow from 'welfare capitalism' went to the more permanent staff of the big corporations or smaller paternalistic companies; not to those workers most in need. Experience showed that capitalism could not, on a firm-to-firm basis, provide workers with protection against the side-effects of economic forces operating through the market. The attempt to do so was a product of prosperity and a casualty of depression.

More significant, because more widespread, was the fact that, in the 1920s, more regular employment and higher real wages were enjoyed by a substantial section of the working class. This brought within the range of an increasing number of families those consumer goods which the economy was turning out in increasing volume. More than any conscious welfare effort or pressure from organized labour, it was the individualistic pursuit of higher consumption levels for the family (and their achievement by many, who set an example), or the prospect of social advancement (achieved at least by some) which reconciled most workers to free enterprise capitalism. This was the main antidote to socialism, together with the higher wages secured by trade union bargaining for the skilled workers, and explains the lack of a major party based upon the working class calling for reform or revolution. It was the reality, or illusion, of ever-improving material conditions through the life-time of the individual, within the existing social framework, which enabled American society to encounter the ordeal of the Depression without revolution or the resort to authoritarian government. If high and stable wages for the employed majority were more important than conscious effort by the corporations to keep the working class loyal to the system, the political left, which aimed to change the system or overthrow it, was weaker and more divided than ever.

The Socialist Party had been a growing political force before the First World War, and it might have been expected that it would become a contender for power after the fashion of its European counterparts. Its candidate for president in 1912, Eugene Debs, had polled 897,000 votes, six per cent of the popular vote. After promising beginnings, the party was torn by dissension over support for the War and then its attitude towards the Russian Revolution. Much of its left wing broke away to form the Communist Party, affiliated to the Third International. The Communists remained a small isolated sect, riven by factional disputes. Many of its members were first-generation immigrants, more interested in the politics of their native land than in what was happening in the United States. At the same time, the main body of the Socialist Party never regained its pre-war dynamism or level of support. Radical unionism, as represented by the Industrial Workers of the World, also became a shadow of its former self. It suffered heavily from legal harassment. Its syndicalist doctrine, concentrating on direct action by workers and opposed to politicians and parties of all kinds, had never had more than a limited appeal, mainly to itinerant workers, miners and the poorly paid. Although there were a few places, such as Milwaukee, where a residual influence of the Socialist Party could be seen, the radical left had virtually been swept off the scene. It survived only in a number of small parties and groups who appeared very much to be swimming against the stream, though they regained some influence during the Depression.

The lack of a mass socialist or labour party was one of the peculiar features of American society compared with Europe, and many explanations have been offered. It may have been that workers saw capitalism delivering the goods: real wages were about twice those in Britain and three times those in Germany. There also appeared to be greater opportunities for upward mobility, especially through education. It may have been because the varied ethnic composition of the working class delayed the formation of a specific class consciousness. Some workers got what they were looking for – a higher standard of living – through trade union bargaining. Assisted by the war, there was a sharpening national consciousness which cut across class lines. The more recent immigrants wanted to be accepted as Americans, not marked out as troublemakers. 'Public opinion', moulded by education, the press and propaganda, was unremittingly hostile to all shades of radicalism at this time, especially after the Bolshevik Revolution made 'socialism' of any sort appear foreign and even sinister. The courts also manifested an evident bias against 'radical' defendants.

Organized labour in the 1920s virtually meant members of those unions affiliated to the American Federation of Labor, still headed by the veteran, Samuel Gompers. He steered the unions away from political commitment and applied the principle of calling on workers, as electors, to punish their enemies and reward their friends. The A.F. of L. unions, with their bureaucracy of paid officials, acted as the business agents of the membership, aiming to sell their labour power at the highest price. They appealed mainly to the skilled workers, often to be found in small shops rather than factories, American-born for the most part, and conservative in their social and political attitudes. The A.F. of L. made little attempt to recruit from the expanding mass-production industries. Union membership had soared during and after the war, taking advantage of the all-round scarcity of labour, reaching a peak in 1920 of about five million. Throughout the 1920s, however, membership fell steadily and was under three million by the end of the decade.

Business was generally hostile to unions. Many corporations would only employ workers who agreed not to join a union (the so-called 'yellow-dog' contract). Active unionists and members of left-wing parties were liable to be sacked and victimized. The aim of most employers was to maintain an open shop and keep union organizers away. They could turn to the National Guard, as well as the police, if a strike actually broke out and were not averse to hiring strong-arm men of their own and bringing in strike-breakers. One device was to bring in workers of a different ethnic origin to that of the strikers, e.g. Blacks.

In their own ways, besides bargaining for the highest wages, the unions did stand for the rights of labour against the employing class and the state. Thus they jealously guarded their autonomy, sought to improve their position under the law and win for labour a higher status in society. With socialism in eclipse and the labour movement in decline, there were few voices critical of American capitalism during the prosperous 1920s, or a large audience for any that were raised. That prosperity was precariously balanced was not evident on the surface, while the expectation of continuous improvement in living standards was deeply rooted in American mythology. It took a major crisis to shake this optimism or complacency, to tarnish the favourable image of corporate beneficence built up in the 1920s and prepare the ground for the imposition of limits upon the free operation of market forces.

THE ORGANISATION OF BUSINESS

The rise and consolidation of the business corporation was at first a response to the depressed conditions of the 1870s and 1890s. Over-investment in the boom periods brought surplus capacity, which put pressure on prices and profits. When competition proved destructive there was a turn towards mergers and combinations, often engineered by the investment bankers. This began with the railroads and then extended into public utilities and large-scale processing and manufacturing industries. Thus there was a tendency for a smaller number of large firms to survive in each field, bolstered by their greater financial viability, their access to raw materials or assured markets. This tendency was most pronounced in new branches of industry needing to invest in costly fixed capital embodying advanced technology. The firms built up in the closing years of the nineteenth century proved to have great staying power; they made up the core of industrial capital and were the forebears of the giant multinational corporations of the following century.

In the scramble for profits and power no holds were barred. The great entrepreneurs who built up the business giants, and particularly the financiers who orchestrated the mergers and combinations, had scant respect for ethics or even for the law; in the achievement of their ends they used force, fraud, bribery and theft. Forthrightly dubbed 'the robber barons' by one historical tradition, others stress their positive contribution, tacitly assuming that capitalism in the United States could not have been built in any other way. From a pragmatic point of view they delivered the goods, even though they were no models of virtue or examples to be emulated. Some of them, the richest and most powerful, like Andrew Carnegie, John D. Rockefeller and the financier John Pierpont Morgan, became household names and their activities achieved wide publicity. The way they spent their money, in some cases, was as spectacular as the way they acquired it. Within a few decades a few hundred men accumulated fortunes comparable with those of the great aristocratic families of Europe. Lavish spending on mansions, yachts, receptions, art collections and rare books symbolized their 'success'.

The large corporation was the sector of American business most suited and eager to adopt new ways of organizing the labour process, and to integrate its workers into the enterprise through welfare schemes. Small and medium-sized firms were still important – the big corporations only accounted for about twenty per cent of the total product value of industry – but key sectors of the industrial apparatus and business structure as a whole were dominated by the corporations.

By a process of horizontal combination and vertical integration in the late nineteenth century, large corporate enterprise had attained its strategic position in the structure of American capitalism. It was the chief producer of primary metals, machinery, chemicals, petroleum, rubber; it governed large-scale manufacturing (notably motor vehicles), food processing (milling, refining, brewing, distilling and canning), as well as tobacco production and meat-packing.

This tendency towards combination and monopoly had roused fears about the dangerous concentration of economic power in the hands of a few corporate magnates. Such fear and hostility goes back to the time of the founding of the republic, when the Jeffersonian ideal of a society of small landowners and entrepreneurs took shape. Revived towards the end of the nineteenth century in the form of populism, it remained a strong tradition in America. Its main achievement had been the Sherman anti-trust law of 1890.

No doubt supporters of this law assumed that it would help to maintain competition and prevent the growth in the power of the big corporations. It declared illegal 'every contract, combination in the form of trust, or otherwise, or conspiracy in restraint of trade among the several states'. It made it a misdemeanour 'to monopolize, or attempt to monopolize, or combine or conspire . . . to monopolize any part of trade or commerce among the several states'. The effectiveness of 'trust-busting' would depend upon the Justice Department bringing cases before the courts and how judges would interpret the law. The initial reaction was one of masterly inaction by the government. Of the many cases later brought, few resulted in any great change in the business structure. Even the break up of John D. Rockefeller's Standard Oil in 1911 came when its market share had shrunk from ninety to sixty-six per cent; and the separate corporations into which it was divided became giants in their own right. The courts used the restraint of trade clause to make decisions which restricted labour union activities. In any case, it was difficult to prove that a corporation had violated the law. Monopoly power was tempered by market forces. The law did nothing about size as such. In fact the tendency was not towards 'monopoly' in the literal sense, but rather the division of the market between a small number of giant firms, without there necessarily being increased concentration; that is 'oligopoly' (a small number of sellers).

In 1914 the Clayton Act was passed, outlawing certain other practices – including price discrimination and interlocking directorates – if the consequence was to lessen competition or promote monopoly. A Federal Trade Commission of five appointees was set up to enforce the act. In practice, the Clayton Act did little to increase the government's powers to enforce competition or limit monopoly power; the FTC was little more than a fact-finding body. The Act did, however, provide some protection for labour unions. Anti-monopoly legislation failed to stop the ever-increasing mergers and the growth in scale and market power of the big corporations. The law may have had some deterrent effect on businessmen, and perhaps the economy would have been less competitive without the acts, but the hope that the concentration of economic power could be checked by state action was illusory. Market forces and technological trends, even economic efficiency, favoured the large scale business. As that meant that only a few firms could survive in industries affected by these trends, competition was bound to be unstable. The working out of the laws of capitalist development weighed heavily against the attempt to curb monopoly power.

Notwithstanding the anti-trust laws, the stronger firms took over or merged with their rivals in the same stage of production in a process of horizontal combination as was the case with John D. Rockefeller's Standard Oil. In other cases they reached back to control inputs like raw materials or intermediate products, or stretched forward into diverse branches of fabrication, or went into the distribution and marketing of the product, selling to other firms or direct to consumers in what is called vertical combination. US Steel had coal mines, coking ovens, iron mines as well as plants producing various types and shapes of steel. The biggest corporations came to have an interest in a variety of generally cognate industries; in time these might be organized into quasi-autonomous divisions of the firm (conglomerates), which brought under the control of one corporation a variety of unrelated businesses.

The typical market situation in an 'industry' dominated by a small number of large firms was 'oligopoly'. The laws of the competitive market no longer applied in their pure form. In an oligopolistic situation each firm watched the market behaviour of the others with strict attention. Instead of competing in terms of price, in obedience to the laws of supply and demand, where the price for each producer was fixed, they sought to exercise some control over the market by restricting supply. They differentiated their products by brand names, packaging and advertising. Prices might be set by subtle forms of collusion, where one or two firms might act as pace-setters for the others, or there might be some tacit agreement about market shares. Firms now sought some kind of security; if possible, prices were based upon cost of production plus the going rate of profit or an approximation to it. Under this kind of 'imperfect' competition, price ceased to be a determinate quantity. Prices, and profits, were presumably kept higher than they would have been under competitive conditions, while output would be lower. In a depression output would be reduced rather than prices.

The characteristics of firms in the corporate sector were basically determined by their sheer size in relation to the industry or to the economy as a whole. They dominated the manufacture of standardized products on the scale made necessary by advanced technology. Not only did they realize the substantial economies of scale often made possible by modern machinery and equipment, but its cost, and the difficulty new firms faced in raising the required capital, discouraged new entrants.

During the 1920s and subsequently, new types of industry emerged based on advanced technologies, new processes and products. In these fields, therefore, newcomers might rise into the ranks of the heavyweights. What is remarkable is that few were knocked out or quit. It was as though the giant corporation had become virtually indestructible, destined to endure as long as the system of which they were an indispensable part. Even the great economic blizzard of the 1930s made little difference; most of the top firms of the 1920s still exist. The names of such firms can be practically taken at random: Standard Oil, Alcoa, Anaconda Copper, Westinghouse, General Electric, Consolidated Edison, International Harvester, R. J.

Reynolds, Firestone, Goodyear, Armour, Union Carbide, Coca-Cola, and so on. Some firms, like R. J. Reynolds (tobacco), may merge with others. Confronted with decline in its original industry, a corporation like U.S. Steel, may diversify into other fields; both have happened in recent years. Firestone has been taken over by the Japanese tyre manufacturer Bridgestone. Durability has become a feature of the corporation. Nowadays it is unlikely that the state would permit a major corporation to collapse: witness the loan, under Federal Government guarantee, extended to the Chrysler Corporation, and the Federal Reserve bail-out of the Continental Illinois bank, in the 1980s.

Typically, the American business, whether a giant firm or a more modest enterprise, is organized as a joint stock company. As a corporation, according to the law, these firms enjoy legal personality; they can sue or be sued as an individual and they enjoy the rights of individuals. The division of their capital into transferable stock enjoying limited liability for the holder makes the joint stock form the most efficient instrument for the raising of long-term capital. Although a firm as big as Ford was for a long time a private, family-owned firm, the scale, capital requirements and risk factor involved in today's large-scale industry makes this a rarity. Through their stock, and the loan capital which they raise on the market, they provide a large part of the negotiable paper which makes up private property in present-day capitalist society.

Today, as in the period of its rise and maturity, while ownership of the corporation is vested in the stockholders, its control typically rests with the professional managers they nominally employ. Independent of their personal ownership stake (which may be considerable or non-existent), the managers have to make the decisions both upon broad questions of policy and about day-to-day matters. This apparent divorce of ownership from control raises many questions about the role of corporate management. Some say that the managers have taken over from the legal owners, the stockholders. Others see them as still bound to take action which coincides broadly with the interests of the stockholders, whose agents they are. Most see the corporate executives as wielding a degree of discretionary power which varies from case to case. Perhaps it is best to regard them as the personification of capital, in much the same way as was the owner-entrepreneur of the nineteenth century. It is in this role that management deals with the hiring and firing of workers, or negotiates with union representatives. Profits still have to be made to justify the stewardship of the managers. Profits are an index of their success, or lack of it, and, as a source of investment funds (and not simply dividends) are a necessary condition for growth. Moreover, a profitable corporation will be able to raise fresh capital or borrow in the bond market more easily. The manager wants to see his corporation grow: it is the source of his salary and of his dividends if he has an ownership stake, as he generally does. Earning power is the basis for the stock exchange valuation of the firm. The executives of a successful, i.e. a profitable, corporation enhance their own marketable value. Meanwhile, although some shareholders may be looking for dividends, a more potent indicator of managerial quality is provided by the stock market and by the creditworthiness of the firm. In any case, managerial control has not weakened the drive for profitability.

The big manufacturing corporations took the lead in introducing the new 'scientific' methods of controlling and disciplining the labour force. Rather than their monopolistic position leading to stagnation, they have had the resources to finance research and development to further strengthen their hold over the market. The managers aimed, and still aim, to control the production process in all its aspects and, as far as possible, the merchandizing and marketing stages as well. Expenditure on Research and Development takes over from the old-style inventor in the drive to make production methods more efficient and to develop new products. As the markets for existing products became saturated, the corporations pushed into new fields in pursuit of profits. The heavy investment in constant capital especially plant and machinery imposed a continuous struggle against the tendency for the rate of profit to decline. Diversification, already evident in the 1920s, was one way in which this could be done.

The same pressures which drove the corporations to seek new product lines and to branch out into new fields at home also led many of them to establish branch plants in foreign countries to serve their markets. The origin of the multinational corporations thus lay in the limitation on the increased profit obtainable by sales in the home market. In addition, while there were frequently tariff barriers to the introduction of American goods into foreign markets, as in Canada, American capital was often welcomed.

The concentration of economic power in the hands of the giant corporations made them, potentially, sources of political power and influence upon government as well. In various ways they looked to Washington for support both at home and abroad. In the empire without frontiers which the United States created in the twentieth century, the corporation became an instrument of American expansion and influence in the world, which could hardly fail to gratify the nationalist leanings of many politicians. In the 1920s there was no doubt that the corporations had the blessing of pro-business Republican legislators and administrations. Although formally adherents of the free market economy and opponents of state intervention, business was not averse to calling upon the state when it needed support against trade unions, political agitators or foreign competitors. Mercantilism was not dead in America; state and business worked together to achieve common purposes.

The prestige of business stood high at this time; it was, after all, bringing prosperity in which all shared, albeit unevenly. There was still the Populist tradition of suspicion of big business and 'monopoly' to be contended with and, in journalism, a 'muck-raking' trend which did not spare business when it was seen to be delinquent. The voice of the political left was too weak to have much influence upon public opinion and there were few native critics of the calibre of the maverick academic, Thorstein Veblen. Thus few Americans recognized the abuse of power possible in a highly concentrated corporate structure, at least not until the Depression, when the prestige of business slumped in line with share prices.

Those in the Populist tradition who thought that capitalism in America could somehow return to its pristine competitive form based on the family farm and the small business were backward-looking Utopians, as the fate of anti-monopoly legislation showed. Corporate capitalism had come to stay. Corporate stock was a major form of property-holding for the wealthy and attracted a growing number wishing to participate in the speculative gains of the bull market in the late 1920s. Talented young men turned out by the universities and business schools sought jobs as executives and managers. A large part of the 'new middle class' was directly or indirectly dependent upon the corporations for their income. Salaries and perquisites available for the successful were the highest in the world. So many of the highly educated and most talented went into business that the inferiority of American politicians and civil servants to their European counterparts was notorious. Many of them could be bought and paid for out of the slush funds of the corporate interests; corruption was endemic in politics at the federal as well as at the state and local level. Organized crime flourished in some cities, while evading Prohibition opened up unheard-of possibilities for illicit business deals and criminal activity.

The prevailing ideology, given credence by 'prosperity', was unqualified support for free enterprise and the market system. There was some incongruity between these professions and the actual practice of the corporate sector which restricted entry, separated ownership from control, created centres of power able to bend and distort market forces and eliminated price competition whenever possible. Moreover, many businessmen saw no contradiction in calling for higher protective tariffs to keep out foreign competition while opposing the trade restrictions of other countries. Meanwhile, competition between capitals for the right to a larger share of the profits continued in oligopolistic situations.

In a sense it could be said that corporate capitalism delivered the goods, and that was evidently how most Americans perceived it; but it also created and perpetuated huge discrepancies in property ownership and income distribution. High pressure salesmanship and the psychological tricks of the advertising man persuaded consumers to buy goods which they did not really need, or did not have the qualities claimed for them. The creation of a mass market was as much a feat of technology as was the production of the goods. Industry needed ever larger and renewable markets. Part of the technique was to make consumers feel dissatisfied with what they already had by insisting that there was now something better on the market, something which their neighbours up the street already had, which they should buy to replace an article which had not yet worn out. Planned obsolescence was becoming a feature of some American consumer goods. Throwing things away before they wore out, waste on a mass scale, seemed to be necessary to keep the wheels of industry turning. No society before had generated so much rubbish. That in itself was the sign of a wealthy society.

While the giant corporation occupied a dominant position in the commanding heights of the economy, lower down there were still millions of small- and medium-sized firms of every variety. They varied from successful and growing firms aspiring to the ranks of the giants to the one-man hopefuls setting out in crowded fields like retailing, petty production or services. Among these firms there was a situation more closely approximating perfect competition: freedom of entry, inability to influence price, lack of product differentiation – and a high risk of failure. Many of these firms had few employees (some depended upon family labour), used little machinery or equipment, were chronically short of money capital and had only a limited capacity to obtain credit from outside sources. Typically, in nineteenth-century fashion, the owner provided the initial capital, took the business decisions himself and supervised his labour force. Failure might throw him back into the ranks of the job-seekers. Many firms of this type produced for, or served, a local market. Some, like the corner store, might enjoy a rent of situation, but the narrowness of the market limited their possibilities for growth.

If the small entrepreneur was not satisfied with a stable income of a given size, he would have to find the means of branching out into a new field or go to another area. Many settled for a respected place in the small-town society which best fostered this type of enterprise. Most small- and medium-sized firms were not threatened by the big corporations, which they complemented in many ways. Retailers sold the branded goods of the giants. Repairmen serviced the machines, appliances, cars and trucks manufactured in giant factories. Small manufacturing firms might work as sub-contractors for a mammoth corporation. They bought their fuel, raw materials, machinery and intermediate goods from the big manufacturers and public utilities. The non-corporate sector, with its many small and medium-sized firms, was not independent of the corporate sector but was interrelated with, and, in some degree, dependent upon it.

Firms in the non-corporate sector came and went; some might survive and grow, others had a brief and unhappy life, terminating in bankruptcy. But the unsuccessful entrepreneur might try something else, somewhere else, later. Such flexibility was an American trait, outcome of a search for making money rather than making a living. It was rare for a small firm to make it into the big time (to use the slang of the period); rare but not impossible. A doughnut stall or a hamburger bar might be the embryo of a business making millions of dollars, to give a contemporary example there was the massive growth of McDonalds from one restaurant in the 1950s to an international fast food giant today. It was a milk-shake machine salesman and not the owners who saw the potential for growth. With such a huge and standardized market a common product like a soft drink (e.g. Coca Cola) might become the starting point for a business empire.

Occasionally smaller firms might be in on the ground floor when some technological break-through was taking place. Before it came to be dominated by three giants, car manufacturing had attracted a small legion of entrepreneurs. New fields generally did attract many aspirants to fortune. The threshhold to success, if not to entry, was the need for finance, control of which was in the hands of the banks and of already established larger firms. A medium-sized firm might achieve some importance regionally or in a specialized field, such as the production of a particular machine-tool. It was more likely to occur outside manufacturing, notably retailing and services. Lack of capital was the main barrier to growth for the small- and medium-sized firms. They might well become the prey of a corporate giant sooner or later, or reach a peak beyond which they could not go.

It should be noted that in the 1920s concentration had not proceeded far in the older-established manufacturing industries with their roots in the previous century. Textiles, clothing, furniture, footwear and other consumer goods industries retained a more competitive structure. They had experienced no major advances in technology, or in the nature of the product, which required big new capital outlays on plant and machinery. They were, in any case, less capital-intensive than the newer, concentrated industries and more dependent upon a stable, and perhaps more skilled, labour force. The market for such firms might still be local or regional rather than national in scope. Their products were distributed by established wholesale and retail channels rather than through their own merchandizing organisation. An expansion of demand was likely to result in a proportionate addition to existing capacity or the entry of new firms. There were few scale economies, so that big capitals were not attracted to these fields. The small producer had the advantage of being able to work closer to consumer demand (of a kind which changed only slowly, in any case) and concentrate on skill and craftsmanship where these were still important. This might hold good not only for fashion goods but also for more sophisticated products, like machine-tools. The giant manufacturing corporation, dependent upon long runs of standardized products, requiring expensive machinery, had to establish a mass market through brand names and advertising. The small firm had few selling costs and might be able to respond more flexibly to changes in demand; merchandizing was left to others and a reputation built up over many years might still sell the product.

The huge scale of the market, the variety and ease of entry to the more competitive sectors of American business, helped to foster the almost complete acceptance of the free enterprise creed. Escape from the working class, desire to be one's own boss, to become established as an American, as well as the search for security and wealth, were among the motives which fired the millions of would-be entrepreneurs. The mythology was the poor boy who made good, the newspaper-seller who became a tycoon, in the style of the once popular author Horatio Alger. Historians have laboriously unravelled the picture and shown that, if such cases can be found, they were exceptional in the extreme. The successful businessman was more likely to come from the class of property-owners. Eventually, the 'corporate elite' became self-perpetuating. Founders of firms also became the founders of dynasties based upon large and enduring fortunes. In the twentieth century the surest way to become a successful businessman was to have a businessman as a father. The result was that hordes of would-be millionaires crowded into fields where their chance of 'success' was negligible. They were excluded from the most profitable and dynamic centres unless they gave up hope of making it alone and joined the ranks of the corporate managers.

As for the small entrepreneurs, their more modest success was often based upon hard work and cheap labour, beginning with that of themselves and their families. Some moved up in the social scale in their local community. Besides success in business, education and training in the professions also provided a ladder for upward mobility increasingly sought after in America. The great increase in the demand for professional services was a sign of growing wealth. Not only did the traditional liberal professions expand, but the corporations also offered employment for the college-educated as managers, engineers and technicians. Through the college or university the boy of modest origins might find a way into the corporate board room. There was no place here for women, and the main source of recruitment was still the established middle class, predominantly Anglo-Saxon still, Protestant most often and, of course, white.

A period like the 1920s fostered the American dream of material success. Many entered the business field, especially retailing and services, hoping to get rich through the old recipe of hard work and thrift, the pursuit of the bourgeois virtues. Others hoped to get rich quick by playing the stock market, encouraged by what seemed to be its permanent upward trend, creating new fortunes. The Wall Street crash and the depression which followed dashed hopes and ruined many, the hard-working and thrifty as well as the speculators out for quick gains. Notwithstanding, the myth of the self-made man survived, to re-emerge in better times.

THE INDUSTRIAL POWER HOUSE

So far little has been said about the actual distribution of industry in the United States. As in other countries, the principal industries were localized in a few regions. Industrialization in the nineteenth century had chiefly taken place in the North-Eastern part of the country from the shores of the Great Lakes, though Illinois, Michigan and Pennsylvania to New York State and New England. By the 1920s these could be regarded as the old industrial regions. They had grown up originally on the basis of the nineteenth-century technologies: coal and steam, steel and engineering, machine-made textiles. While by this time some of the older areas had declined in absolute terms, as well as relatively, new industries had been moving in. The automobile and rubber industries had risen to importance within very much the same region as the older industry, in the North-East. What are today called the 'smokestack' industries (in the disaster areas of the 1980s) were concentrated around the major cities in this region: Chicago, Cleveland, Pittsburgh, Akron, Buffalo; these were the throbbing heartlands of the world's industrial giant.

Industry had been drawn to these areas because of the accessibility of the basic, heavy, bulky and dirty materials of nineteenth-century industrialism, such as anthracite coal and iron ore. Crucial in their location, too, was the availability of means of transport to shift these materials long distances at modest rates. Hence the importance of the Great Lakes and rivers as well as canals and railways and, by the 1920s, the highways for motor traffic. Abundant space, the right resources in large quantities, the ability to attract a mobile and largely immigrant labour force gave flexibility to the location of new plants in the formative stages of industrialization and encouraged their construction on a large scale, often dwarfing the mines and plants of Europe. Growing centres of population provided growing markets for lighter, consumer goods industries and a host of service trades. But a primary business of this region was to provide the heavy plant and machinery that made up the capital stock of American capitalism and helped to account for its power.

Necessarily, therefore, the North-Eastern industrial region became the main field for the manufacturing operations of the big corporations. Indeed, in the 1920s, outside the extractive industries, few really large plants were erected anywhere else. The massive industrialization of the West coast was still in the future. Industry had not yet penetrated the South to any significant extent. Small-scale industry was well represented in parts of the North-East, especially in New York and the industrial parts of New England, and everywhere else it was practically the only type of industry to be found. The Mid-West, as well as the South, indeed the small towns in all the predominantly agricultural states, remained the preserves of small business with little large-scale industry; here there flourished the capitalism of Main Street, not of Wall Street.

The existence of such a wide geographical arena for small enterprise helps to explain its relative vitality in the 1920s. It centred very much upon the small towns which dotted the landscape of rural America. Such towns still had close links with the agriculture round about for which they depended for their trade. This made up a type of capitalism still reminiscent of the nineteenth century rather than of the new forms associated with mass production and the giant corporation. In the co-existence of these two contrasting structures, the United States did not escape a form of 'economic dualism' of the sort found in Europe.

The economic power of the United States was based upon the great manufacturing industries built up in the period of industrialization between the Civil War and the First World War. Their strength rested upon their ability to provide the basic materials of modern industry and to pour out long runs of standardized products at low unit cost using advanced technology, the rational organization of labour power and trained management.

Most of the leading firms of the 1980s were already well-established by the 1920s; newcomers were mainly to be found in fields which did not exist then or were in their infancy, such as aviation and electronics. The main industrial trends were increasing total output, rising productivity and higher profits. The main force for growth lay in a high rate of investment, in new, technologically advanced plant and machinery, giving a high ratio of constant to variable capital (that is to say, outlays on wages). Year by year there was more horse power and more machinery per employed worker, especially in the great mass production industries. New methods were devised of getting more out of the worker in a given time. The drive for productivity was an outstanding characteristic of American industry; it was pushed to levels never before achieved and much higher than in other industrial countries. Wage incentives were devised to gear the workers to the goal of ever increasing output at lower unit costs. The virtues of the 'high' American wage were extolled by the ideologists of the boom, and impressed foreign observers. As the productivity of labour rose, corporate industry increased its profits and tended to plough back a larger proportion into new investment. This provided the real basis for the rise in stock market prices which gathered momentum in the late 1920s. The growth in the productive power of industry, evidence of general prosperity, and the rise in stock market prices boosted confidence, enhanced the authority of businessmen and reinforced public support for the American free enterprise system and faith in its future.

The number of production workers employed in American industry in this decade exceeded eight million; they formed the most homogeneous portion of the labour force, with the attributes of a classic industrial proletariat. It was not so much degrees of skill which differentiated the mass of industrial workers as their diverse ethnic origins. Many were new immigrants or first-generation Americans, still conscious of their national origins, often regarded with hostility or suspicion by members of other ethnic groups. They competed with each other for jobs. Employers could take advantage of such rivalries and antagonisms. American newcomers to the labour force came often from rural communities. An increasing number was made up of black migrants from the South who suffered discrimination on account of their colour in the Northern cities where they congregated in insalubrious 'ghettos'. The diverse ethnic and cultural origins of the industrial labour force hindered the development of a solidarity based upon class interests. Ethnicity continued to be a powerful binding force despite the homogenizing effects of factory work. A specific class consciousness was slow in developing. Few workers in factory industry belonged to trade unions until the great organizing drives of the 1930s. Trade union membership as a whole was falling and the leadership of the American Federation of Labor showed little interest in building unions in the mass production industries.

Capital per worker in manufacturing rose by thirty-six per cent in the period 1919 to 1929, while value added by each worker jumped, on average, by seventy-five per cent. The increase in the amount of power and machinery behind each worker was greatest in the more concentrated industries dominated by a few giant corporations. Mechanization was pushed forward most rapidly in the great new mass production industries turning out automobiles, machinery and consumer durables.

A main thrust of technology was in the design and application of more specialized machines and machine-tools which required only minimal skills to operate. In plants where they were installed the bulk of the workers could be described as semi-skilled; almost any physically fit and mentally normal person could become proficient in the job after a short time. Skilled craftsmen would be confined to the tool shop and to the repair and maintenance of machinery. There was no need for apprenticeship or trade training as far as the mass of the labour force was concerned. Workers could move from one job or from one plant to another without much difficulty. The actual operations performed by the workers were reduced to a required sequence worked out in advance by time-and-motion study experts. The pace of work was determined by the rate at which the different parts and components were fabricated and passed from one stage of production to another, typically by means of a conveyer belt.

In the large plant the work force was heavily supervised by foremen, who transmitted the orders of management to the factory floor. They had to ensure that the manufacturing process operated smoothly, that workers were kept at their task as constantly as possible and that output and quality were maintained. The foreman might have the power to transfer a worker to another job or to another department or even have him or her sacked for unsatisfactory work or infringing labour discipline. He would probably be a 'native' white American, or of a different ethnic origin to the workers under him. Evidently he played a key role in the management structure and in the success of the drive for maximum through-put needed to reach targets of profitability.

In factory jobs, like those on the assembly line, workers became interchangeable, like the parts of the commodities they produced. They could easily be replaced by newcomers to the labour market – immigrants, Blacks, unemployed people. This was a spur to effort and hard work, a reason not to question the decisions of management or foremen. Traditionally, workers had tried to impose their own idea of what was a fair day's work or an acceptable tempo of production. One of the aims of 'scientific management' was to break up this kind of 'workers' control' of the workplace. It was implicit in the approach of the founder of 'Taylorism', Frederick W. Taylor. One of the aims of 'Taylorism' was to return to management undisputed control over the workplace, a common aim of management in any case, and a reason for opposing union organization. It did not succeed entirely. Workers did not give up trying to enforce their concept of work, while employers were constantly devising new ways of dealing with what they considered to be workers' interference with the prerogatives of management. At the same time, they sought worker co-operation through incentive payments and welfare schemes intended to make them identify their own interests with those of the firm. It was difficult in practice to reconcile the drive for productivity with the welfare of the workers. When trade unions came on the scene, one of their main functions was to handle the many grievances of individual workers, or groups of workers, which arose from the impersonalized and alienating ways in which the labour process was organized in large-scale factory industry.

Under the kind of factory organization described as 'Fordism', mechanically-driven production lines carrying vehicles at various stages of completion were manned by individual workers or teams at fixed points to carry out a given operation. This was a working out of the 'detail' division of labour about which Adam Smith and Marx had written. Indeed, passages from *Capital* Volume One read like an anticipation of the automated plant foreshadowed by Fordism. It only remained to eliminate the worker from the process altogether, as was to happen with the development of automation and robotization thirty years on.

If scientific management ordered the worker what to do, the assembly line set the pace of work above and beyond any possibility of control by the worker. As with Taylorism, Fordism seeks the limits of the physically (and psychologically) possible for the human element in the production process. For effective operation, this kind of industry required a continuous supply of mostly young and robust workers able to support the physical and nervous strain involved. It could be argued that such workers not only could work fewer hours than under more traditional systems, but that they needed a higher intake of nutritious foods and stimulants and thus a higher wage. To recruit a sufficient supply of workers and to reconcile them to the discipline of the assembly line, Ford offered a wage well above the ruling average. Nevertheless, although Ford employees were relatively well paid, many could not stand the pace for long and labour turnover tended to be high.

More generally, 'Fordism' was used to describe the strategy of high wages and high consumption which advocates of business counted upon, in the 1920s, to reconcile workers to capitalism and act as an antidote to class solidarity. The extent to which it was applied then or later is a matter for debate. A victim of the depression, the economy of high wages was resurrected after the Second World War.

Wages had been pushed up during the period of labour scarcity in the First World War and, in conditions of low unemployment, these gains were retained. This helped to account for the acceptance of Fordism before the depression. Another factor was that labour on the factory floor in the mass production industries was still unorganized. After a burst of industrial militancy during and after the war, both the political and industrial wings of labour went into decline. Its left wing, especially the Communist Party and the syndicalist Industrial Workers of the World, were subject to severe government repression in the post-war 'red scare'. The courts were hostile to labour organization; court injunctions were used to end strikes, particularly sympathetic strikes, boycotts and mass picketing. Effective trade union action was therefore limited, especially in the mass production industries. The conservative American Federation of Labor was mainly confined to the better-paid craft workers and did not seek a conflict with the state.

AGRICULTURE: THE SIMMERING CRISIS

Agriculture was the one sector of the American economy which appeared to be ailing in the 1920s. Although overall the United States had been transformed in the period from the Civil War of the 1860s into a highly industrialized country, with only about fifteen per cent of the gross national product (GNP) coming from agriculture in 1920, some twenty-nine per cent of the occupied population was still employed on farms. In that year, no less than 31,614,000 Americans lived on farms out of a total population of 106,466,000. There were approximately 6,518,000 farming units of every type and dimension. About fourteen per cent of all farmers were black, mainly in the South and generally among the poorest of all.

There was a steady decline in farm employment and in the contribution of agriculture to GNP relative to the non-farm sectors and this trend continued during the 1920s. During that time the farm population decreased by over one million and the number of farm units fell by almost 160,000. In fact, although few probably appreciated it at the time, if American capitalism was to continue to expand, more manpower and resources would have to be shifted out of agriculture into the urban sectors. In no country has such a process taken place without opposition from the farm community and without social tensions and, in some cases, a major upheaval. In the United States, however, the constitution placed disproportionate voting weight and political influence in the hands of the rural population. This influence was used in the Senate and in Congress to maintain agriculture in opposition to the forces of economic development tending to bring about its decline. This meant serious contradictions and problems which have not been resolved down to the present time.

Agriculture, and rural life in general, had played a special role in the history of the country and there was a strong ideological bias in their favour. Even sophisticated urban people and politicians paid tribute to the virtues of rural life and the need to preserve a healthy agriculture. Though for many this may have represented lip-service or was necessary to win farmers' votes, perhaps in most cases it was sincere. The pioneering, self-reliant and hard-working farmer who had opened up the West was part of American mythology and a valuable asset for those who bargained, at state or federal level, on behalf of the farming interests. A strong prejudice thus existed in favour of some kind of state support for agriculture, which found particular expression in the New Deal and in Roosevelt's own attitude.

Although the ancestors of most American farmers, with the obvious exception of the Blacks, had been European peasants, by the twentieth century there was a wide difference between the American farmer and the peasant. Both tilled the soil and raised livestock, were subject to the rhythm of the seasons and the whims of nature, but their aims and methods, their relationship to the land and to the society in which they lived represented, it might be said, two different eras. American farmers were caught up inescapably in the mechanism of the commodity market: they needed to sell their produce at a profit rather than provide directly for family needs. Even the idealized 'family farm' was essentially a business unit. What this term generally meant was that the farm was of such a size as to be run by the farmer and his family without the use of hired labour. Regardless of the amount of land held, whether it was owned, rented or held on a share-cropper basis, all or most of what was produced was destined for the market. Practically all farmers had to purchase most of their household needs, as well as many necessities for the cultivation of land and the raising of livestock. Some kinds of farming could not be carried on competitively without expensive machinery which had to be hired or bought. Farmers, large or small, were typically debtors, which increased their sensitivity to price fluctuations and market changes. Their products had to be transported by rail and stored and sold by merchants, underlining still further their dependence upon market forces.

Thus even the family farmers were small businessmen, strikingly different from the typical peasant of the nineteenth century still operating on the fringes of the exchange economy. Moreover, by the 1920s there was a steady growth of 'agri-business' – highly capitalized cereal cultivation, ranching and fruit growing, using the techniques of mass production as far as they could be adapted to the needs of the enterprise. Not only was the farm sector distinctly capitalist in its structure and purpose (to make profits), but capital intensity was tending to increase. As in industry, machinery was being substituted for labour and technical change was making possible substantial increases in productivity. This inevitably meant that more and more farmers would become superfluous; but the working out of economic laws was resisted by the social and political weight of the farm interests, for whom it was a question of livelihood and survival.

As pointed out, American agriculture was far from being homogeneous. Consisting of over six million business enterprises, as it were, it was normal that there should be an enormous variety of productive units to be found under the general heading of a 'farm'. The amount of land farmed and its quality, the nature of the outputs, the ratio of labour and machinery to land, the level of efficiency of the individual farmer and the basis on which land was held were among the factors which contributed to this variety. Some farmers lived in dire poverty and were among the poorest people in America. A small number were rich and powerful. There was no typical American farm or farmer. So far as the mythology of the family farm had a basis in reality, it is to be found in the fact that in the great agrarian regions such as the mid-West there was a preponderance of middle-sized farms and middle-income farmers, employing little or no hired labour. Even within this broad grouping there were considerable variations.

American agriculture had been able to supply the growing needs of an increasingly industrialized and urbanized population with a relatively high income per capita. In addition, sections of it were geared to world market demand. The income of the farm population was dependent upon fluctuations in demand, and thus on market prices. It was also sensitive to the price of inputs, services and household requirements. When the rest of the economy expanded, receipts and income would rise, in real terms, although some costs might also go up. In a time of slump, agriculture would probably be disproportionately depressed: nothing could be done to hold up prices, while fixed costs such as rent, interest and mortgage payments would take up a disproportionate share of income. Responding to falling prices by increasing output in the next season, as many farmers were tempted to do, might make things worse. Farmers were generally protectionist, but many depended upon foreign markets in which they had to face competition from other producers. The role of exports varied from one region to another, but the history of the expanding agricultural frontier had been inseparably associated with overseas demand for the staple products of American farmers, especially cereals, cotton and livestock products. The prosperity of the regions specialized in such commodities was thus inextricably linked with world market trends. The farmer was pitted not only against natural forces, which determined the amount and quality of his product from year to year, but also against the spontaneous forces of the market over which he also had no control. As a purchaser as well as a seller, he was at the mercy of market forces. No wonder then, that farm interests in some way sought to exercise control either by co-operative action or by calling on the state for assistance. The larger and more highly capitalized farmers would be in a better position to anticipate, if not to influence, market forces. The smaller farmers might feel that banks, railways and merchants were in some kind of conspiracy against them. The fundamental point is the farmers' deep and inextricable involvement with the capitalist market economy, one which, over time, was bound to condemn many farmers to extinction.

Some kind of agriculture was, and is, carried on in almost every part of rural America where land is suitable for cultivation or the raising of animals. Around the main centres of population, vegetable production and market gardening (truck farming) are carried on in the open or under glass. A series of highly specialized regions developed as transport facilities improved and became cheaper. Dairy farming and the fattening of livestock for slaughter generally required proximity to local markets, unless the products were to be canned or preserved in some other way. Climatic conditions made California and Florida favoured areas for the large-scale cultivation of fruit crops and vegetables. A similar specialization was characteristic of parts of the North-East. Areas like Wisconsin, south of the Great Lakes, became noted for their cheese, butter and other dairy products. Apart from such regional specialization, American agriculture in the twentieth century has been dominated by three great commodity belts: wheat, corn and cotton. It is these regions which have been most vulnerable to variations in domestic and foreign demand and to the price swings which they have generated. It is here that, as methods of production improved, the problem of surplus output was to arise in its most acute form. The 1920s already showed signs of a problem which was to become endemic.

The North-West Prairie land, like those across the border in Canada, was the great region for wheat-growing. The Central states made up the Corn Belt, though much of the corn is fed to pigs and other animals, making this also a meat-producing area. The Southern states, where in the 1920s the black population was still concentrated, comprised the Cotton Belt. Although there were no hard and fast dividing lines, this division was, and remains, of considerable economic significance when considering disparities in income levels as well as types of farming.

On the whole, wheat is the crop which has lent itself best to large-scale production using expensive machinery and thus large capitals. Farms in the Corn Belt have tended to be of a more modest size, more mixed in their output, raising pigs and poultry and cultivating other crops besides corn. In the South, in the 1920s, cotton was still king though tobacco was also an important cash crop. In place of the *ante-bellum* plantations, the land was tilled in small share-cropping farms run by Blacks or poor whites. This region made up the poorest and least developed part of the United States. Within each of these regions, and in the other smaller, specialised areas of agriculture, considerable variations were to be found in the size of farms and the efficiency and income of the cultivators. Besides the importance of the accessibility of markets, prices did not move in the same way or to the same extent for the various agricultural commodities. The response to market fluctuations might be very different as far as the various sections of the farm population were concerned, with sharp contrasts in the same locality. Farmers at a distance from their market, like the Western wheat-growers, were more susceptible to changes in storage and freight charges than those who sold mainly in a nearby urban market. Share-croppers suffered from special disabilities because of their poverty and weak bargaining position, and those who were black from racial discrimination as well, for example, in obtaining credit. Some farmers were more dependent than others upon food-processing firms which had established a monopsonistic position in some product markets.

Before 1914, with a rapidly growing internal market, agriculture, although declining in relative terms as a contributor to national income, was reckoned to be enjoying a prosperous time. This continued as a result of the First World War, which brought an insatiable demand for American products and sent prices zooming upwards. As invariably happens under such conditions, farmers were encouraged to expand the scale of their operations by extending their acreage, by renting, or by buying land with loans and mortgages and by purchasing additional machinery. Mechanization was indispensable on the larger cereal farms on the prairies. New and improved machines were coming on to the market and they could now be hooked to the versatile tractor – almost 250,000 were in use by 1920 and by 1930 that figure had risen to 920,000. Farmers were also making use of trucks on a comparable scale. There were 139,000 motor trucks on farms in 1920 and 900,000 by 1930; cars in use already numbered over two million and rose to twice that number by 1930. Farms were thus becoming increasingly mechanized and motorized. Rural isolation was being broken down with the increasing use of the telephone and the radio, while electricity was becoming available in more rural areas.

Most of these technological changes favoured the larger farmer with capital of his own or a good credit rating. He could then produce a cash crop at lower unit cost and find the money to finance a larger-scale operation to meet market demand. The smaller farmers, especially those with little or no capital, or the handicap of poor soil, were less able to afford machinery, fertilizers and pesticides. Their methods tended to be routine and they had to work themselves and their families hard. Indebtedness was a perennial problem for the small farmer. Higher prices for their produce, like those which ruled during the First World War, encouraged borrowing, but mortgage and loan charges could become crippling when prices fell again. In such periods, of which the 1920s was one, the stronger farmer might have to take a cut in income – and complain bitterly, individually or through one of the farm organizations – to his congressman or senator, but he could more easily hang on and await better times. The over-borrowed small farmer could face ruin. This was the fate of many when the post-war depression hit its low point in 1921, and of many more in the 1930s.

The technical advances making it possible to raise production and productivity on the farm meant that supply tended permanently to outstrip demand. Exports were necessary to keep agriculture prosperous; but output had increased in other countries, growing economic nationalism meant more tariff barriers and hungry people in other countries could not afford to buy American food. In retrospect it may be seen that the small American family farm, like the European peasant holding, the cynosure of the agrarian mythology, was under sentence of death. The agony was to be long drawn out, but the United States had to face a problem which arises invariably in the course of capitalist development: how to reduce the size of the rural population. This process underlies all the problems from the First World War onwards in the agricultural sector.

Meanwhile the change in the world position of the United States, by making it the major international creditor, worsened the prospects for exports. Foreigners sought to expand their sales in the United States as part of the process of servicing their debts. United States' exports now tended to be linked to the outflow of funds; when foreigners could not borrow they were unable to buy American products. Output, especially of wheat, had expanded during the war, but the post-war market was clogged with the excess production of Canada, Australia and Argentina. In addition, the boosting of production had, in some parts of the United States, been accompanied by bad farming practices, which had stored up trouble in the shape of soil erosion and dust bowls. Technical progress steadily reduced the demand for labour in the areas of extensive farming because of the reduction in the labour time necessary to produce a given amount of wheat or other product. Control of disease made it possible to raise more pigs, poultry or cattle; better feed increased the yield of meat or milk, and hens laid more eggs. If technology, advancing on many fronts, appeared to be solving the problem of production, other trends were limiting the expansion of demand. In the United States and in all of the wealthier countries, per capita consumption of the basic food, like cereals, was in steady decline. Prosperity in the rest of the country or an upturn in the world economy did not necessarily mean good times for agriculture, as it had done in the past. Poorer countries could have consumed more basic foods but lacked the means to pay for them. Those branches which did best were those producing the higher-quality foods, such as fruit, fresh vegetables, dairy produce and prime meats. Intensive methods prevailed here, with room for family farms (such as the Japanese in California) but often involving the employment of hired labour, perhaps on a casual and seasonal basis.

Given the inelasticity of demand for basic foods there was little chance of a big increase in the domestic demand for the staple products. Although the industrial countries of Europe had to import food and raw materials in large quantities, they did not have to buy them from the United States. In the case of cereals, cotton, and even tobacco, there were alternative sources of supply. During the 1920s cotton retained its position as the United States' most important export, sales abroad accounting for about half the crop. In this case the world price was governed by the cost of producing, transporting and handling American cotton. It was still produced largely by small farm units in the South, which were highly labour intensive. Production remained fairly stable during the 1920s and disaster did not strike until the depression became worldwide. The role of US cotton in the world market, however, was being undermined by the rise of new areas, the difficulties of the old manufacturing centres and the competition of artificial fibres. Later, machinery was to appear to threaten the share-croppers' position.

Although many American farmers suffered some decline in real income compared with the period of rising prices before 1914 and its prolongation in the war-time boom and were vocal in expression of their grievances, agriculture had not yet become a disaster area. For those who could read the signals, and for the historian with hindsight, it was clear that farms would have to shed an increasing proportion of their labour force and would either have to find new markets for their output or curtail it, in some branches quite significantly. Few read these signals. They were disagreeable to farmers, ran contrary to the mythology which favoured a large population of independent tillers of the soil as the salt of the earth, and posed the question of major economic readjustments which policy-makers did not want to face. Meanwhile, year by year, a certain number of rural people, mainly the younger men and women, were succumbing to the blandishments of urban life. The car and the bus brought rural people closer to the city and made them more familiar with its amenities. The War had shaken established social patterns by taking young men out of the rural environment and showing them new aspects of life. War-time jobs had attracted many, women as well as men, to the industrial centres with the lure of high wages. The first big shift of Blacks from the rural South to the Northern ghettos had begun. In the longer run, with population continuing to grow as well, the problem would be whether the number of urban jobs would increase fast enough to absorb the surplus labour from the countryside. As it happened, just as this problem was becoming more acute the depression struck, bringing a catastrophic shrinkage of the urban job market. This brought to the surface the submerged crisis in the agrarian sector which was simmering in any case and was, in a sense, independent of the depression.

Economic liberalism was the prevailing orthodoxy in the United States at this time. There was a reluctance to see the state interfere with the free operation of market forces and the right of the individual to do what he liked with his own. On the other hand, many people, especially those who were the victims of the vagaries of the market, called on the government to take action to shield them from its effects. They did this on a piecemeal basis rather than on doctrinal grounds. They sought government aid to deal with social disruption and distress, or simply to shore up acquired positions which came under threat. There was no clear-cut or consistent policy for agriculture, though the government did administer schemes to assist farmers to be more efficient and increase production mainly through education, research and information. At the same time, rival agricultural associations used pressure-group tactics to influence agricultural policy as particular problems arose.

The principal problem already was unsaleable surpluses, actual or potential. One proposal to deal with this, named after its Congressional sponsors McNary and Haugen and first put forward in 1924, was to combine tariff protection with government purchase of surpluses and their sale abroad. The claim was that the American producer would receive a price higher than that ruling in the world market, raising total farm incomes above the level determined by market forces. The scheme was to be financed by a levy on output. Despite the weaknesses of McNary-Haugenism – a US tariff on farm products would be ineffective, foreigners would impose retaliatory tariffs – the plan had some success with public opinion in appearing to offer a simple remedy for an intractable problem. Proposed to and passed by Congress on two occasions, the last time in 1928, it was vetoed by President Coolidge as an interference with the free market. It did not die then; it was still being discussed during the depression and certainly influenced the shaping of New Deal policy.

The Republican administration, biased towards business and the interests of industry, tried to uphold the free market; it proposed co-operative marketing as a way out for farmers dissatisfied with low prices and incomes. After the election of Hoover, an Agricultural Marketing Act was passed in 1929 which, besides giving more assistance to co-operative marketing, also set up a Federal Farm Board endowed with $500 million of government funds. Its task was to assist the farm co-operatives and help stabilize prices by keeping surpluses off the market. The aim of the Act, inconsistent with the free market ideology, was the organization of producers in each market through producers' self-government in the shape of co-operatives, national or regional in scope, able to influence prices by limiting supply. In practice, the powers granted were insufficient. If prices fell, individual farmers tended to produce more in order to maintain income, thus frustrating the purpose of the marketing scheme. More draconian intervention would be required if supply were to be controlled. In any case, the Federal Farm Board was set up to deal with the problems of the 1920s, not the far more acute problems which arose when the depression struck. Hardly had it been set up when it found itself confronted with bulging stock piles and crashing prices. Striken farmers demanded more effective remedies which, in turn, meant more direct control over production. If the Hoover administration had already opened a breach in the non-interventionist policy, it was to be widened spectacularly by its successor when the alternative seemed to be the ruin of a large part of the farming population.

THE BANKING SYSTEM: A WEAK LINK

The banking system inherited serious weaknesses from the past, exposed by the Wall Street crash of 1929 which brought it to the brink of collapse. It was characterized by the existence of a large number of banks whose activities were confined to one state or even to one office, so-called unit banks. There were almost 30,000 banks in the early 1920s, though the number then fell gradually by merger or by failure. This fragmentation contrasted with the tendency towards concentration in other forms of business and the domination of a few large chains in countries such as Britain or Canada.

Investment banking and merchant banking were mainly concentrated in New York and were dominated by a few firms which had consolidated their position in the late nineteenth century. Such firms did not do across-the-counter business but operated on a large scale for corporate and governmental bodies. They provided finance for large-scale industries, engineered mergers and consolidations, raised international loans (as during the First World War) and acquired a dominant position in the long-term capital market. The post-war reconstruction needs of Europe gave further scope for firms like Morgans, which became an international power to which governments had to defer, reflecting the new-won creditor position of the US. Thus the question of reparations payments and inter-allied debts, as well as the financial needs of post-war Europe, invariably involved American finance. At the same time American finance was pushing into Latin America and other parts of the world which had formerly been the preserve of Britain or other European countries.

Banks were formed and operated under different sets of rules, according to whether they were chartered by the state or the federal government or had no charter at all. The terms under which charters were granted made branch banking difficult if not impossible, and confined each bank's activities to a single state. Federally-chartered banks, set up under the National Bank Act of 1864, were permitted to issue notes but in other respects were subject to more stringent regulations than state-chartered banks. Instead of national banks taking over the bulk of banking as had been expected at the time of the passage of the act, state banks (and private banks) multiplied, and this was further encouraged by the states' easing restrictions and by the growth of the banking habit. During the 1920s the banks moved into investment in securities, stocks and bonds, or set up affiliates for that purpose.

Under a system of fractional reserve banking, where only sufficient reserves are held to meet day-to-day needs, and some multiple of deposits can therefore be lent out, there is always a risk of failure if many customers seek to withdraw their deposits at the same time, whether because they have lost confidence in the bank's ability to pay or need cash for some reason. Because the banks were closely linked to the local or regional economy, they were particularly susceptible to runs. Even if they were solvent if might take time to call in loans; or bad management might have led to risky and unsound investment. Both to facilitate inter-bank clearing and to put their reserves to the most profitable use, small-town banks usually had deposits with the larger city banks and, in the case of the national banks, this was an obligation. From the 1830s until the setting up of the Federal Reserve system in 1914, the banking system had operated without a central bank. There was widespread distrust of the concentration of financial power that such a bank was supposed to represent.

The impetus for the setting up of a new type of central bank was provided by the serious financial crash of 1907. The Federal Reserve Act was the product of several years work by the National Monetary Commission, culminating in a special session of Congress in the spring of 1913. It provided for a privately-controlled system of twelve regional reserve banks, topped off by a Federal Reserve Board with seven members appointed by the President. While they were, in effect, government officials, the management of the twelve Federal Reserve Banks was drawn from regional business and banking circles. The Board itself was responsible to the Federal government, while the interests of bankers, a group generally suspicious of government intervention, were expressed through the Reserve Banks.

The National banks were obliged to join the system, while state-chartered banks had the option to do so by purchasing stock in their Regional Reserve bank and by holding their reserves with it. When the system came into operation, the Federal Reserve Board assumed the functions of a central bank: it acted as a bankers' bank, was a lender of last resort and became the arbiter of the money supply. The object was that it should use its control over the supply of money and credit to even out fluctuations and prevent the recurrence of financial crises like that of 1907. How it should do this was left vague and ambiguous. It was supposed to set discount rates 'with a view to accommodating commerce and business' and to maintain sound credit conditions. That is to say, by setting the rate at which it was ready to discount bills for the commercial banks, it could raise or lower market rates generally, thus reducing or increasing the supply of credit. The Fed was thus to exercise more power than the government in the determination of overall economic policy. The fact that the state-chartered banks were not obliged to join, however, weakened the Federal system from the outset. The majority of such banks did not join because it meant conforming with more stringent capital and reserve requirements. The Fed could thus do nothing to remedy the inherent weaknesses of a fragmented banking structure.

The monetary theory on which the Federal system was based was the 'real bills' doctrine, which claimed that if banks only discounted those bills which resulted from a genuine commercial transaction there could be no over-expansion of credit. However, a steadily decreasing proportion of trade was financed with bills while, in any case, continued discounting of bills might lead to an over-expansion of credit, for example to build up stocks. Before it could acquire experience in normal conditions, the outbreak of war in Europe, followed by the entry of the United States, created new problems, notably the breakdown of the international gold standard, the flow of gold from Europe and finally the financing of the government's war requirements.

The war was followed by a speculative boom which culminated in a crash and depression in 1920–1. When put to the test, the Fed had obviously failed; it neither curbed the inflationary boom nor prevented the depression which followed. Indeed, it was accused of keeping interest rates low when they should have been raised and keeping them up for too long when signs of depression had become apparent in the latter part of 1920. Agricultural interests attacked it because of the sharp fall in prices which hit farmers.

Meanwhile the Fed had discovered a new method of controlling the credit situation that could be more effective than manipulating the discount rate. In 1923 it set up the Open Market Investment Committee, with powers to buy and sell securities, formalizing a practice which had grown up in the previous years. By buying or selling securities on the open market, the Fed could, in effect, force the banks to expand or contract credit. Equipped with this more powerful weapon the Fed was in a much stronger position to shape what today would be called macro-economic policy. One consequence of the 'discovery' of open market operations was that the 'real bills' doctrine became less important as a guide to policy.

The question now was how effectively the new weapon would be used, given that it depended upon the Board's estimation of the future course of the economy. For most of the 1920s it appeared to be mastering the new technique. It intervened to moderate a downturn in 1923–4 and again in 1926–7. Stable prices and stable monetary growth in these years seemed to show that the Fed was successful in its main aim of financial stability, without checking the prosperous upsurge of the economy. More controversial is the policy which the Fed pursued from late 1927, when it lowered discount rates and made large purchases of securities on the open market, just when the stock exchange bull market was getting under way. The object of the Board, under the influence of Benjamin Strong, Governor of the Federal Reserve Bank of New York – the most powerful figure in banking circles at this time – was to encourage a movement of gold from the United States to facilitate the return of gold to Europe and thus the restoration of the gold standard mechanism.

Meanwhile, abundant supplies of money were flowing into stock market speculation. Banks were channelling funds into the stock market and also encouraging their customers to buy securities and stocks, including those of foreign governments, which was a highly lucrative business. The Federal Reserve Bank of New York sought to bring the situation under control by raising discount rates, but the Federal Reserve Board resisted on the grounds that this might bring the prosperity to an end. The upshot was that the system did not act decisively enough to avert the Wall Street collapse in October 1929.

Until late 1927 it can be said that the underlying prosperity, with only minor recessions, gave the Fed little to do but take the credit for growth with stability. The functions it fulfilled were never clearly stated or defined in public. Its main object was sound money and financial stability, even if that meant economic slowdown, agricultural depression and unemployment. That was inevitable given the composition of the boards of the member banks: few saw the signs of impending doom in the late 1920s amid the prevailing euphoria. In any case it is not certain that the Fed would have been able to prevent the crash even had it acted more decisively.

In a strange kind of posthumous hero worship, an exception has been made for Benjamin Strong, claiming that had he lived (he died in 1928) he would have been able to dampen down the speculative fires without provoking a general economic downturn. He had warned a colleague shortly before his death of the dangers inherent in the speculative frenzy, while urging that the Fed should stand ready to manufacture liquidity in order to maintain confidence and confine the extent of the damage when it came to an end. There was much opposition to Strong within the system and there is no means of telling whether, had he lived, he would have been able to impose his policy on his colleagues or whether it would have had the desired effects. As it was, the Fed failed to rein in the stock exchange speculation or provide liquidity to soften the shock when the crash came.

CHAPTER 3

A decade of crisis: 1929–1939

By its unexpectedness, its scale and its duration, the Great Depression of the 1930s had a traumatic effect on all sections of American society. Coming as a sequel to several years of prosperity which had led business spokesmen and leading economists to forecast a new era of crisis-proof expansion, it proved to be the longest and deepest in history.

For three and a half years following the Wall Street crash, the economy continued on a downward plunge, ruining millions of small businessmen and farmers, condemning one quarter of the labour force to unemployment and almost destroying the banking system. In what Americans proudly assumed was the richest country in the world, the living standards of many unemployed workers and poor soil farmers fell to 'third world' levels. The blow to the 'American dream' was so sudden and severe that the reaction of many was one of disbelief and passivity rather than of anger. There was no sharp turn to the left by a segmented working class, no mass middle-class support for a far-right saviour – though both tendencies were later to appear.

The explanation of the Great Depression poses many problems for economists and it is not surprising that no consensus should exist. Many were, and still are, reluctant to attribute it to some organic weakness of capitalism, looking rather to extraneous circumstances, mistakes in government policy or wrong decisions by the monetary authorities.

THE GREATEST DEPRESSION

Most accounts of the Depression begin with the Wall Street crash, so that the beginning of the Depression can be exactly dated to 24

October 1929. It is unlikely that the crash would have been followed by such devastating consequences had there not been about this time the coming together of various factors making for a slump. The crash, while particularly severe, was a financial panic of a classic type familiar in the financial history of European countries as well as the United States. Its form was a rush into liquidity by those holding shares, and later, other types of paper – bonds, securities, bills of exchange – bringing prices crashing down. In the previous months share prices had been rising at an extraordinary rate, the result of excessive speculation in which large numbers of people, including many newcomers to stock-market transactions, had been participating. In such speculative manias, a time comes when confidence in the continued upward movement of stock-market prices begins to break. Some feel the urge to sell before the fall begins, or become overcommitted and have to sell to settle payments elsewhere. Once selling generates a fall there is a good chance that the movement will spread until it becomes an avalanche. Weaknesses and frauds are exposed, and it becomes virtually impossible to reverse the trend.

Behind the stock-market boom were the business expansion and high profits of the late 1920s: large-scale investment in manufacturing industry, power generation and construction of all kinds. To finance this investment there was a considerable increase in the volume of shares and loan capital traded on the market. Money seemed to be readily available to purchase new issues and to trade in existing paper. Promoters took advantage of the situation to push new holding companies, investment trusts and foreign securities, some of which were highly speculative. A wider circle of investors was attracted to Wall Street by the ease of borrowing and the lure, not so much of dividends, as of capital gains: prices seemed to be moving permanently upward. Moreover, investors could buy on margin, which meant that they put down in cash only a fraction of the value of the stock they bought, or they could borrow from the banks. As long as prices continued to rise this practice seemed to be justifiable, but it meant that the whole exercise became a speculation and investors were encouraged to over-extend themselves. The interest on the borrowed money exceeded the income which could be expected from the earnings of the assets acquired. Only the prospect of capital gains motivated those who were playing the market. They bought in order to sell again at the right moment. Prices were pushed up artificially and had no relation to the real value of the assets they represented. Speculative markets of this kind always come to grief sooner or later; perhaps the participants in the bull market of 1929 were vaguely aware of this. But no one could know when the peak had been reached; everyone hoped to get out at the right time.

Whatever finally pricked the bubble, confidence gave way in the week beginning 21 October 1929 and a wave of selling began. On Black Thursday of that week the bottom dropped out of the market. Wall Street saw its biggest trading day: panic selling drove prices down to levels which meant heavy losses, if not ruin, for many who had bought on margin or with borrowed money. In an attempt to restore confidence, businessmen and bankers issued reassuring statements, to no avail. The process of liquidation went grimly forward into the following week. In his graphic description of events, *The Great Crash 1929* (1955), J. K. Galbraith writes: 'Tuesday, 29 October, was the most devastating day in the history of the New York stock market, and it may have been the most devastating day in the history of markets.' Another huge fall in prices lopped millions of dollars off the paper wealth of many of America's richest people, and the decline continued with little abatement until mid-November, when at last prices levelled off. They rose a little in the first quarter of 1930, only to falter once again and resume another protracted decline which did not come to an end until June 1932. By that time the state of Wall Street mirrored that of the economy as a whole: America was in the icy grip of the greatest depression in its history and the heady days of the stock market boom of 1928–9 seemed an age away.

Not only America but the whole capitalist world was afflicted with the economic equivalent of the bubonic plague of the sort which had paralysed medieval Europe. Everywhere production declined precipitously. Falling prices cut farmers' incomes, and factories closed or cut down production for lack of customers. Bankruptcies rose and unemployment everywhere reached record levels. The star performers of the boom suffered badly; car sales dropped from 4,455,000 in 1929 to only 1,103,000, in 1932. This spectacular decline was repeated over a large swathe of industrial America.

The connecting links between the Wall Street crash and the subsequent depression are by no means easy to establish. In a sense it acted as a detonating force which ignited combustible material accumulated ever since the First World War. The after-effects of that war were still apparent in the shape of inter-Allied war debts and the reparations problem. Europe as a whole had been weakened by the war at the same time as the world role of the United States had been enhanced, especially as a creditor country. In several European countries, but especially in Germany and France, there had been much investment in plant and machinery during the 1920s, encouraged by an influx of

American funds. Short-term funds from the US had come to play a vital part in the financial system in Europe. The new industrial capacity was, by 1929, probably reaching the limits of the existing markets and international competition was growing.

Competition from countries which had devalued their currencies in the 1920s hit Britain, which had returned the pound to gold at pre-war parity, particularly hard. There were signs of a slowdown in France and Germany by mid-1929, before the Wall Street crash. The pressures on the British economy increased with an over-valued pound, leading on to the financial crisis of 1931 and the devaluation of sterling. European governments tended to blame the United States for what followed, but it does not mean that their economies could have continued on an upward trajectory. As it was, American funds did begin to leave Europe to participate in the Wall Street boom and were repatriated still faster when it collapsed. Meanwhile tariffs and quotas began to hit American exports to Europe and elsewhere.

If a common cause is to be sought for the downturn in production from which the major capitalist countries suffered in the 1930s, it may be found in the exhaustion of new opportunities for profitable investment of the kind which had fuelled the boom. Existing capacity could no longer be profitably employed, so there was no point in adding to it. This affected the capital goods industries most of all; they had been equipping growing industries which now ceased to grow, or even contracted. Thus there was a disproportionate contraction in the means of production industries: iron and steel, coal, engineering, shipbuilding particularly. Likewise, there was an all-round contraction in international trade and a raising of tariff barriers so that export industries and those sections of agriculture dependent upon exports were badly hit, and this was clearly the case in the United States. Increased protection (such as the Hawley-Smoot tariff of 1931) aggravated the problem by inviting reprisal measures by America's customers.

In theory, after a time the market mechanism would generate forces making for recovery. Costs would fall, such as wages and raw material prices. Inventories would fall to an abnormally low level and would have to be built up again. Plant and machinery would wear out or become obsolete so that some would have to be replaced. Interest rates would fall and excess funds would be looking for profitable employment. Businessmen would come to the conclusion that rock-bottom had been reached and begin to see the future in a more rosy light, searching out profitable fields in the new conditions. The hope that the depression would right itself in this way was general among orthodox economists and the supporters of capitalism, who commonly expressed the view that the American economy was basically sound. The worrying thing was that the self-righting mechanism did not seem to be working or was taking an inordinate time. Meanwhile, the economy continued to wind down alarmingly, with an unacceptable increase in unemployment and an enormous toll in human misery which have made the 1930s the locust years of American social history.

It was the intolerable character of the social costs, and the fear of the political upheaval which might follow, which made it inexpedient to leave market forces to work themselves out. In this situation it is difficult to see how an interventionist reaction could have been avoided. Indeed it began under the Republican administration of President Herbert Hoover, which was backed by the majority of the business community and was doctrinally in favour of free market forces.

The severity of the depression and then its prolongation tended to discredit the orthodox economic view, while the remedies it prescribed did not work or seemed to make matters worse. Of course, as interventionist policies became more positive and systematic under President Roosevelt it was possible to argue that they prolonged the depression, either because they were inept or because they undermined business confidence. Indeed this is a favourite view of conservatives in America today, who see Roosevelt's resort to state action as the beginning of all evil. Others recognized an historical tendency for mature capitalism to raise productive power in excess of the effective demand of consumers, while claiming that the gap could only be filled by government expenditure. The appearance, or at least the widespread acceptance, of such a viewpoint was itself a product of the depression, which orthodox theory had failed to anticipate, explain or propose remedies for.

Most explanations agree that the slump was a result of a fall in capital investment in plant and equipment, as well as a decline in house building and other construction. The problem is why capital investment and other outlays were reduced in this way, since once investment fell it is easy to explain how, by the fall in demand for the factors of production, there should be a cumulative downturn. Obviously, therefore, those who took decisions about investment were pessimistic about future prospects, notably the return on new capital investment. In other words, they curtailed investment because they did not think that it would yield a profit, taking the risk factor into account. Into this estimation went actual costs and anticipated profits based upon expected prices for final output. Thus the question of costs and the condition of market demand was also crucial. Moreover, if already existing capacity was more than adequate to meet actual demand, only a belief that for some reason demand would rise in the future could justify increased investment in the here and now. That elusive factor 'business confidence' comes in here; if the climate were generally pessimistic, it would reinforce the other factors tending to dampen down economic activity. Recovery would not come until, for some reason, businessmen revised their future expectations in an optimistic direction. Such states of mind were not autonomous but reflected real developments, namely the actual relationships between costs and prices, and thus anticipated profits. New investment would not be undertaken unless it was expected to yield profits. Business decisions were, of course, influenced by many factors not directly hinged to markets, such as government policy, labour relations and the international situation.

Costs included wage rates and the rate of interest on borrowed money. Some have argued that if wages could have been brought down sufficiently, the check to investment would have been short-lived. In fact, in the early stages President Hoover appealed to employers not to cut wages and further cuts would certainly have met with resistance both from organized and unorganized workers. Interest rates depended upon the policy of the Federal Reserve Board, which has been blamed for permitting excessive expansion of credit in 1929, and curtailing the supply in 1930 when it should have been pumping more money into the system. Thus the fashionable monetarist view sees monetary stringency as the reason for the severity of the depression and especially the collapse of the banking system. If such a view is accepted, then an awesome power resided with the monetary authorities and their misjudgements had far-reaching and catastrophic effects. Such an attempt to divert blame from the workings of the capitalist system and to place it on the shoulders of a few individuals in the central bank is, to say the least, simplistic.

If wages had been drastically reduced without a sharp deterioration in labour relations, the question remains as to what effect this would have had upon market demand. And even if investment had subsequently gone forward at a higher level, would that not simply have postponed the problem? Sooner or later an increased supply of goods would come onto the market without there being purchasers. In such circumstances profit rates would again be squeezed and businessmen would again revise their expectations downwards. Likewise, while it is plausible that an increase in the money supply at the right time would have reduced the immediate number of banking and business failures, and might even have raised the floor of the depression, it does not follow that it would have provided the basis for renewed prosperity. In any case, we are concerned with what did happen; with hindsight it is always possible to be wiser than contemporaries.

The failure of the Fed to act as its critics subsequently argued that it should have done added one more factor to a number of others conspiring to drag the economy down. Signs of overproduction were visible by mid-1929 in some industries. The number of new house starts had already fallen off, and that influenced the demand for consumer durables. Similar trends were also visible in Europe, where some prices had already begun to come down. The fall in share prices left many middle-class investors and speculators with debts which they could not meet, or with depleted bank balances and incomes. They had less to spend on luxury and semi-luxury goods. It was significant that much of the increase in production in the 1920s was in goods (like consumer durables) which did not have to be replaced regularly, but could be kept in use longer if income fell. Banks and financial houses now held bad debts, and the general demand for liquidity, also reflecting the decline in confidence, undermined the structure of debt built up by the boom in house construction and public utilities in the previous years.

Orders for new capital equipment fell off badly in 1930, as did sales of motor vehicles (see above) and consumer durables in general. The extent of the stock market crash had caused apprehension in government circles that a depression was on the way. It was in the autumn of 1929 that President Herbert Hoover reiterated his belief that 'the fundamental business of this country, that is production and distribution of commodities, is on a sound and prosperous basis'. The distinction between 'production' and the goings-on on Wall Street is implied. The intention was to minimize the latter and boost the confidence of the business community. Other exhortations followed, to little effect. Individuals, firms and institutions were concerned with their own survival and took decisions accordingly, often making things worse for everybody else. It was generally believed (or hoped) that the depression would be short-lived; in reality the economy was in the grip of an accelerating downward spiral. Instead of recovery being round the corner, the years 1930–2 were to reveal new horrors.

The general deflation of the Great Depression was accompanied and partly caused by the near collapse of the banking system. The existence of the Federal Reserve system, which had been counted upon to provide greater stability and a barrier against deep depression, did nothing to remove fundamental weaknesses which were exposed after the great crash. The small unit banks which made up a significant part of the banking structure were susceptible to shocks even in the best of times. There were over five thousand bank failures between 1921 and 1929 (classified as 'suspensions', so many may have subsequently re-opened); those in rural areas were especially affected by the fall in agricultural prices and thus in farm incomes. There were 1,352 suspensions in 1930, 2,294 in 1931, 1,456 in 1932 and a record 4,004 in 1933.

A high volume of indebtedness had been built up during the 1920s boom, which meant that many banks were in an exposed position when the economic situation changed. When farmers could no longer meet their mortgage payments, businessmen failed to pay off their loans, and shareholders were unable to realize their shares at prices which enabled them to meet their obligations, the banks were bound to be in trouble. As depositors got wind of this their natural reaction was to withdraw their funds but, as the figures show, all too many banks were unable to pay out because a large part of their assets were tied up in now worthless paper. There were several waves of bank failures following runs, notably in mid-1930, in the latter part of 1931 and in early 1933 just after President Franklin Delano Roosevelt took office. Millions of Americans saw their savings evaporate as banks collapsed and their other assets fell catastrophically in value. Runs on the bank and the overnight ruin of individuals and firms added to the nightmarish quality which the depression assumed in the course of 1931–2. The jobless totals rose inexorably from 1.5 million in 1929 to 4.3 million in 1930, over 8 million in 1931 and over 12 million in 1932; it was still 7.7 million in 1937.

There was no general system of unemployment assistance, only voluntary effort and local relief. Millions thus became helpless victims of the blind forces of economic disorganization. Poverty ravaged not only the city slums and ghettos but also many rural areas as well. Most farmers produced not for household needs but for sale in the market, concentrating on one or two cash crops or livestock products. Falling prices sharply reduced income available to buy food as well as other things. Consequently, even farmers' families were reduced to a near-starvation diet in many places. In some areas the plight of the farmers was made worse by soil erosion and drought. With overall farm income falling to less than half its pre-depression level, a large market for industrial products disappeared. The great industries which had led the expansion of the 1920s were now working at a fraction of their capacity and a large part of their work force had joined the army of the unemployed. Firms operating under oligopolistic conditions

Table 3.1: The economic impact of the Great Depression

	Unemployed		*GNP*		*Business Failures*	
Year	*Total (in thousands)*	*As % of civilian labour force*	*Billions (1958 prices)*	*Annual % Growth Rate*	*per 10,000 businesses*	*Bank Failures*
1929	1,550	3.2	203.6	6.7	104	659
1930	4,340	8.9	183.5	–9.8	122	1,352
1931	8,020	16.3	169.3	–7.6	133	2,294
1932	12,060	24.1	144.2	–14.7	154	1,456
1933	12,830	25.2	141.5	–1.8	100	4,004
1934	11,340	22.0	154.3	9.1	61	61
1935	10,610	20.3	169.5	9.9	62	32
1936	9,030	17.0	193.0	13.9	48	72
1937	7,700	14.3	203.2	5.3	46	83
1938	10,390	19.1	192.9	–5.0	61	80
1939	9,480	17.2	209.4	8.6	70	72
1940	8,120	14.6	227.2	8.5	63	48
1941	5,560	9.9	263.7	16.1	55	16

were, however, able to keep up prices despite falling output.

The statistics of national income, industrial output, new investment, prices and employment all show a precipitous and unprecedented decline in those years as the depression gripped the economy (Table 3.1). National income, which had been growing at the rate of 5% per annum in the period 1922–9 went down at the rate of 14.4% between 1929 and 1933; output of manufactures fell by half, and in 1933 private domestic investment was only one-eighth of what it had been in 1929. The general price level fell by 25%, while the prices of farm products were less than half what they had been in 1929, a sharp fall having begun in the following year. The fall in prices cut incomes severely and thus contributed to a further decline in demand for manufactured goods. New housing starts (outside the farm sector) had been on the slide for several years before 1929; in that year they were still over half a million, by 1933 the number was down to 93,000. Unemployment, the grimmest figure of all, rose from 3.2% of the labour force on official count for 1929 to no less than 25% in 1933; probably an underestimation of the real position and not including short-time working general in many industries.

One result of the general fall in prices and a lower cost of living was that consumption fell less than income and output. Indeed, some people might have been better off than before; but they were a minority. The general fall in income meant a disproportionate fall in the demand for house space (as housing figures show) and for durables.

HOOVER'S RESPONSE

The Republican administration headed by Herbert Hoover was very much a product of the optimistic 1920s; it now had to handle a situation as intractable as it was unforeseen. Hoover was a man of moderation; a friend of business and a believer in market forces, he did not want to see either organized business or the state become too powerful. A competent administrator, his deep belief in the virtues of capitalism conditioned his initial response to the depression. Thus the budget had to be balanced and financial orthodoxy maintained; not the state, but rather business itself, could fight the depression. The administration had to assist it by building confidence, not by intervention in the market. The essence of his policy was belief in the self-righting mechanism of free market forces.

Hoover could not be accused of inactivity in the early stages; he saw his role as boosting business morale and preventing anything which might aggravate the decline. He called on business to maintain employment and avoid wage-cutting, but he did not resist the growing protectionist reaction, especially among farmers, approving the Hawley-Smoot tariff in June 1930, against his better judgement, in the face of impending Congressional elections. The result was the opposite of that sought; retaliatory tariffs by other countries hastened the decline of American exports, aggravating the depression.

As time went on, Hoover had to authorize rescue operations which required a certain amount of state intervention and expenditure, but he doggedly resisted proposals for large-scale public works or relief for the unemployed. Veterans of the First World War who gathered in Washington to demand bonus payments in advance of the due date met with a stony reception and were finally dispersed by the military.

The near collapse of the financial system in 1931 forced the administration's hand; a National Credit Corporation was set up, enabling the stronger banks to assist those in trouble. Its resources were limited, however, and its effect was practically nil. More far-reaching was the Reconstruction Finance Corporation, set up in January 1932 to deal with the continuing problem of bank failures. This time the federal government put in money amounting to $500 million and the RFC could borrow additional funds to enable it to make loans to banks, insurance companies, and savings and loans associations (similar to British building societies) in difficulties; local and state governments were later added to the list. Other measures were taken to shore up stricken sectors of the economy on the same lines. A certain amount of financial aid was extended to agriculture through the Federal Land Banks. In July 1932 a system of Federal Home Loan Banks was set up to assist financial institutions in the mortgage business. The lending policy of the Federal Reserve Board was liberalized by the Glass-Steagall Act of February 1932. Previously, Federal Reserve notes had been backed by forty per cent gold and sixty per cent eligible paper (mostly lending to member banks) or gold. Under the new act government bonds could be used to make up the collateral, thus making it possible to enlarge the extent of the Federal Reserve Board's open market operations. Nevertheless it remained reluctant to embark upon a policy of credit expansion which might have been able to counteract the deflationary trends in the economy as a whole. Expert opinion is divided; on the whole it is looking for a scapegoat based on the assumption that there was nothing basically wrong with the economy.

In view of the scale of the disaster, these measures were little more than palliatives. The state backing which they gave to financial institutions went about as far in intervention in the market as it was possible for the administration to go consistent with the ideology of the President and his supporters. They proved to be totally inadequate and the banking and financial system continued its march to the abyss with an election looming. The pledges given by businessmen on employment and wages, when prodded by the President, soon became the victims of the inexorable logic of the balance sheet. Orders continued to fall and prices moved downwards. Prospects for profit-making became increasingly gloomy and business reacted accordingly. First, short-time working cut earnings; then more and more workers were made redundant; and finally wages were cut. When United States Steel imposed a ten per cent wage cut in October 1931, it was symbolic of what was happening throughout industry. At Ford the seven-dollar day became the four-dollar day; the economy of high wages only worked when the demand for the product was high, otherwise wages were a cost which had to be reduced just like any other. Many of the much-vaunted welfare schemes of the 'New Era' were likewise a casualty of the depression. As it deepened, so the prestige of businessmen slumped as badly as their order books. They failed to do what Hoover urged when it was inconsistent with their profit-and-loss accounts. As they sought to do what was best for their own firm, they made matters worse for all.

Voluntary effort was proving its impotence in the face of remorseless economic decline. Exhortations had been tried and failed. To protect their investments and profits businessmen had to take defensive action, regardless of the overall situation. Market forces unrestricted seemed to threaten the self-destruction of the economic system. Even Hoover was having to move away from voluntarism towards some degree of public intervention and control; but his administration moved slowly and reluctantly amid a growing clamour that something should be done to stop the rot. By the middle of 1932 belief in the self-righting forces of the market had fallen to a low ebb; pragmatic Americans were ready to try something else.

As the underpinning for the ideology of economic liberalism received more hammer blows, new concepts, or old ones taken out of the drawer, began to gain support. That most conservative part of the ideology, economic theory, began to be challenged. Some of its practitioners themselves began to take a new direction as they sought explanations for the depth and duration of depression. In short, an increasing number saw it not simply as a business cycle downturn like those of the past, but as a product of long-term factors inherent in American capitalism. Perhaps its expansion was at an end, or would have to be revived by new policies which only the state could implement. Though only a feeble minority called for socialist planning, many now believed that if capitalism was to be saved from itself it would have to look to the state, not to unchecked market forces.

ROOSEVELT AND THE NEW DEAL

The changing ideological climate reflected the spread of crisis from the economy to society as a whole. As the depression spread it left no sector of the economy standing upright and blighted the lives of masses of people who had hitherto given unquestioned obedience to the dream of American prosperity. Although the left-wing parties gained adherents and new far-right movements began to gather strength, the overwhelming majority still believed that salvation would come through the two-party system in a constitutional manner. Naturally, the incumbent administration came in for a heavy share of blame; business and its political friends were under a cloud. It was obvious that Hoover had failed to rise to the occasion; he found neither the language nor the policy to match the growing sense of national emergency. Nothing that the administration had done seemed to make the slightest impression on the sinking economy or offer any hope for the future. The sweeping victory of his Democratic Party rival, Franklin Delano Roosevelt, in the presidential election of 1932 was not therefore a great surprise.

During the campaign, and the usual war of words, it seemed that what was at issue was a choice between different styles of government rather than a clear-cut alternative between policies for overcoming the depression. Programmes and policies put forward by the rival candidates were almost interchangeable. The heavy shift in the popular vote towards the Democrats expressed dissatisfaction with Hoover and a desire for a change: it did not signify positive support for an alternative programme, which Roosevelt did not have and did not campaign for.

The unprecedented character of what had become, by the beginning of 1933, a national economic disaster nevertheless gave the election of Roosevelt a dramatic significance. The ground had been prepared for a break with the old methods and the time was ripe. If market forces had failed to bring about recovery, that automatically posed the question of what the government could do to promote it. Hoover himself had moved tentatively in that direction, but without great conviction and lacking personal charisma. In his economic ideas, such as they were, his successor was no less conservative. During the election Roosevelt too had promised government economy and a balanced budget; he sought to reassure business and win its support, especially because many of them distrusted the Democratic Party. On the other hand, besides his personal appeal, people looked to him to find a way out of the depression. Taking office at the very nadir of the depression in March 1933, he accepted the challenge and sought a new approach. Having few ideas of his own, he turned to others to provide them, new men, unknown to Washington before, university economists, bright young lawyers, publicists and reformers of various kinds. During the campaign Roosevelt had spoken of a 'New Deal'; its content had still to be worked out, what it would represent in concrete terms was unclear even to him. But it became the catchword of his presidency, and symbolized the change of course in American social and economic policy with which he was to become identified.

The New Deal was thus not a programme drawn up in advance and implemented once Roosevelt took office. It was worked out in a pragmatic way, while dealing with particular problems. It lacked a unifying theoretical basis or even any guiding principles, it suffered from contradictions and inconsistencies. The test of any particular measure was whether it did the job that it was intended to do, and in this respect it was profoundly American in its nature, as well as bearing the stamp of Roosevelt's own personality. But there was never a 'Rooseveltism' which could be distinguished, defined and copied elsewhere, like Socialism or Nazism.

The object of the New Deal was not to project an alternative to corporate capitalism of the American kind but rather to create the conditions for its survival by saving it from its own excesses, of which the Depression was the most self-destructive expression. Government intervention was to be limited by the need to uphold the basic institutions of capitalism; nationalization of key industries or central planning were never considered. Belief in private property, free enterprise and the market economy was as much part of the creed of Roosevelt as of Hoover.

As far as there was any attempt to diagnose what had gone wrong with American capitalism to plunge it into such a disastrous depression, New Dealers found the answers in the machinations of bankers, the excesses of monopoly power and the destructiveness of unchecked market forces. As much as Hoover, Roosevelt believed that the economy was basically sound, but its fate could not be left to businessmen alone; they were too apt to follow sectional and selfish interests at the expense of the public good. They had to be checked and controlled, but also encouraged. The democratically elected government was entitled to use its countervailing power to enable capitalism to function better. Its intervention was not motivated by hostility to private profit-making and there was no question of the state making inroads into private ownership. The object was not to end private profit-making but to harmonize its pursuit with the public good. Excessive profits, backed by monopoly power, led to the unequal distribution of income and thus the lack of purchasing power which had brought on the depression and led to its prolongation. So far as there was a New Deal theory of the depression, it was an under-consumptionist one and a number of its measures were designed to raise purchasing power.

It dealt rather with symptoms than with causes; it never legislated to deal with the concentration of economic power or ventured on a head-on collision with business. Even in dealing with symptoms, Roosevelt was handicapped by his adherence to financial orthodoxy, particularly his reluctance to run a budget deficit which the less conventional economists began to argue was necessary if depression was to be overcome. Even when New Deal measures began to be implemented, any increase in government expenditure was looked upon as a short-term emergency and not seen as part of a permanent cure for the instability of capitalism.

Thus, at any rate in its early years, the New Deal owed nothing to the 'deficit-spending' and 'pump-priming' remedies for depression of the sort proposed by the British economist J. M. Keynes and advocated also by American economists like Alvin Hansen. Keynes showed that a market economy does not necessarily bring about the full employment of labour and resources because of the deficiency in demand which it tends to generate. Government spending can, and should, fill the gap; by its overall regulation of demand, the state can thus bring about a higher level of employment than would result from the free operation of market forces. Hansen was the best-known advocate of these theories in the United States, urging that fiscal policy should be used to prevent depression. These ideas gradually made their way in the economics profession, achieving the status of a new orthodoxy from the 1940s until the 1970s, when they came under increasing criticism. Roosevelt was not a follower of Keynes, but the British economist did have some influence on the thinking of the New Dealers. The recession of 1937 (see below) appeared to be a confirmation of the Keynesian analysis and the policy of government deficit spending as an anti-cyclical remedy.

Immediately after his inauguration, Roosevelt had to deal with the breakdown of the banking system. His response was to declare a national bank holiday and secure the passage of an emergency banking act to prop up ailing banks with state funds. The public having been reassured by the first of his broadcast 'fireside chats', confidence in the banks came back and they were re-opened within a week. Roosevelt followed this with an economy measure: ex-servicemen's pensions and the pay of federal employees were cut. Prohibition was ended and the breweries and distilleries were back in legitimate business. Thereafter, during the rest of the first hundred days of his administration, a stream of legislation was passed, constituting the first version of the New Deal. The new economic policy was represented above all by the National Industrial Recovery Act (NIRA), the Agricultural Adjustment Act (AAA) and the Securities Act. Drawn up in haste and under pressure, they received widespread support and were taken as an indication that the administration intended to deal with the depression as a national emergency.

The set-piece of the recovery programme, hailed by the President himself as 'the most important and far-reaching legislation ever enacted by the American Congress' was the National Industrial Recovery Act of 1933. In essence an enabling act, the NIRA gave the President broad powers to deal with the economic emergency; so far as it had a precedent it was to be found in the controls administered by the War Industries Board set up to manage the economy during the First World War. As in war-time, it sought to build a broad national consensus by offering something to a wide variety of interests and currents of opinion. In part it was a spending programme aimed directly at what seemed the source of the depression by financing public works, to be paid for with new taxes rather than deficit spending. In part it was a programme of industrial self-government, backed by the state, to enable business to make its own contribution to overcoming what were supposed to be causes of the depression.

Particular trades and industries were granted powers to draw up and enforce codes of practice aimed at promoting co-operative action, eliminating 'unfair' practices and reducing unemployment. It attempted to enlist the support of the working class by providing for maximum hours of work and minimum wages; the famous clause 7a recognized the trade union having the support of the majority of workers in an enterprise as their rightful bargaining agent. Although not easy to enforce where employers were hostile, it was the basis for the big breakthrough of trade union organization in the large-scale manufacturing industries as recovery began. The position of the trade unions was reinforced by the Wagner Act of May 1935 (not supported by Roosevelt himself), officially called the National Labour Relations Act. Not sponsored by the administration until it had passed Congress, it was a response to pressure from organized labour and its friends. It had an enduring effect in linking the new unions of mass-production workers organized in the young and more militant Congress of Industrial Organizations (CIO) to the Democratic Party in a new political alliance. It meant the virtual end of company unionism and gave workers a clear right to organize. The union which enjoyed the support of the majority of workers was to be the legal bargaining agent, certified as such by the National Labour Relations Board, the agency set up to administer the Act. In practice the Wagner Act helped to canalize labour militancy into orderly channels of negotiation by strengthening the hands of the central leadership, generally more moderate than the shop floor.

Other provisions were aimed at stopping destructive wage and price cutting, gave the President powers to control imports, prescribe the necessary rules and regulations and give collective bargaining agreements the force of law. The business-labour-state partnership envisaged in the NIRA justifies it being described as a form of corporatism. In that respect it was something new in American experience.

Despite widespread support to begin with, as its contradictions became obvious it began to be criticized from all sides, and most vigorously by business.

The National Recovery Administration (NRA), with its blue eagle emblem, was the agency set up to administer the recovery programme. Its first task was to supervise the drawing up of codes by representatives of the various industries and trades covered by NIRA. In practice, this generally meant that the larger firms exerted disproportionate influence in shaping the codes. The anti-trust laws were waived to enable minimum prices and agreed regulations governing marketing practices to be formulated and enforced by the bodies representing the firms in each industry. Smaller firms complained that their interests were being neglected and efforts were made subsequently to take this into account. Observance of the clauses favouring labour was often little more than nominal. Consumers, too, had little say; although their spokesmen were placated by the setting up of a Consumers' Advisory Board, it did not have much influence on the codes. The NRA codes operated to restrict competition and keep up prices; in the more organized industries they resulted in officially-sponsored cartels. The theory was that higher prices would raise the rate of profit and encourage business revival. The NRA was criticized by many small businessmen, who thought that the codes favoured their bigger rivals.

Even New Dealers mistrusted the power granted to business and feared the growth of monopoly power backed by the state. While many sections of business at first showed enthusiasm towards the NRA recovery programme, they became increasingly critical of the growing bureaucracy needed to administer it and disliked the labour provisions. Business hostility to the New Deal and to Roosevelt himself was to grow. While the codes were enforceable, in some cases the price schedules were difficult to apply, especially where there were many small firms. In some respects NRA was more of a showpiece than a real factor in recovery.

Although the economy began to climb out of the trough of depression in 1934–5, it was difficult to claim that NRA had made a significant contribution. Enthusiasm for NRA soon evaporated. For the left and labour it seemed like a business racket, a step towards a corporate order, smacking of fascism. For an increasing number of businessmen any advantages they may have gained seemed to be overshadowed by the fear of bureaucratic intervention. Beseiged by many conflicting interests, lacking a definite objective or a guiding ideology NRA failed to project a clear and consistent policy. It did not constitute an economic revolution or a middle way between capitalism and socialism. Big business used it at the beginning to consolidate its position and welcomed the waiving of the anti-trust laws, but opposed any kind of economic planning or state intervention which would have limited its freedom of action. As a partnership between business and government it proved to be a failure and the attempt to extend it to labour met with strong opposition from most members of the business community. In short, the American environment proved to be inhospitable for corporate experiments.

Within a year of its birth NRA was already practically at stalemate despite the adoption of codes by over 500 trades and industries. Difficulties of enforcement and of interpretation, continuing conflict over its objectives and growing criticism from many directions had made it a political liability. Finally, a test case concerning a firm of poultry dealers named A. L. A. Schechter Poultry Corporation was taken to the Supreme Court. The firm was accused of violating the codes for the poultry industry, including the sale of diseased birds. The judiciary decided that the code-making power conferred by the NIRA was unconstitutional. This meant that all the codes became unenforceable as a matter of law; the Schecter decision of the Supreme Court thus put an end to the experiment and placed a question mark over the rest of the New Deal.

What the NIRA was supposed to do for industry, the Agricultural Adjustment Act (AAA) aimed to do for farmers by raising prices and purchasing power. By 1932 farm product prices were below half of the 1929 level and total cash receipts had fallen to not much more than forty per cent of their pre-depression level. In many areas farmers faced disaster. Given the competitive nature of primary product markets there was little prospect of raising prices except through state action using plenary powers. Farmers would not voluntarily limit production unless they could be sure that all other producers of the same commodity would do likewise. There was always the problem that some producers might be tempted to break a voluntary agreement by trying to raise income by selling below the agreed price. To deal with such problems the Act of 1933 set up an Agricultural Adjustment Administration to organize production control schemes for the major commodities. Producers agreed to limit production in return for cash payments from the government; the necessary funds were to be found from a levy on processors, which would, of course, be passed on to consumers. Emergency programmes, such as the slaughter of pigs and the ploughing in of cotton, were launched in 1933 to get rid of unsaleable surpluses which bore down upon market prices, causing something of a public outcry.

As time went on such schemes became more difficult to operate. They were criticized because they involved the destruction of products which millions of people were unable to afford to buy, as well as for not doing enough to raise farm incomes. Total cash receipts of farmers did begin to rise slowly but did not reach the 1929 level until 1941. Thus the AAA did not have spectacular success though it may have prevented a worse disaster for the farm population.

Other New Deal measures were taken to deal with farm debts and stem the tide of foreclosures, notably through the Farm Credit Administration and the Federal Farm Mortgage Corporation. The processing tax levied to finance the crop restriction schemes was declared unconstitutional by the Supreme Court in January 1936 but this did not bring the activities of the AAA to an end. A new means was found of controlling production and continuing to subsidize farmers through the Soil Conservation and Domestic Allotment Act. Crucial here was the problem of soil erosion dramatized by the dust bowls and droughts of 1932–4. The new Act offered farmers cash payments for not sowing soil-depleting crops and for leaving land idle or cultivating soil-enriching crops. In addition, payments might be made to farmers who made use of soil-conserving methods aimed to combat soil erosion. While the soil-improvement features of the Act were widely approved, it was clear that it was mainly a device to enable government to continue to restrict agricultural output and to subsidize farmers.

Although the New Deal programmes went some way towards alleviating the immediate problems of the depression by helping to raise prices and farm incomes, they did not tackle the long-term problems of American agriculture. Rather did they inaugurate a new period, not yet at an end, in which the agrarian sector was to be dependent upon state support. Henceforth, state agencies helped to determine the quantity of the major crops which would be produced, which land should be cultivated and how and what the income of farmers would be. To a significant extent, and for an indefinite period, American agriculture was to be shielded from the full operation of market forces. Backed by the widespread belief in the special virtues of rural life and the farm people who lived it, the agriculturalist received a specially favoured position, although he probably did not see it that way. In any case, as time went on, the main beneficiaries of New Deal farm policy were the larger farmers. As they had the most land they received the biggest payments for land left uncultivated or turned over to soil-conserving crops. They gained more from the effect of crop reduction and price supports than the smaller farmers. When a second Agricultural Adjustment Act was passed in February 1938 the control provisions were retained. The main innovation was the 'ever normal granary' intended to maintain stocks at a given level from year to year. In fact, such was the productivity of American agriculture with the new techniques that it employed that surpluses continued to mount in the late 1930s despite the compulsory marketing quotas under the Act.

The Second World War came along in time to rescue agriculture from another excruciating problem of overproduction. It had been found, between the two prosperous wartime periods, that the social costs of allowing market forces to operate unchecked in the agricultural sector were too heavy and dangerous (as well as being politically inexpedient) to be acceptable. American capitalism had to pay the price in an over-sized agriculture with a permanent problem of surpluses, dependent upon government support, in which the larger and more efficient units were increasingly favoured, but retaining a large number of smaller, high-cost producers who were only slowly to be squeezed out in the following decades.

Some of the emergency measures taken in 1933 to shore up the financial and banking system were to become permanent. In May 1933 the controversial Securities Act was passed, followed a year later by the setting up of the Securities and Exchange Commission, aimed at preventing the kind of stock market speculation which had led to the crash of 1929. Provision was made for the regulation of stock-market dealings, the prevention of unfair practices, the control of credit available for stock-market transactions and greater publicity for the protection of investors. Bitterly contested at the time as unwarranted interference by a section of the financial community, the Securities and Exchange Commission soon became part of the accepted institutional structure of American capitalism.

Equally pressing, in 1933, was some means of restoring and regulating the banking system which was literally falling apart when Roosevelt took office. The Banking Act passed in June of that year was an emergency measure to restore banks' liquidity and solvency and thus the confidence of their depositors. In the longer run it did so by increasing the powers of the Federal Reserve Board to supervise and control the operations of the private commercial banks, whose activities were to be separated from those of investment banks. An insurance system administered by the Federal Deposit Insurance

Corporation was set up in 1935 to guarantee repayment of bank deposits up to a given maximum per customer in order to prevent the recurrence of the kind of panic and collapse which had brought the banking system into disrepute in 1933. Despite the rather hostile reception accorded to it by the bankers, it became clear that this kind of intervention was necessary to establish stability in the banking system and in stock-market dealing. It was a case of saving the stock market and the banks from their own excesses, and the measures were strictly conservative in intent and efficacious in practice.

When the Depression struck, the United States lacked the kind of social security system which had existed for some time in most advanced industrial countries. There was no national system of old-age pensions, very little public provision of any kind for the unemployed and the destitute, and what there was came from local or state sources on poor relief lines. The massive growth in unemployment revealed the inadequacy of existing provisions; moreover, local and state revenues fell off at the same time. Roosevelt disliked 'dole' as much as did Hoover. The attempt was made, therefore, to link income relief with the provision of work and to deal with unemployment on an emergency basis with the hope that, before long, private industry would create more jobs.

The Federal Emergency Relief Act of May 1933 provided Federal funds, while calling on local and state governments to take the initiative in works projects. Part of the funds went into direct relief, part went to new bodies set up to organize public works schemes, notably the Civil Works Administration (CWA) and the Works Progress Administration (WPA). The CWA launched a variety of socially useful projects and employed, at its peak, some 4.3 million people; it was succeeded in the spring of 1934 by the Emergency Work Relief Program and then by the WPA. These make-work schemes in effect disguised unemployment, but had the merit of giving many of the unemployed the sense of doing something useful. Since the usual public works projects required mostly unskilled manual labour, while the unemployed included people with a variety of specialized skills and training, the WPA sponsored a wide range of schemes employing writers, artists, actors and other professional people. Partly inspired by the idea that outdoor life was healthy and morally uplifting, many of the younger unemployed were mobilized by the Civilian Conservation Corps (CCC) into work in forests and national parks.

The New Deal period marked an historic watershed in the development of American capitalism. While Roosevelt was not a great innovator, he was ready to experiment; his pragmatic approach, however, was bounded by his basic confidence in the institutions of capitalism. He never sanctioned a move towards central planning and the measures he promoted were supportive of private ownership and the business system. His object was to save capitalism, not to supersede it. He accepted that emergency measures, breaking with national tradition, were necessary if the fabric of American society was not to be ripped apart by the economic crisis. Although he was an experienced and wily politician, Roosevelt's knowledge of economics was scanty and in the formulation of policy he depended upon the advice and counsel of those who could win his ear, drawn from the motley crew of New Dealers who gathered in Washington in 1933.

Sharing the popular suspicion of financiers, Roosevelt nevertheless sought to win the support of businessmen, a majority of whom were traditionally Republican supporters. Although in confronting the emergency there was little alternative but for the state to take the initiative, he wanted to see business itself work out the details of policy, as under the NRA codes, and sought the agreement of farmers to the restrictionist policies of the AAA. Most of the New Deal policies were based upon ideas already canvassed and in that sense were not really novel. Just as the limits of Roosevelt's pragmatism were set by the need to uphold the property relations of capitalism, so it was necessary to try to win over, or conciliate, disparate and conflicting social forces: bankers and farmers, creditors and debtors, employers and workers. The concessions which had to be made to labour, to the farmers and to the populist moods of sections of the population; the inevitable extension of the powers of the Federal government; new financial measures and restrictions imposed upon business, all contributed to business distrust of the New Deal. The President's sallies into populist rhetoric dismayed Wall Street and nervous investors.

Essentially, however, the New Deal was intended to bolster up capitalism, not to weaken it, to put state policy at its service, not to oppose it. There was nothing in it to which business could not adapt. Undoubtedly, in the 1930s, business was under a cloud. It had lost the self-confident air of the previous decade and was sensitive to the critics who made it responsible for the Depression. Businessmen also regarded with suspicion the emergence of a rival power centre in the Washington bureaucracy and its potential for extending bureaucratic intervention and control. Business advocates claimed, and continue to claim, that recovery would have come in any case after the Depression had hit its low point in 1933 and that the contribution of the New Deal was negligible, or, by undermining business confidence, negative. This is to take a narrowly economic view and to overlook the morale-building effect of the New Deal on wide sections of the population, some of whom might otherwise have looked for more radical, anti-business solutions to what was a crisis of American society as a whole.

The New Deal was in the first instance a counter-cyclical policy; it sought to deal with the urgent problems created by the economic blizzard: mass unemployment, rural distress and urban poverty. It went on to attempt, through legislation, to make the economy proof against a repetition of depression on that scale. This meant that the state was called upon to play a more positive role, supplementing and moderating market forces but not superseding them. It also began to elaborate the rudiments of a social policy designed to deal with the individuals and families who were casualties of the market system: the unemployed, the destitute, the sick and the aged.

The Democratic administration continued to move away from *laissez-faire* policies already begun tentatively under Hoover. The New Deal was not qualitatively different: it left industry in private hands, reinforced rather than broke up the power of the big corporations and, while its advocates often claimed that lack of purchasing power was a causative factor in the depression, it did nothing to redistribute income. It sought, after all, to facilitate recovery through the revival of profitability, while interfering as little as possible with the basic institutions of American capitalism: private ownership of the means of production, and the free market. For Roosevelt and his supporters, at any rate in the early years of the New Deal, the desirability of government economy and a balanced budget was axiomatic. The New Deal at this stage was not a Keynesian type, deficit-spending programme.

A large part of the business community, especially the smaller entrepreneurs, bitterly opposed Roosevelt and maintained their support for the Republican Party (and some supported far right movements). This seems paradoxical in the light of what has been said: if the New Deal set out to save capitalism, why did it not gain the wholehearted support of the capitalists? Of course, the business community was not monolithic, and some sections of corporate management welcomed parts of the NRA programme which regulated competition and virtually legalized cartels. That did not make them political supporters of the Democratic Party or admirers of Roosevelt himself. Business as a whole resented the regulation of hours and wages and the recognition of trade union rights, which seemed to threaten management's prerogatives. If business confidence was slow to return after 1933 there were other factors, besides the New Deal, which can be held to be responsible:

Table 3.2: Index of manufacturing production 1929–1940

	(1947–49 = 100)
1929	58
1930	48
1931	39
1932	30
1933	36
1934	39
1935	46
1936	55
1937	60
1938	46
1939	57
1940	66

(*Historical Statistics of the United States*, 1960)

the international financial crisis, protectionism abroad, the policy of the Federal Reserve Board and the simple fact that market demand was slow to pick up.

Slow and partial recovery was the story after 1933. Sales of passenger cars steadily rose, but with just under four million in 1937 they were still half a million below the 1929 peak. By 1932 steel output was down to 13.68 million tons compared with the 1929 peak of over 56 million tons; it then rose steadily up to 1937 when it was up to 50.56 millions tons, slumping to 28.34 million tons in the following year. The index of manufacturing production brings out the overall trend shown in Table 3.2. Unemployment, after reaching a high point of almost twenty-five per cent of the labour force in 1933, began to fall, as shown in Table 3.3. These figures show the gradual nature of the recovery and underline the fact that the depression had not been overcome before the next war in Europe began to have its effects on the American economy. The year-to-year growth rates of the recovery period, however, were high, continuing from 1934 until the spring of 1937. Industrial production by then, had risen above its 1929 level but over seven million remained unemployed (on the year's average).

Roosevelt had been re-elected in 1936 for a second term, but, although there was no sign that he intended to extend the sphere of the state at the expense of the private sector, businessmen remained hostile. A sharp reminder that the depression was not over was provided by the recession of 1937–8. Industrial production fell by one-third and unemployment topped nineteen per cent again in 1938 (yearly average).

Table 3.3: Unemployment, 1934–1940

1934	11.3 million	21.7 per cent of labour force
1935	10.6	20.1
1936	9.0	16.9
1937	7.7	14.3
1938	10.4	19.0
1939	9.4	17.2
1940	8.1	14.6

The renewed down-turn suggested that the New Deal policies had not got to the root of the trouble. Keynesians, and their American cousins such as Alvin Hansen, thought that the responsibility for the recession lay with the fiscal policies of the Federal government. Contrary to some assumptions, deficit spending was no part of the New Deal; the deficits that did appear were inadvertent, and spending was heavily cut in 1937. Taking local and state budgets together with that of the Federal government there was a small overall surplus during the year. At the same time, the Federal Reserve Board also pursued a restrictionist policy by raising member banks' reserve requirements. According to the Keynesians, deflationary budget policy and credit restriction amply accounted for the recession. When spending rose again in 1938, during the spring a revival began; 'pump-priming' appeared to have succeeded. Before it could be seen whether such a policy could be efficacious in the long run, as well as being acceptable to business and public opinion, the war in Europe began to exert its influence. The prospect for long-term recovery would have depended upon the willingness of corporate enterprise to borrow and invest on a much larger scale than they had done up until 1937.

Although the primary aim of the New Deal was to deal with the catastrophic situation brought about by the depression, it initiated an important structural change in the American economy. It did this by endowing the state with a permanently enhanced role and initiating the so-called 'mixed economy'; an inaccurate term in so far as the nationalization of industry was not an issue. What it meant was that the state, or its agencies, aimed to correct malfunctions in the market mechanism (right-wing critics would say that it impeded its proper functioning). At the same time, public spending greatly increased and provided a lever for influencing the level of economic activity. Federal spending doubled between 1929 and 1939 as a proportion of Gross National Product. Increased public spending also required an expansion of the functions performed by local and state governments. This theme will be taken up later; for the present it provides one of the keys to the understanding of the long-term historical significance of the New Deal.

Towards the end of 1939, the business magazine *Fortune* organized a 'round table' of seventeen businessmen, politicians and economists to consider the question: 'How Can the U.S. Achieve Full Employment?' It reflected anxiety about the continuance of depressive trends in the economy. The participants, though disagreeing on some matters, agreed that 'government expenditure should make provision for the unemployed even if this involves deficit financing, and should meet other generally accepted social needs'. This was a marked change from the commonly accepted pre-depression views of such people. They placed considerable stress upon removing 'deterrents' to production and investment erected by business, labour, agriculture and 'by certain government policies'. Failure to do so, they thought, 'will be to provoke sooner or later a crisis in our national life even more serious than that following 1929'.

> Conceivably this country can continue indefinitely in its present state of stagnation – a condition under which 10,000,000 remain unemployed, the budget continues to be out of balance, and the national income remains below the pre depression figures. But every patriotic American must look with concern upon such a gloomy possibility. For this means that a large proportion of American youth will be doomed to a life robbed of opportunity and that a large minority of people must subsist on an emergency standard of living. If such conditions long continue, some demagogue not yet on the horizon may organize a movement of the underprivileged to overturn our present system on the ground that it has betrayed the chief justification for democracy, namely equality of opportunity.

Although concluding with an expression of faith that if business showed the initiative and fortitude of 'our forefathers', and individuals and groups subordinated their special interests to the public good, unemployment and other social problems could be overcome, the deliberations of this 'round table' reflected an underlying anxiety typical of the times. The depression had not gone away; it had not been overcome; and that in itself contained serious dangers for the political and social order, the threat of 'a movement of the underprivileged'.

THE DEPRESSION: A SUMMING UP

At a theoretical level, the Great Depression posed new questions about the future of American capitalism, a debate which still goes on and has been given renewed topicality by the end of the post-war boom and the series of shocks it has experienced since 1971. Orthodox supporters of capitalism gloss over the problems and see its depth and duration as indicating that it was no more than a sharp cyclical down-turn aggravated by mistaken monetary or fiscal policies. They echo contemporary critics who blamed the New Deal medicine for the failure of the patient to recover earlier and more fully.

A new school of economists, influenced by Keynes or thinking along the same lines, suggested that the old expansionist forces had run out of steam and that a new era of permanently reduced investment opportunities had begun. They saw the depression as indicating fundamental flaws in capitalism which could only be overcome through the fiscal policy of the Federal government. Basically under-consumptionist, they saw that dependence upon market forces alone would not ensure that outlays on consumption and investment together would be sufficient to ensure continued growth at 'full employment' levels. It was thus the task of government to fill the gap by deficit spending adjusted to the current state of the business cycle. This type of economic management would involve a more systematic interventionist policy than anything conceived of under the New Deal. While it was not ruled out that some new stimulus to profitable investment might appear, in the shape of another round of technological innovation or a growth in population, without them the prevailing trend would be towards stagnation.

In fact, as will be seen, the Second World War and the new world role of the United States after 1945 opened the way for the operation of new forces of expansion, appearing to overcome whatever had caused the Great Depression. In the long view, however, these new forces were only of limited duration and partial efficacy, and within thirty years at the most the underlying contradictions which had manifested themselves in the 1930s once more broke surface. The basic problems had not been dealt with, while the techniques of Keynesian-type economic management had produced cumulatively some additional, equally intractable problems, notably inflation, monetary instability and an ominously growing public debt.

The collapse of the investment boom of the 1920s meant that the industries producing means of production, like iron and steel and heavy engineering suffered a heavy fall in demand. Gross investment (which includes cost of maintaining existing plant and machinery as well as new investment) which peaked in 1926 and remained at a high level until 1929 had fallen almost to zero by 1933, indicating that during the trough of the Depression there was net disinvestment. After reaching high levels in the 1920s, GNP fell from 1930 to 1933, in 1931–2 by as much as 14.7 per cent. High rates of business failure were reported, while bank failures reached a record total of over 4,000 in 1933. Corporate profits had reached a high of $9,990 million in 1929. Not only did profits fall to about one-third of that figure in 1930, but became negative in 1931 and 1932 (Table 3.4). The 1929 figure was not exceeded until 1940. Prices, wages, production, profits and employment embarked upon what was to appear as a remorseless downward trend. On the other hand, people had to eat. Total consumption expenditure in real terms was relatively well maintained by drawing on savings, going into debt, depending on relief and cutting back on other forms of expenditure. Hence people employed in the consumption goods sector suffered less from the Depression than workers in the capital goods industries and construction. Also, the deflation meant that prices of food and other essentials went down. Those who kept their jobs and whose wages and salaries were maintained could actually have lived better in the 1930s than before. None the less, for the majority, the Depression, even if it did not mean real hardship destroyed for the time being that typically American expectation of a continuous rise in incomes and living standards, the basis of 'the American Dream'.

Table 3.4: Fall of corporate profits during the Depression

1924	$9,990	millions (not exceeded until 1940)
1930	3,697	
1931	–372	
1932	–2,309	
1933	956	
1934	2,346	
1925	3,590	
1936	6,340	

The Great Depression was a traumatic experience for all classes of Americans. It revealed the essential instability of the institutions of capitalism and left the haunting fear that something like it could occur again. While economists favourable to capitalism have argued, with varying degrees of confidence, that it could not, Marxist and other critics have implied that a repetition in some form was possible, if not inevitable. Even sixty years after the great Wall Street crash the trauma has not disappeared. After the crash on 17 October 1987, the events of 1929 were instantly recalled, raising the question of whether it would be the prelude to another depression. As it happened, history did not repeat itself; action taken by the Fed to boost the supply of money and credit appears to have provided a counteracting force. With similar policies activated by the other major countries a depression, or even a recession, was avoided, but at the price of further inflationary pressures. The question of whether a repetition of the Great Depression is possible still remains open.

CHAPTER 4

The economic impact of the Second World War

The Second World War did what the New Deal had failed to do: it geared the economy to maximum production and brought about full employment. For the United States, direct involvement in the war began with the Japanese attack on Pearl Harbour on 7 December 1941, and ended with the surrender of Japan in August 1945. Its own territory was immune from attack, and battle casualties, at 291,557 (with 113,842 deaths from other causes in the armed forces), were modest compared with those of other belligerents. Apart from those killed, injured (670,846) or bereaved – that is, for the majority of Americans – the war was not a bad experience, especially when compared with the depressed 1930s.

The excess capacity and unused resources were such that, despite the voracious demands of the military, the goods and services available for the civilian population also grew. Not only did unemployment disappear, strengthening the bargaining power of wage-earners, but, with many families having more than one wage-earner, the money available for consumption or savings grew substantially. Although there were still many low-paid jobs, many workers now had the opportunity to move up the wage scale, especially if they possessed scarce skills. True, money would not always buy what the recipients wanted. Some goods such as new cars and consumer durables, were no longer available; others were rationed or disappeared into the black market. All the same, people had money in their pockets, held growing cash balances in banks or bought government bonds, thus building up a pent-up purchasing power, potentially inflationary, which would be released on to the market after the war.

The war was thus a period of prosperity; in particular it meant an abundance of jobs and of money compared with the depression years. Not only was unemployment absorbed, but despite the call up of over 10 million men, the civilian labour force increased from 56.1 million in 1940 to a war-time maximum of 66.3 million in 1944. This resulted from the entry of women, retired people and school and college drop-outs into the labour force in large numbers. Huge labour armies were assembled in what had been remote places to work in newly-built war plants near Omaha, Tulsa or Morganton and Institute in West Virginia. Vast army camps sprang up in formerly quiet rural areas, especially in the South. Military bases, naval ports and airfields expanded or were newly created in many parts of the country. Much new industry went to the West coast and parts of the South.

Farmers now found that their surpluses disappeared; they could sell all that they could produce, at remunerative prices. Many Blacks left the rural South, attracted by the job prospects in the war plants of Northern cities. Many of them had to accept the lowest-paid jobs; segregation and discrimination continued, in the armed forces as in civilian life. Although there was still poverty and the war made little difference to the distribution of income, large numbers of Americans were better off than they had ever been. Paradoxically, for them the war meant jobs, spending power and better living standards; a new version of the American dream.

At the same time the war was good business. With contracts pouring in, the great corporations worked at full blast to satisfy the insatiable needs of the war machine. Smaller firms, though not without complaining that they were not getting a big enough share of the pie, benefited as sub-contractors or from the expansion of civilian purchasing power. War turned out to be a profitable affair; corporate

Table 4.1: The labour market in wartime

	Unemployment (% of work force)	*Armed Forces (in millions)*	*Civilian Labour Force (in millions)*
1939	17.2	.3	55.6
1940	14.6	.5	56.1
1941	9.9	1.8	57.7
1942	4.7	3.9	60.3
1943	1.9	9.0	64.9
1944	1.2	11.5	66.3
1945	1.9	12.1	66.2

The average number of hours worked in manufacturing industry rose from 38 in 1940 to 48 in 1944.
(Historical Statistics of the United States)

business, like the population at large, accumulated liquid assets on an unprecedented scale.

Nevertheless, the experience of the depression had left deep scars. Even while appreciating the economic benefits of war-time, people were asking the question: will there be a return to depression after the war? This feeling of insecurity was manifest in business circles, too. In the early stages of rearmament, before the United States was involved in the shooting war, some firms had been reluctant to commit themselves too far to war production; by 1943, they were beginning to worry about the cessation of war orders and about how they could reconvert to normal production and recover their markets. There was, indeed, a fairly general conviction, shared by economic experts as well as ordinary folk, that the end of the war would lead, perhaps after a short boom, to a return of unemployment and slump.

One apparent lesson of the war, many felt, was that government spending on a sufficient scale could eliminate unemployment and create prosperity. Keynesian prescriptions and analysis, which had already begun to gain ground as a result of the 1937–8 recession, won new adherents; it was becoming the 'new economics'. On the other hand, experience with war-time controls did not necessarily mean that business had become reconciled to state intervention; rather the reverse. Business wanted to return as far as possible to a free market system, if not in its pristine nineteenth-century form, at least freer than it had been under the New Deal. In any case, by the late 1930s little remained of the original New Deal measures and the New-Dealers were scattered or in disarray.

Meanwhile the huge outpouring of military hardware of which American industry was capable, its ability to meet the most ambitious targets, greatly enhanced, or restored, the prestige of business. In the organization of the war economy the main features of corporate capitalism were retained, despite the inevitable apparatus of control needed to allocate resources and secure the appropriate product-mix required by the war machine. It was significant that, unlike in Europe, there was no widespread demand for the nationalization of industry either during or after the war.

THE WAR MACHINE

During the war, of course, the demands of the armed forces had priority. In the peace-time economy the armed forces had made little demand upon industry or the Federal budget. The military hierarchy was strictly professional, with little or no political influence. Of the armed forces, only the navy was of world class and Roosevelt gave it priority (out of romantic attachment as well as because of the danger from Japan). The role of air power was only beginning to be appreciated in the 1930s and the United States itself did not seem to be vulnerable to the bomber of pre-1939 vintage. The army, a professional force of volunteers, was of modest size for a country as large as the United States, hardly adequate to do more than defend American interests in the Western Hemisphere. Isolationism still had a powerful hold, especially in the mid-West. It was based upon opposition to involvement in foreign quarrels that might put American lives at risk. War was thought by many to be bad for business. Public opinion was generally confident that, through naval power, 'fortress America' was immune to foreign attack and should do nothing to provoke one. The corollary of this outlook was that the war industries were small in the inter-war period, reflecting the modest size of military contracts, often more for prototypes than for long runs of a standard product.

By the late 1930s, however, Roosevelt's policy began to change as the war dangers increased, both from Nazi Germany and from Japan. As the arms build-up abroad continued, neutrality might remain desirable, but preparedness was prudent. The outbreak of war in Europe in 1939 and the overrunning of France in May 1940 underlined the point. Before long industry felt the pull of war orders from Britain and France and the administration, still cautiously, began to lay the foundations of a war economy.

Although the stance of neutrality was at first maintained, only three weeks after the outbreak of war Roosevelt persuaded Congress to permit the United States to supply arms to the belligerent countries on a cash-and-carry basis. That is to say, purchases had to be paid for at the time of delivery and carried in their own ships; a one-sided arrangement designed to favour Britain and France. Meanwhile the American defence budget, which had only accounted for 12.2% of Federal spending in 1939, went up to 16.5% in 1940, leaping to 45.7% in 1941. Thus, well before the Japanese attack on Pearl Harbour (base of the Pacific fleet on Hawaii) in December 1941 rearmament had begun on a considerable scale. From barely a third of a million men under arms in 1939, that number exceeded 1.8 million in 1941. A noticeable acceleration of military spending and recruitment had followed the fall of France. Besides stepping up expenditure on the 'two-ocean navy', Roosevelt called for an annual production target of 50,000 war planes.

As well as an increase in the number of combat troops, provision was made for a reserve army of 800,000 men.

During 1940–1 foreign (i.e. British after the fall of France in June 1940) war orders, as well as the Federal government's own big contracts began to stimulate industry. Existing plants were nowhere near able to produce at the level that the government was now projecting. The government thus had to take the lead in financing and constructing new plants able to turn out war material on an unprecedented scale. New shipyards had to be built, too, for the enlarged navy, and the aircraft industry had to be expanded at a dizzy rate. Many of the new plants and shipyards had to be built away from established industrial centres where space was available; in such cases a whole new infrastructure, including housing, had to be provided, requiring further government expenditure.

With the defeat of France, the German occupation of most of Europe, as well as growing tension with Japan in the Pacific zone, opinion in the United States began to veer towards possible American involvement. Roosevelt took a major step in that direction with the passage of the Lend-Lease Act of 11 March 1941. While making it possible to supply 'any country whose defence the President deems vital to the defence of the United States', the main aim was to supply Britain with arms, food and raw materials to carry on the war against Germany. This represented a growing feeling that the United States could not afford to see Nazi Germany become the permanent master of Europe and a world power as well, which would have been the consequence of the defeat of Britain. Lend-Lease meant that supplies necessary for Britain to carry on the war would be purchased by the US government and sold, leased or given to Britain, or any other beneficiary. It was a step on the road to involvement in the shooting war. Expenditure on Lend-Lease supplies was to mount steeply, but was soon dwarfed by the rising scale of America's own war preparations.

The sharp increase in the export of goods to Britain under the Lend-Lease Act, together with the growing scale of war orders from the Federal government, fuelled a boom. Unemployment began to fall, though slowly at first. By 1940 it was down to 8.1 million (yearly average) from 10.39 million in 1938; in 1941 it had fallen to 5.56 million, still far short of full employment. Nevertheless, more people had jobs and the economy was moving again. The car industry was now booming and although it was the most suitable mass-production industry for turning over to war production, showed no hurry to do so. It was selling more of its new models, now in fresh colours, and many equipped with the increasingly popular automatic transmission.

Government-built plants were now being completed and opened for war production, run, not by government officials, but by the big corporations. They were coming on-stream in 1941, even before the massive conversion of existing plants to war production which began only after Pearl Harbour. In the interim period, civilian and war industries were competing for scarce supplies, skilled labour, machines and machine tools, driving up prices. The administration would soon have to accept the logic of total war: namely that an apparatus of controls and directives, centrally organized, would be necessary to allocate scarce supplies, giving top priority to the needs of the war effort and determining the relative priorities of other needs. The conditions of an armaments-generated boom were different from those created by a boom dependent upon business investment and consumer spending. Beginning in 1940, armaments began to play a permanently larger role in the output of American industry. Government demand for war material had an imperative nature backed by reasons of state. It could not be left to compete in the market and bid against civilian demand, forcing up prices and raising costs. The state therefore had to intervene in such a way as to give its demands priority, on grounds of national security; it had finally to create a mechanism, other than market forces, for the allocation of scarce resources. As its demand was additional to those otherwise existing, it would tend to push prices upwards; thus price controls also became necessary. Inevitably, once the war economy had become established, civilian demand would have to be directly curtailed by further interventionist measures. Moreover, the goods acquired by the government for the armed forces would not re-enter the productive cycle, either as investment goods raising future output, or as consumer goods to be bought with the incomes created. In addition, as more men were drafted, their needs, as well as those of their dependents, had to be paid for by the government. A whole 'unproductive' sector was brought into existence which was not responsive to the needs of the market but whose output was designed for destruction. At the same time, it was not separated from those sectors in which the laws of the market continued to operate, but was connected with them by many links.

Economic management in the years of the New Deal had never contemplated centralized agencies for the allocation of resources or intervention in the market on the scale required by the war economy. Opposition to the relatively mild interventionist measures of the New Deal had been powerful on the part of business, fearful as it was that more and more economic decisions would be made by bureaucrats intent on increasing their own power at the expense of private enterprise. The argument that state intervention and controls were necessary in the national interest in war-time was difficult to resist. The question was not so much whether the government should intervene, but what the limits of its intervention should be, and how much compulsion or coercion it could legitimately use. In any case the extension of government intervention and control, although it was to require the creation of a large new bureaucracy, especially in Washington, was to be staffed, at the highest levels, largely by business executives seconded by the corporations, conservative lawyers and orthodox academics. These 'dollar-a-year men' (receiving a salary from their employers, the dollar symbolised their status of government employees) were not fearsome radicals of the New Deal type, allegedly hostile to business. Their outlook and background were identical with those of the executives who remained with their firms, which were now subject to the controls they established. In that way, businessmen controlled other businessmen. Likewise, the temporary bureaucrats found a similar identity of interest with the military procurement officers with whom they worked. What was later to be described as 'the military-industrial complex' began to take shape in the 1940s, under war conditions.

Roosevelt seemed reluctant to create a strong central body to run the war economy which might rival his own authority. Consequently, the tendency was to set up a special agency whenever a new problem arose, or to appoint 'czars' with wide powers to sort out a particular difficulty. After Pearl Harbour, Roosevelt was granted virtually dictatorial powers. Then, to deal with economic mobilization as a whole, he set up the War Production Board in January 1942, headed by Donald Nelson, head of the Sears, Roebuck mail order and retailing giant. In and around this body, as well as the other agencies set up to handle particular aspects of the war economy, a struggle of interests took place. Besides the big corporations, with their men in Washington, organized labour, small business and liberal planners all sought to influence, or win control over, war-time economic policies. In the end, however, victory went to the military and their corporate allies; and it was really this alliance which determined the outcome. Strategic needs, reflected in the procurement policies of the armed services, asserted priority.

Interested above all in the rapid fulfilment of contracts, the military favoured granting them to the big corporations which had the plant and the surplus capacity and were accustomed to large-scale manufacturing. With automobile and consumer durable industries brought to a stop from February 1942, this meant that the master contracts went to the corporate giants in these industries – General Motors, Ford, Chrysler. It remained to allocate raw materials and labour on a priority system, keeping essential production for the home front going at the same time. By concentrating civilian production in a few designated plants, additional capacity was released for military needs.

Military procurement officers and the dollar-a-year executives in the bureaucracy thus saw eye to eye. Two-thirds of the military contracts granted during the war went to a hundred companies: nearly half were won by a mere thirty-six of the corporate giants. Chrysler built tanks, A.C. Spark Plugs manufactured machine-guns and Ford turned out more bombers than the air force could use. Although there were some newcomers, such as Henry Kaiser in shipbuilding or Reynolds in aluminium, perhaps inevitably, the dominant firms secured the lion's share of the war contracts. At best, small firms could hope to win sub-contracts. Those employing less than 100 workers obtained only 3.5% of such contracts; those with less than 500 workers only 12.6%. The big new plants custom-built by the government, such as the famous Willow Row near Detroit, were run by the big corporations, in this case Ford. As additional encouragement, costs of expanding and re-equipping existing plants for war production were underwritten by the government. War contracts were paid for on generous cost-plus terms, meaning guaranteed profits; capital outlays could be amortized for tax purposes over five years. Although an excess profits tax was levied, it would be recoverable if a firm made losses after the war. For the corporations, this eliminated all risk from war contracts and ensured high and steady profits throughout the war period. Anti-trust laws were waived to permit inter-firm co-operation, and existing suits for infringement were ended. The big corporations thus did exceedingly well out of the war, extending their capacity at government expense and accumulating liquid assets which could be turned into productive capital after the war was over.

An essential feature of the American war effort, then, was that the big corporations were permitted, even encouraged, to make money out of the process. They came out on top in the endemic conflict of interests which went on behind the front of national unity. That is not to say that the actual shaping of the war economy was not determined by strategic needs as perceived by the service chiefs; in that sense, the corporation played a subordinate role. Nevertheless, the inevitable physical controls and priority directives were designed to enable the corporations to serve the war effort on the best possible terms. Corporate business accepted controls when they meant full order books and a high rate of profit, with the government financing capital expenditure and taking the risks.

The great conversion of industry to war production took place in the course of 1942. Temporary unemployment appeared as the great car factories were re-tooled and re-organized to make tanks and planes. The newly-built government plants also began to come on full stream. In the next two years phenomenal increases in output took place as American industry turned over to what it could do best: churning out a vast quantity of standardized, manufactured goods. Indeed the most impressive aspect of the American war machine was its sheer capacity to produce. Targets which seemed over-ambitious, like Roosevelt's call for 50,000 planes per year, were to be surpassed with ease.

The movement from prototypes to mass production brought problems in its wake. Quality might be sacrificed to a rapid increase in output; early products were not of advanced design or a match for the enemy's weapons. Fighters sent to the Pacific were not capable of dealing with the Japanese Zeros and those sent to Europe were no match for the German Messerschmitts. The Catalina flying boat was not adequate for the patrol duties to which it was assigned in the Pacific zone. American tanks were out-gunned by Rommel's armour after the landings in North Africa in November 1942.

Even worse, there were a number of scandals where contractors supplied defective or even dangerous material. Aero-engines manufactured by the Curtiss-Wright Corporation, holder of the second largest war contract, proved to be unsafe, causing planes fitted with them to crash. There was proof that tests had been falsified, records destroyed, and inspection skimped. On testing, twenty-five per cent of the engines supplied by one plant turned out to be defective. Another leading corporation, Anaconda Wire and Cable, supplied defective cable and communications wiring to the forces from a plant owned by the government. In July 1943, a newly-delivered freighter broke its back and sank off the West coast. It was found that the hull had been made of sub-standard steel supplied by the giant United States Steel Corporation. These were among notable cases publicized by a Senate enquiry in 1943.

With the Japanese invasion of South East Asia, the principal supply of natural rubber from Malaysia was cut off. It was vital, therefore, to increase the output of synthetic rubber. One of the many international cartel agreements entered into by US firms before the war, however, was that by which Standard Oil agreed not to embark upon the large-scale manufacture of synthetic rubber, by agreement with the

German combine I.G. Farben, holder of the main patent. When this became known, Standard Oil was fined a nominal $50,000, the government took over the German patents and constructed fifty-one synthetic rubber plants, to be run by the existing rubber manufacturers.

The economic problem in war-time was one of maximizing production of the appropriate assortment of goods to feed the war machine and provide for the essential needs of the civilian market. It was no longer, as in the 1930s, to deal with over-production. This reversal created new problems, both of deciding upon the strategic priorities, a matter for the service chiefs, and of allocating scarce goods to the civilian sector while maintaining morale. Means had to be found, therefore, of seeing that those goods which could be spared when war needs had been met were fairly distributed.

The first step in this direction came with the setting up of the War Resources Board in November 1939, on the recommendation of the military. Roosevelt soon regretted the step and the Board was to have little effective power. With no acute scarcities and plenty of excess capacity as well as surplus labour, it was premature. Subsequent practice, reflecting the President's influence, saw the setting up, as the war proceeded, of a multiplicity of authorities with over-lapping powers. Thus some scarce commodities had to be rationed and price controls were introduced to prevent rationing by the purse. Price controls were administered by the Office of Price Administration set up early in 1942. A series of scarce commodities, such as petrol, coffee and sugar, were rationed. Rationing conflicted with the American myth of abundance and with belief in market forces. Not surprisingly, therefore, a black market sprang up as speculators saw the chance to make a fast buck. Nevertheless, backed by war patriotism, the broad intentions of the rationing programme and price stabilization policy were achieved.

Despite a big increase in money income, in the money supply and in the liquidity of the population, prices remained remarkably stable from 1942 until the end of the war. Wholesale prices went from 78.6 in 1940 to 105.8 in 1945 (1926 = 100), but when farm products are excluded the rise was more modest, from 83.0 to 99.7. The overall consumer price index went from 59.9 to 76.9 (1947–9 = 100). The post-war rise was to be much steeper.

Even before American entry into the war, the principle of conscription to the armed forces was adopted in the Selective Service Act of 1940. On 16 October 1940, 16.5 million men between twenty-one and thirty-six were registered. Under the Act, not more than 900,000 men in any one year could be called up for service in the armed forces; a limitation that ended with America's entry. Throughout the war, however, labour and wealth escaped conscription.

THE LABOUR MOVEMENT 1939–1945

The labour surplus of the depression, which survived into the early 1940s, had disappeared by 1943 when the unemployment rate was 1.9%, compared with 14.6% in 1940. For skilled workers, such as tool- and die-makers or turret-lathe operators, a chronic scarcity had appeared much earlier. At the same time, not only were fit men mobilized for service in the armed forces until, by 1945, over 12 million men were under arms, but also the labour force had increased well above its peace-time level and stood at 52.8 million in that year, compared with 47.5 million in 1940 (both figures exclude the unemployed). These figures do not bring out the recomposition of the working class which took place during the war years. A large proportion of male workers of military age disappeared from the civilian labour force. The increase in total employed came from new additions to the labour force. While experienced and older workers not called up could move into better-paid and more responsible supervisory and skilled jobs, a huge army of raw recruits poured into the labour force. They came from the worst-off rural areas and the share-cropping South, as well as from the urban unemployed. Many retired people returned to paid work. Drop-outs from school or college joined the labour force prematurely, seeing it, perhaps, as a patriotic duty. Women made up the largest labour reserve and, by 1944, the proportion of women in the labour force had gone up by thirty per cent. Some five million women were employed in war industries, usually doing work formerly done by men. Although 36.3% of American women participated in the war-time labour force, making up one-third of that force at the height of the war, the figure was not as significant as Britain's, where over 70% participated. Most of them, like the legendary heroine of the film 'Rosie the Rivetter', quickly returned to domestic life after the war. Blacks moved into better-paid jobs and formed a substantial part of the manual labour force in some areas, though not without racial tensions (there were race riots, notably in Detroit in 1943).

Overall labour scarcity considerably improved workers' bargaining power; the war thus saw a growth in the importance of the trade unions, especially those in mass-production industries affiliated to the Congress of Industrial Organizations. After Pearl Harbour, both the CIO and the AFL leaders agreed to give full support to the war effort, including a no-strike pledge. By that time, following the German attack on the Soviet Union in June 1941, the Communist Party, members of which held important positions in some unions, had adopted a super-patriotic attitude after having strongly opposed entry into the European war in its early stages. The main exception to the policy of full support for the war by union leaders came from the President of the United Mineworkers, John L. Lewis. In 1940 Lewis had switched allegiance from Roosevelt to the Republicans; in October 1942 he pulled his union out of the CIO, and remained a truculent opponent of the government's war-time labour policy.

Rivalry between the CIO and the AFL continued. While the CIO had become the mainstay of the Democratic Party in the major industrial cities, strongly backed Roosevelt, and was in full support of the war effort, the more conservative AFL doggedly upheld the trade union rights of the skilled craft workers, even in war-time. During the rearmament period, state mediation of industrial disputes had been introduced through a body known as the National Defense Mediation Board. After Pearl Harbour a more powerful body was set up, the National War Labor Board, a twelve-member body of employer, labour and government representatives. The object was to settle labour disputes by discussion instead of strikes and to enforce the Board's decisions by law. It became, in fact, a means for imposing government wages policy on the unions. It adjudicated 14,000 disputes during its three years of existence; it strengthened the hand of the trade union bureaucracies and reduced the autonomy of the locals.

The most notable act of the NWLB was to work out a formula to take into account the rise in the cost of living, which was causing widespread dissatisfaction among workers and was a potential source of strike action in support of wage demands. Applied first of all to the steel industry, and known as the Little Steel formula, it allowed for a fifteen per cent wage rise based on the cost-of-living increase from 1 January 1941 to May 1942. This provided a yardstick for settling wage demands in other industries.

It was followed by another decision of considerable importance for the unions. Many new workers in the war plants had no tradition of trade unionism, and with wage increases limited by the Little Steel formula and the no-strike pledge, it had become difficult for the union officials to collect dues. As a reward for union support for the war, the NWLB worked out what was known as the 'maintenance of membership' formula. Workers entering a plant for the first time, or becoming subject to a newly negotiated contract, were given fifteen days to leave the union. If they did not do so, they were considered to be members and union dues were deducted from their pay packets by the management for the duration of the contract. This ensured the growth of union membership under war-time conditions and meant secure, rising incomes for the unions. They could now embark on recruitment drives in the war plants and were amply provided with funds.

During the war, membership of the CIO almost doubled; total union membership, by the end of the war, embraced about one-third of the labour force. Many of the new dues-paying members, however, with no tradition of organization, took little interest in union matters. Militancy was frowned upon by the union leaders, who were able to consolidate their power, within certain limits, and played an essential role in gearing the working class to war demands. Unlike in Britain, union leaders were not accepted into government and their political influence was small. Calls by well-known union leaders, such as Walter Reuther of the United Automobile Workers, for greater worker participation in industry and for more 'equality of sacrifice', went unheeded by the administration. Union hopes that as a reward for their part in the war effort, war-time planning would continue and lay the basis for a post-war reshaping of society on social-democratic lines proved to be illusory.

Meanwhile, from late 1942 the government pressed for the adoption of incentive pay schemes, and the elimination of the customary time-and-a-half pay for Saturday and overtime working with double time on Sundays. While the CIO leaders accepted these proposals and put them through the unions, they met with opposition from the traditionally-minded AFL. Members of the UAW (the CIO affiliated auto-workers' union) also opposed it. At the Buffalo plant of Curtiss-Wright, a majority of the workers voted to leave the CIO and to join the AFL union of machinists which had refused to give up premium pay. In September 1942, the issue was dealt with by a presidential order banning premium pay for overtime work on Saturdays and Sundays, but granting it when work went on for seven consecutive days. This followed strong pressure from the UAW. The question continued to rankle with union members and was finally resolved by a series of rulings made by the National War Labor Board. By appealing to the state, the CIO weakened its hand in collective bargaining and became involved 'in an ever more complicated bureaucratic tangle', as one labour historian writes (see

Nelson Lichtenstein, *Labor's War at Home*, on which this section is based).

Labour discontent mounted during the later years of the war and there were numerous strikes, in defiance of the no-strike pledge made by trade union leaders. John L. Lewis led the miners into a head-on collision with the government in 1943–4 and claimed a substantial wage-increase. One outcome was the passage of the War Labor Disputes Act (known as Smith-Connally), intended to prevent strikes which might disrupt the war effort by imposing a thirty-day 'cooling off' period, followed by a secret ballot on strike action. The Act passed over Roosevelt's veto, based on the fear that it would provoke further labour dissatisfaction. It indicated the growing strength of the anti-union backlash in Congress.

THE COST OF THE WAR

War production continued to climb rapidly, reaching its peak in the course of 1943 in preparation for the final battles in which industrial might was to prove decisive. Industrial production rose to 268, taking the 1939 average as 100; this was achieved partly through additions to the labour force, partly from higher productivity. Spectacular advances were made in particular branches of industry, notably in shipbuilding (both naval vessels and cargo ships, like the famous 'Liberty' ships built in record time) and plane-making. The results of the gearing-up to war of the most powerful industry in the world were seen on the beaches of Normandy, and in the naval battles and landings in the Pacific war zone.

At its peak, the war commanded about forty per cent of GNP. To pay for this enormous outlay the federal government had to find new sources of revenue. Roosevelt wanted to cover as much as possible of war costs from taxation; but there was a limit to how much could be raised in that way and it produced only forty-six per cent. Various indirect taxes were raised as the war went on, and by the Revenue Act of 1942 practically all income-receivers were brought into the income-tax net by a withholding (pay-as-you-earn) system. Thus the state was able to claw back part of the increased money incomes resulting from war-time activity. The withholding system was to become the foundation stone upon which the permanently higher government expenditure of the post-war period was to be based. Excess profits taxes and corporate taxes were also increased but, as pointed out, the corporations were treated gently. The Revenue Act of 1944 brought Roosevelt into collision with Congress, which passed a more lenient measure than he had called for over his veto. Although income taxes generally took less than twenty per cent of the average taxpayer's income, they raised forty-three per cent of the federal government's tax revenue by 1945.

The rest of the cost of the war was met by borrowing. By the end of the war the national debt had risen five-fold, to over $250,000 million. Part of this was held by banks and financial institutions, part by the public in the shape of securities and war bonds. Borrowing from the banking system was, to all intents and purposes, the creation of fresh money at the disposal of the government. Bond sales to the public, at least in part, represented the mopping up of purchasing power which might otherwise have had inflationary consequences. A great deal of ballyhoo went into the regular drives to sell war bonds, to convince the purchaser that it was a patriotic duty. Some twenty-five million wage and salary earners agreed to have payment for bonds deducted from their pay-packets. Bond holdings represented a great deal of pent-up purchasing power, held in check by war-time controls and the lack of goods consumers wanted. For the institutional investor, government bonds were a sound long-term investment, providing security and liquidity. The liabilities of the government were held by the bondholders whose interest payments represented a transfer payment from the pockets of the taxpayers, often the same people. The inflated national debt proved not to be so frightening after all, particularly in view of the growth in GNP (which doubled in current prices between 1940 and 1945) and the inflation which reduced its real value.

In the course of 1943, too, the apparatus of war-time controls reached its final form. Conflicts of interest within the directing agencies continued unabated and a number of new bodies was set up. In an effort to overcome the resulting difficulties, Roosevelt created, in May 1943, the Office of War Mobilization with wide powers to resolve disputes between the military and the civilian agencies. Headed by James Byrnes, a former Senator and Supreme Court judge, it possessed adjudicating powers which made it the final authority over the allocation of resources among competing uses.

As minds began to turn towards what would happen when the war was won, the War Production Board became the theatre for a major struggle over the pace of reconversion to peace-time production. Throughout the war, in Washington and in business circles, there was concern about what would happen to industry when government expenditure dropped back to normal: would there be a quick return to depression and unemployment? There was a strong case for preparing for orderly demobilization and staged reconversion. Nelson of the War Production Board took the view that civilian production should be spliced in as military demands on industrial capacity were scaled down. Projects to this effect were put forward in mid-1943, when Nelson was already in disagreement with the military over the whole question of procurement. The military feared that resuming civilian production too early would have an adverse effect upon arms supplies. Firms would become anxious to re-organize their production lines to take advantage of civilian demand. The big corporations, heavily involved in major war contracts, supported the military; small business and organized labour were favourable to an early start being made in the re-conversion process. In the end the military secured the President's backing, on the grounds that until the invasion of Europe had succeeded it would be too risky to resume peace-time production. After D-Day (6 June 1944), Nelson presented a worked out re-conversion programme and resigned when it was rejected. His successor, Julius Klug, while personally more acceptable to the military, also took the view that the WPB should plan ahead for a smooth transition to civilian production. As the war dragged on into 1945, however, the re-conversion issue was postponed until after the defeat of Nazi Germany. Then the services acted and began rapidly to cancel their contracts. By the summer of that year various controls and most rationing schemes (which, unlike the British rationing of essential foods and clothing covered only some items in short supply) had been ended. The movement out of war jobs took place rapidly; many people left the labour force altogether, especially women and older workers. The abrupt cancellation of contracts meant that some factories had to scale down production or close entirely; anticipating a consumer boom, the corporations began hastily to re-tool and prepare their production lines to meet it.

DEMOBILIZATION AND RECONSTRUCTION

The running down of government demand was soon to be compensated for as the purchasing power built up in the years of war scarcity began to be unleashed. Businesses had the liquid funds to finance the switch to peace-time production while consumers, deprived of so many of the attributes of the American way of life, spent readily on new cars, refrigerators, washing machines and other items as soon as they became available again.

Meanwhile the armed forces shed over ten million men between the VE and VJ days (1945) and the end of 1947. These demobilized ex-servicemen had spending power from gratuities or accumulated pay, and were entitled to various financial benefits, such as government grants to set up small businesses or to pursue further education. The advent of new families created a demand for new houses; there was a construction boom and an expansion of the service trades. The average American now had twice as much money income as in 1939, and every incentive to spend it. Families, often with two or more bread-winners, had money to spare. Although unemployment rose in 1946–7, it did not reach the level of the 1930s, as many had feared; instead it remained under four per cent, a modest figure considering the scale and rapidity of demobilization and re-conversion.

The general consensus is that the mighty power of American industry ensured the Allied victory in the Second World War. Friend and foe alike were impressed with the material equipment of the American forces. During the war, not only was the excess capacity left over from the Depression mopped up, but there was a considerable extension of the industrial base. While some parts were of little use in peace-time, others could more or less rapidly be brought into civilian use. Particularly important was the growth of the aircraft industry, which enabled the United States to play the leading role in the development of civil air transport after the war and to extend it still further in the jet age. Not only was there a large domestic market to be tapped, but also American planes were bought by foreign companies. Great new plants had been built to turn out war-planes, largely at government expense, in areas such as Seattle and Southern California. While some plants in aircraft and other industries became superfluous, many were sold off on favourable terms to the corporations which had been running them. Government surpluses, including machinery and vehicles, were also disposed of at low prices.

Big business had done well out of the war and it intended to do as well, if not better, out of the peace. It welcomed rapid de-control and demobilization, hoping to cash in on the consumer boom. Thanks to lucrative war contracts, low taxation and government hand-outs in the shape of low-priced plant and equipment, it was poised to recapture the home market and to expand its sales abroad. Part of war-time demand had come, via Lend-Lease financed by the federal government, from America's allies in Europe. The ending of this agreement in August 1945 put those countries in a difficult position and placed a question mark over America's foreign trade. The American market remained highly protected, so that even if these countries could produce goods so soon after the war, to exchange for machines and supplies urgently needed for reconstruction, they would have difficulty in getting past the tariff barrier. Already a creditor before the war, the United States was now virtually the only source from which funds could come to finance the reconstruction of the war-stricken countries. Both France and Britain had to obtain loans from the United States as soon as Lend-Lease ended. The proceeds of these loans ran out more quickly than had been expected, so that by 1947 there was danger of economic collapse in Western Europe, creating the conditions for social discontent or even revolution. By this time the Cold War had begun, dividing the world into two blocs behind the principal protagonists, the United States and the Soviet Union. A new and ominous factor had entered the international scene.

Meanwhile, despite the growth in consumer demand, the threat of over-capacity seemed to be looming for war-bloated American industry; agriculture once again faced the problem of unsold surpluses. The Economic Recovery Programme, generally known as the Marshall Plan, provided a ready response to domestic American as well as international problems created by the war and its sequel, economic disorganization in Europe and the threat, as it was perceived, from the Soviet Union. The United States was to become permanently involved in Europe in a way which could hardly have been foreseen before the war. It began, with Marshall Aid, in ensuring the recovery of the Western European countries.

The redundancies which followed the ending of military contracts in the summer of 1945, a feeling of insecurity about the future job situation and the fact that real wages were being eroded as overtime disappeared and prices rose, created the conditions for a wave of strikes. More days were lost in 1946 than in any year since 1919; it was to be the peak of labour militancy for some time. Although the labour leaders formally rescinded the no-strike pledge in August 1945, they found themselves embarrassed by such militancy. Co-operation with the government in the NWLB had fostered the belief that an era of industrial peace was opening, and that organized labour would have a higher status than before as a reward. The Communist Party, and trade unionists influenced by it, supported the view that three-power unity in the international arena would have its parallel in continued class peace in industry (on such grounds the CPUSA was dissolved and reconstituted as the Communist Political Association). The thinking of the reformist leaders ran on similar lines, especially in the CIO, greatly influenced by Reuther, while John L. Lewis and many AFL officials wanted an early return to collective bargaining. Detroit was the stormy centre of the early post-war strike wave which developed spontaneously in the turmoil created by re-conversion.

These strikes were at first strongly opposed by Walter Reuther of the United Automobile Workers, the main union involved. Sensing the atmosphere, however, he called a strike against the General Motors giant, aimed at establishing the principle of a thirty per cent wage increase without any rise in the price of cars. The GM strike lasted from November 1945 until March 1946. Reuther aimed to put pressure on the administration, now headed by Harry Truman, to accept the union case, while keeping working-class discontent in check. The UAW firmly opposed the spread of the strike to other car-makers in order to intensify the pressure on GM to get its production lines moving again by accepting the union's demands. Reuther aimed at, and succeeded in, keeping control of the movement out of the hands of the rank and file. It ended with a negotiated settlement which placed the whole emphasis on wages on the same lines as the agreements made with other car-makers without strike action. In return, the UAW agreed to oppose wild-cat strikes, implicitly accepting management's right to manage (and thus restricting shop-floor rights) in return for the wage increase plus some fringe benefits and a dues check-off by the firm. In fact, the model for such agreements had been set earlier by the settlement between the United Steelworkers' Union and US Steel in February 1946. Here the unions agreed, and the Office of Price Administration accepted, that a wage increase should be linked to a rise in the price of steel for which the company had fought. Truman extended this principle to other industries which were strike-bound or facing wage demands. The decision in the steel industry thus represented a breach in the price control policy, now become untenable. By 1946 the OPA had ceased to function; firms now felt free to put up their prices, allegedly to meet higher labour costs. The floodgates were open and prices began to take off as they had never done during the war; by 1948 wholesale prices were double their 1940 level. The inflation soon absorbed the wage gains made by the militant strike wave of 1946. The unions began to slip back into a bureaucratic torpor. Meanwhile, the anti-union backlash, sharpened by the anti-Communist witch hunt, culminated, in 1947, in the passage of the Taft-Hartley Act limiting union power (see below). Labour had lost the war at home.

THE WAR ECONOMY AND THE DEVELOPMENT OF AMERICAN CAPITALISM

The scale of the economic effort of the Second World War, the changes it wrought in the United States and the country's role in the world economy, mean that it cannot be treated as a temporary interruption of a normal process. It represented a permanent change which can be seen in many fields. Most obviously the war brought the depression to an end in a way in which the programmes of the New Deal had been unable to do. It inaugurated a long period of expansion, and allayed fears of secular stagnation expressed by leading economists in the 1930s. But the major and essential feature of the post-war epoch was the enhanced role of the state (that is federal, state and local governments) as an employer and as a spender. The United States had become a 'mixed economy' and the overcoming of the stagnationist tendencies depended upon the maintenance of state spending at a high level.

War-time controls quickly disappeared: there was no longer need for rationing, price controls or a manpower policy. The market took over; war-time allocation procedures did not grow into anything like a planning system. Nationalization was not an issue, as it was in European countries where there were strong Socialist or Communist parties. Nevertheless a distinct shift had taken place in the relationship between the state and the market system. The public authorities were now drawn into a supportive role and accepted responsibilities in the social field requiring large financial outlays.

At the same time, the war-time experience basically confirmed the structure of the American economy as it had taken shape in the earlier part of the twentieth century. The big corporations retained their dominant position in the strategic centres of the economy. After the doldrums of the 1930s, the war had been a positive stimulus and they emerged strengthened from the experience. They could claim that it was the phenomenal capacity and productivity of American industry which had made victory possible. The status of businessmen, many of whom now had experience in government, had been basically restored and with it went a growth in their self-confidence. No longer entirely hostile to government intervention, they saw it as a back-up for the private sector but resisted, as before, any extension of state intervention which seemed to conflict with the interests of the corporations.

The effect of the war on organized labour was more ambiguous. Ostensibly it had grown considerably in scale and had gained greater recognition from government and business as a valid interest to be consulted. Its effective power could not match that of the corporations and the apparent strength of the union bureaucracy rested upon insecure foundations. The great era of the unionization of the mass-production industries had passed. The CIO leaders of the post-war years now resembled their AFL counterparts. They had become respectable business agents, bargaining on behalf of their members, most of whom simply paid dues, mainly concerned with higher wages and greater job security. They no longer represented a challenge to management in any real sense. With the purge of the Communists they became fervent supporters of the Cold War and of US foreign policy as a whole. The outcome of the post-war strike movement was that industrial discipline was restored and, with the Taft-Hartley Act (1947) the rights of the unions were severely curtailed.

On the international stage, the United States now had to shoulder the burdens associated with being the leading capitalist power faced with a dangerous competitor for world influence. This meant, among other things, that it had to accept the financial responsibility for preventing the collapse of West European capitalism in the post-war years. The United States was now an economic and military *superpower*: this meant a correspondingly enhanced role for the military, now in possession of weapons with unlimited destructive potential as shown by the use of the atomic bomb to end the war with Japan in August 1945. The maintenance of military strength to back the new world role demanded the continuous technological development of weaponry and a powerful industrial base provided by the great corporations. With the onset of the Cold War, the military-industrial complex came into its own as a peace-time fixture.

Alongside the enormous industrial power of the United States went some alarming signs of vulnerability. This was shown, for example, in the crisis which developed over synthetic rubber during the war. A similar problem was posed by magnesium and other metals needed for the production of machines and weapons of war. It was clear, too, that America had a vital interest in opening up and controlling supplementary and alternative sources of petroleum for strategic and commercial reasons (the giants in the oil business were almost all

American). Thus there was now a more compelling expansionary thrust to ensure supplies of vital raw materials and energy sources and to deny them to an enemy, and consequently enhanced interest in developing and controlling mineral production in Latin America. The United States became a contender for influence in the oil-rich Middle East and in the colonies and semi-colonies of its war-time allies.

Likewise, to keep the great industrial machine working it was necessary to expand world trade and to remove restrictions and impediments imposed by other nations. The big corporations were thus more concerned than before with opening up foreign markets and ensuring the flow of raw materials needed from abroad. At the same time, the limitations of the home market meant that the scope for profitable investment was also limited, just when capital was available in considerable amounts. Thus the pursuit of profits drove the corporations into finding new outlets by establishing branch plants abroad, benefiting from cheaper raw materials and labour, and in closer proximity to the consuming market. Before long American capitalism was spreading out into new as well as long-established fields of influence and investment: an empire without frontiers, or, more strictly, one bounded by the frontiers of the Soviet Union and its allies (including, from 1949 mainland China).

Not only had the American economy grown absolutely during the war, but at its end the relative international preponderance of the United States reached its apogee. The United States had not suffered destruction or loss of life on its own territory. Civilian society had experienced inconveniences of a relatively modest kind. The war period was one of unexampled prosperity, with higher living standards for the majority of the population. Of the more than 12 million mobilized into the armed forces the official death toll was 405,399; the figure, large enough in itself, pales into insignificance compared with the casualties of the Soviet Union, China and Germany. In the case of the latter, battle deaths alone amounted to 3.5 million. While other countries were exhausted by the war, their industries ruined and countryside devastated, with shortages of every kind, a huge backlog of investment and a mammoth task of reconstruction, the United States was richer and more powerful than ever before.

CHAPTER 5

The post-war economy: the 1950s boom

The Second World War opened a new phase in the history of American capitalism, launching it on a long-term expansion which encountered no major setback until the late 1960s. The factors which now propelled it were different from those responsible for the 1920s boom and it did not end in a crash or a slump of the 1930s type. History did not simply repeat itself, as many people at the time expected. There was no post-war slump and the feared return of the depression did not happen. On the contrary, as early as the mid-1950s, and certainly during the early 1960s, there was a confident feeling that the expansionist trend would continue indefinitely with only the mild and short-lived recessions experienced up to that time since 1945. The business cycle seemed to have been brought under control and the stagnationist hypothesis demolished. But these views were premature. American capitalism had by no means overcome its problems; but they were the problems of a new age and a different world from that of the 1920s.

To understand why there was no return to depression or stagnation it is necessary to look at the changes wrought by the war, both in the domestic situation and in the relationship between the American economy and the world market. Corporate business had waxed fat on war conditions; it had built up capacity while making high profits. It was able greatly to reduce its debt burden; it was now more liquid and vastly more self-confident than it had been in the 1930s. It had the means and the technology to turn out goods on an immense scale for the civilian market as it had been doing for the war machine. Favouring the investment of liquid funds in new plant and machinery was the fact that civilian investment had been curbed by the war, following on years of low, or negative, investment during the Depression. Although clearly these factors do not account for the long-term expansion of the 1950s and 1960s they certainly inaugurated the post-war boom.

As a result of the war, the industrial capacity of the other major industrial countries had been partly destroyed; they had fallen behind in technology and in investment, lacked the means to pay for indispensable materials and plant, and thus could not immediately restore pre-war levels of production. The world was crying out for the manufactured goods which only the United States could supply, as well as for food and primary products. The problem was that even the advanced countries which needed goods from the United States could not afford to buy them. Moreover, there was a worldwide food shortage, whereas American agriculture had available surpluses. The hunger for American products was translated into a general scarcity of dollars.

On the domestic front there was the enormous task of demobilizing the armed forces and reconverting industrial capacity to peace-time production. Although there was some immediate dislocation as war-time plants were closed, re-tooled or re-equipped, and unemployment shot up in the areas affected, it proved to be relatively short-lived. Many people, especially women and pensioners, who had entered the labour force during the war now left it. Individuals and families had built up liquidity during the war, which aided re-adjustment and also enabled them to appear in the market as purchasers as soon as consumer goods, especially durables, became available in normal quantities again. Likewise, demobilized servicemen had gratuities and qualified for loans, mortgages and further education at government expense. Pent-up purchasing power in the hands of consumers, coupled with the money paid out in the demobilization process, as well as the liquid funds and credit available to business, helped fuel demand in the early post-war years.

Although military spending came down from its bloated war-time level it did not fall back to the peace-time norm even at its lowest point, in 1948, and it soon began to climb again under the pressure of the Cold War and the shooting war in Korea, which began in June 1950.

Price controls lasted until July 1946; with their removal, the barriers to inflation crumbled away and prices rose more rapidly than they had done during the war. Before the end of the year the consumer price index had gone up from 133.3% in June to 153.3% (1947–9 = 100). By 1951 the annual average for wholesale prices stood at 103.1% compared with 78.7% in 1946 (1947–9 = 100).

One result of the increase in prices was growing labour militancy. The close of 1945 and the early part of 1946 saw bitterly fought strikes at General Motors and in the steel industry. Although wage increases were won, they were soon swallowed up in the price increases which followed de-control. Other sections of workers joined the strike movement in 1946, with little success in increasing real wages. One significant result was an anti-labour backlash, which prepared the ground for the Taft-Hartley Act curbing the rights of the trade unions passed in the following year.

THE ROLE OF THE STATE AFTER 1945

Post-war America was still deeply influenced by the traumatic experience of the depression and the fear that it would return. During the war, Keynesian thinking had made some headway among economists and more generally among opinion-formers and some policy-makers. Its main implication was that state spending could avert or alleviate recessions and that fiscal policy, including budget deficits, should be used to keep the economy on a stable course. Hostility to the kind of state intervention required by such a counter-cyclical policy remained strong both in the Democratic and the Republican Parties and was bound up with the traditional fear of government spending and Federal budget deficits.

There was, however, a growing recognition that the state would have to play a more positive role, especially through the prevention of unemployment on the scale of the 1930s. Backed by the New Deal coalition, or what remained of it, a bill to this effect was introduced into Congress in January 1945. It met with stiff opposition and turned into a watered-down version of the original. In what became the Employment Act of 1946, all reference to 'full employment' had been excised and the fear that such a measure would give the government unlimited powers to spend was assuaged. As finally passed, the Act was vague and full of qualifying phrases. It read more like a commitment to free enterprise than to 'full employment'. The Employment Act stated:

> This Congress hereby declares that it is the continuing policy and responsibility of the federal government to use all practicable means consistent with its needs and obligations . . . to co-ordinate and utilize all its plans, functions and resources for the purpose of creating and maintaining, in a manner calculated to foster and promote free competitive enterprise and the general welfare, conditions under which there will be afforded useful employment, for those able, willing and seeking work, and to promote maximum employment, production and purchasing power.

Nevertheless, a concession had been made to Keynesian-type thinking in so far as the government was now endowed with some responsibility for maintaining employment. The Act gave the government no new or effective powers to cope with a depression of the 1930s sort. It was no doubt intended to signal that the United States government would try to prevent such a depression from disrupting the new international monetary system, based on the dollar as the key currency, which had been set up at Bretton Woods in 1944. The Act also established a Council of Economic Advisers to report to the President on the progress of the economy and the Congressional Joint Committee on the Economic Report. While the Act was not exactly the landmark it has sometimes been seen as, there is no doubt about the acceptance of an increased role for government in regulating the economy. In the post-war world, economic policy assumed a new importance, with a corresponding enhancement in the standing of the economics profession.

If the fear of a renewed depression continued to influence policy and haunt the minds of ordinary people, the reality of these early post-war years was of a welcome, if inflationary, boom. Indeed, signs of renewed vigour on the part of American capitalism somewhat weakened the argument for more government support for the economy. Before long, however, the onset of the Cold War brought it back into the arena as a big spender, this time in a cause to which business and its allies could not take exception: defence of the free enterprise system against world Communism. Expenditure on armaments went virtually unquestioned.

At the same time, the big corporation – whose reputation had been tarnished by the depression – was now being rehabilitated as the centre-piece of the business system. It could guarantee the outpouring of material things which would ensure prosperity for all. The secret of well-being, the true American way, was not to be found in increased state intervention, or in the redistribution of income, but by increasing the size of the cake: then everyone would have a larger slice. The concentration of wealth and inequality of income found their justification in a high rate of investment and the incentive to produce more for general consumption. While in Europe the experience of war had brought an anti-capitalist tide, nationalization of basic industries and greater government intervention, the current in the United States ran the other way. Although a return to *laissez-faire* was out of the question, what came to be called the 'mixed economy' did not include a state sector but rather increased state spending, which acted as support for private capitalism. As the supposed new power and threat from the Soviet Union was perceived and the Cold War began, domestic policy also became more conservative. There was soon to be a rampant anti-Communist campaign, which was to assume hysterical proportions in the time of Joe McCarthy. Its first, and most important, success was to drive Communists from those unions in which they held key positions. It was also reflected in a more aggressive posture on the part of corporate management towards the unions, however moderate and conservative their leadership.

THE BRETTON WOODS SYSTEM

The death of President Roosevelt in April 1945, shortly before the victory which was partly of his making, brought into the White House his Vice-President, Harry S. Truman a Democratic Party stalwart and career-politician. Consequently, it was he who gave orders for the use of the atom bomb and who conducted delicate negotiations following the conflict. He also presided over the containment policy towards what was seen as Soviet expansionism which required a permanently higher level of arms expenditure, a major reason for the continued presence of the state as a factor in economic development. It also made necessary military support and economic aid for America's allies and a quite new overseas commitment in the shape of military garrisons and naval and air bases in Europe and Asia. This was a new drain on resources, represented by an outflow of funds in the balance of payments. The scale of this involvement consecrated the international economic hegemony, which remained unchallenged for over twenty years. Needless to say, the whole post-war economic-strategic structure was held together by the real power of the American economy, its continued ability to maintain its world leadership in industrial technology and thus its superiority in output and productivity. It was thrown into further relief, in the early years, by the eclipse of the other major industrial powers. On the domestic front the Truman administration saw a re-affirmation of confidence in free-market capitalism, which had been shaken by the Depression, and thus the prestige of corporate management. At the same time, the New Deal was laid to rest and a liberal-conservative consensus emerged which was to endure for two decades. It was underpinned by the new-found vigour of the economy. It took for granted America's role as the military protagonist of 'the free World' and the high level of military expenditure which went with it. It accepted greater involvement by the Federal government in the economy and the commitment of the Employment Act and thus a degree of economic management along Keynesian lines. While many Republicans chafed at state regulation of the economy the consensus was not finally challenged until Ronald Reagan took office in 1980.

The new constellation of world forces brought about by the war compelled the United States to assume the leadership of the capitalist countries economically and strategically. This included restoring some kind of order to the international monetary system which had disintegrated during the Depression. The classic gold standard had operated for a relatively brief period. The United States did not unequivocally adopt it until the Currency Act of 1900. Under the gold standard the value of each currency was fixed in terms of gold and the amount of gold governed the domestic money and credit supply. As long as a country observed 'the rules of the game' it would reduce the supply of money and credit if it lost gold, owing to a balance of payments deficit, and would increase the circulation and make credit easier to obtain if it had a surplus. The standard was thus supposed to operate automatically and impersonally. The gold standard broke down on the outbreak of the First World War and, partially restored in the mid-1920s, was a victim of the monetary breakdown of the Depression years.

In its heyday the gold standard had, effectively, been operated by Britain as the major creditor and financial centre. The Bretton Woods agreement, drawn up by the allied countries in July 1944, was intended as a substitute for the gold standard without the disadvantages which had led to its collapse.

Determined by the interests of the United States as perceived by its leading officials at the time, it linked other currencies to the dollar at a fixed rate which could only be changed under special conditions. The value of the dollar in terms of gold was established by the obligation of the United States to sell gold at a fixed rate, set at $35 per fine ounce. The management of the new system was in the hands of two institutions, the International Monetary Fund (IMF) and the International Bank for Reconstruction and Development (later known as the World Bank). The IMF, financed by contributions from member countries according to the strength of their economies, saw to the regulation of exchange rates, decided when, owing to a 'fundamental disequilibrium', the value of a currency could be altered and made loans to tide over temporary balance of payments difficulties. The Bank was in the business of making long-term loans to member countries in need of assistance and became increasingly involved with the financing of 'developing' countries.

In practice, the Bretton Woods system became an instrument for the attaining of American aims in the world economy. High among them was a universal open door policy: breaking down national barriers to the free movement of goods and capital, assumed to be in the interest of the United States. A major aim was to bring about the dismantling of the preferential tariff and currency systems erected by America's allies, Britain and France. These countries had preferential tariff systems with their colonies and managed currency blocs in which the currencies of their colonies and satellites were tied to their own currencies (the sterling area and the franc bloc). At this time the United States was still a highly protectionist country, but as the dominant economy it was to be expected that its spokesmen now saw an advantage in lowering tariff barriers, beginning, of course, with those of other nations. At Bretton Woods, American opposition had prevented the setting up of an International Trade Organization; by 1947, however, the United States had become a leading proponent of the General Agreement on Tariffs and Trade which looked forward to a general lowering of tariffs.

THE COLD WAR

While the United States government was thus advocating the opening up of the world market through lower tariffs and the breaking up of preferential trading systems, it found, to its chagrin, that a large part of the world was being closed to it, first by the extension of Soviet influence into Eastern Europe and, from 1949, in Asia by the success of the Chinese Revolution. The Iron Curtain was above all a barrier to trade and investment, while the Soviet system seemed poised to advance westward by military, as well as political and ideological, means. As the antithesis of free enterprise and market choice, it appeared to pose a threat to the fundamental bases of the American way of life. What is more, it appeared to have a fatal attraction for malevolent, or misguided, people in other countries and even in the United States itself. With the Soviet economy battered by the war and the enormous destruction and loss of life, it is doubtful whether the Red Army was in any position to move westward. Indeed, Stalin's policy, as expressed at the Yalta (February 1945) and Potsdam (July 1945) conferences, was a division of the world in which the Soviet sphere of interest would be recognized and guaranteed. The failure of the Americans and the British to reach agreement with Soviet representatives about the future shape of Europe, in an atmosphere of gathering mistrust during 1946–7, provoked partly by American possession of the atomic bomb, provided the breeding ground for the Cold War. A new era of international affairs had opened, with the division of the world into two antagonistic power blocs with incompatible social systems. It was now assumed, on the American side, that the Soviet Union was prepared to take by force what it had failed to secure by negotiation. Free market capitalism thus faced a challenge which would have to be met with military means. The United States now became committed to the possession of superior military force both in conventional weapons and in the new means of mass destruction of the nuclear age.

Resistance to the real or imagined expansionary goals of the Soviet Union could not be successful without the support of the other capitalist countries: former enemies as well as allies from the Second World War. Cold-War strategy required that American troops should be stationed on European territory and that the European countries should contribute their own contingents (formalized by 1949 in the North Atlantic Treaty Organization, NATO). In the period immediately after 1945, the West European countries, including the victors, were having an increasingly hard struggle to revive their economies. The defeated countries (including Japan) were grappling with enormous problems of reconstruction. The earlier American policy of reducing their industrial potential was abandoned under the pressure of the Cold War. The victor powers had to overcome the results of pre-war depression and war-time destruction and dislocation. They lacked the means to finance recovery and modernization principally because they could not afford to pay for necessary imports of raw materials and capital goods. With the abrupt ending of Lease-Lend, both the British and the French governments had sent envoys to Washington in 1945 to negotiate loans intended to tide over the first years of reconstruction. Because of price rises and the scale of the needs, however, the dollars obtained were soon exhausted. The prospect of a drastic reduction in the already straitened living standards of Western Europe, or even of economic collapse opening the way for revolution or Soviet intervention, now seemed to be on the cards. Whether or not such fears were too cataclysmic, it was evident that it would take some years of austerity before there could be any hope of rebuilding the European economies. In the meantime they would not be able to buy American goods nor would they be attractive to private American capital. The chaos and conflict caused by inter-Allied war debts and reparations in the inter-war period may have played some role in influencing expert opinion. Prolonged economic difficulties would compel European countries to raise tariffs, control trade and generally revert to the bad habits of the 1930s which Washington wanted to change. The prospect of a drying-up of the American export trade to Europe raised the spectre of depression. The United States needed Europe perhaps as much as European capitalism needed the United States for its survival.

As a preliminary, in May 1947 President Truman authorized financial aid to Greece and Turkey as part of the containment policy, directed against the Soviet Union, known as the Truman Doctrine. Work on drawing up an aid programme for Western Europe began shortly afterwards, and was publicly announced by Secretary of State George Marshall on 5 June 1947. He proposed that the European countries should draw up proposals for using American aid as part of a general programme for European recovery to include the revival of Germany.

While at first it appeared that American aid might be forthcoming for the Soviet Union and its allies in Eastern Europe (the Czechs especially were interested), it was soon clear that the terms attached, amounting to the opening of their economies to Western business, were unacceptable. In that respect, the Marshall Plan helped to divide the continent into two incompatible economic areas in the post-war years. In the atmosphere of mutual mistrust, little else could be expected.

It was some time before the Economic Recovery Programme launched by General Marshall took a concrete form. Criticized in the American Congress and Senate as a mis-spending of American taxpayers' money, the funds voted were less than the original proposal and there was no real sense of urgency until after the Czech 'coup' of February 1948, which brought the Communist Party to power. Marshall aid appropriations were voted in the following month and the aid soon began to flow across the Atlantic. For a country which had just spent lavishly on a major war and which was now committed to heavy military expenditure, the amount devoted to European economic aid did not represent an enormous burden. Presented to the public as an altruistic and humanitarian gesture, the plan was anxiously pushed through Congress by Truman, and in fact was based upon the need to counter the political and military threat assumed to be posed by Soviet expansionism. Its attraction for industry and agriculture was that it offered assured markets for goods which might not otherwise be sold. In the short run – with fears of renewed depression still alive – it was a counter-cyclical policy of government spending.

In the longer run it was aimed at opening the way for permanent trade links and secure investment prospects in a prosperous Europe, with a renascent Germany at its centre able to provide troops and bases for the containment policy. Doubtless no one foresaw the time when re-invigorated European economies would challenge American predominance and rival American industry. It has to be seen in its time and international context as an intelligent blend of altruism and self-interest, having a political-strategic as well as an economic dimension. It was a potent weapon in the struggle with the Kremlin for influence in Western Europe, as well as being an indispensable basis for the rebirth of capitalism in that area.

PROSPERITY RETURNS

Meanwhile, the domestic economy digested the change-over to civilian production without major upsets. Price rises in 1947, while reducing real wages, helped the adjustment to the increased money supply resulting from war finance. Unemployment rose to 3.5% average for that year, climbing to over 5% by 1950; both modest figures by the standard of the 1930s. There was a mild recession in 1949, but generally civilian demand remained buoyant; new-model cars continued to attract more customers, and for the first time sales exceeded five million.

The recession was over by the time that the Korean war broke out in June 1950; arguably it prevented a full-scale depression in the early 1950s. Military outlays were already well above pre-war levels, while the Marshall Plan and other aid programmes financed by the government helped to provide outlets for industrial production. The Korean conflict was a 'small' war and, unlike the later Vietnam War, it was financed largely through taxation without heavy borrowing and only mild inflation. Expansion had begun before the outbreak of the war mainly in civilian demand. However, there was a rapid increase in government expenditure rising to some 279 per cent of the low point in 1947. Military expenditure rose from 6 to 11 per cent of GNP between mid-1950 to mid-1952. There was a leap in civilian expenditure on the anticipation of shortages and price rises. In addition, through the Office of Defence Mobilization, the government undertook a programme of stock-piling of raw materials, which had a world-wide impact. The assumption was that in the event of war supplies from foreign sources would be cut off.

Housing starts had reached a record 1,396,000 in 1950. Predominantly these were one-family homes, many in suburban areas. Expenditure on household equipment and furnishings rose accordingly. The war imposed no sacrifices on the civilian population. With 1.25 million men mobilized, the job market was tight, unemployment falling to a low 2.5% in 1953. By the middle of that year, however, the slowing down of war production and civilian demand resulted in a mild recession which lasted into 1954. After a recovery in business investment as well as in sales of consumer durables and cars there was a more serious recession in 1957–8, a result mainly of a fall in investment in the durable goods industries. The new role of government spending was indicated by the way in which 'automatic stabilizers' came into play: government payments rose while receipts fell slightly. Consumption was well maintained and this helps to account for the mildness and brevity of the recession with only eight months of contraction.

Good times had returned for Americans; or so it seemed in the booming 1950s. While the superpowers froze into frightening Cold War postures, American capitalism was both able to build an expensive military machine with world-wide connections and provide unprecedented prosperity for a sizeable proportion of the population. The mood was one of self-congratulation and restored confidence. Fear of depression gave way to a new orthodoxy: it could never happen again; as in the 1920s there was a feeling that prosperity would last indefinitely. With hindsight we know that it lasted a long time, but not that long.

ANTI-UNION BACKLASH

It was under Truman that an end was put to the seemingly irresistible growth in the power of the trade unions from the time of the great organizing drive of 1936–7. This took the form of the Labor Management Regulation Act, better known as Taft-Hartley, which passed Congress in May 1947 and then became law over the President's veto. Truman was influenced by the Democratic Party's dependence upon union backing in many areas, but the Republican Congress passed the Act with support from Southern Democrats.

Taft-Hartley was very much a sign of the times; it may even be seen as one of the foundation stones of the post-war social order in America. It was the culmination of an anti-union backlash which had been building up for some years. It was a powerful counter-attack on the positions of strength which organized labour had apparently achieved with the help of the New Deal and the chronic labour scarcity of the war period. A severe defeat for the unions, Taft-Hartley was a comprehensive legal code aimed to curtail union rights and enhance the powers of management. It prohibited outright a number of practices, such as secondary boycotts and mass picketting, which had been invaluable in spreading trade union membership among hitherto unorganized, low-paid workers. The law empowered the President to seek an injunction to put an eighty-day moratorium on any strike which would, in his opinion, 'if permitted to continue, imperil the nation's health or safety'. Strikes by government employees were made illegal. Trade union organization by foremen and supervisory workers was made virtually impossible. Trade unions could be made corporately liable for acts performed by their members and agents. Union officials had to sign an affidavit affirming that they had no association with the Communist Party. Where state laws were more stringent, on matters like the union shop, they were to have priority over the terms of the Act. These and many other detailed clauses, if fully applied and administered, would have left the unions virtually impotent. About the only type of union activity not prohibited or curtailed under the Act was the basic one of collective bargaining, and then only so long as the union was accepted as representative of the workers.

Not only was Taft-Hartley a serious blow for organized labour after many years of growth, but the campaign for its repeal failed. Instead, court decisions over the years further limited the scope of union activities. The rank and file was unable to fight back without the leadership, and the unions, of the CIO as well as the AFL, were ruled by a conservative bureaucracy which had no taste for a confrontation with the state. Instead it settled for bargaining within each industry to win wage increases and other concessions which kept their members happy. If necessary the leadership would enforce the contract against recalcitrant members, among whom shop-floor organization was generally weak or non-existent. Although workers, especially in large-scale industry, won a series of fringe benefits over the years, covering sickness, retirement and unemployment (covered in other countries by state Social Security systems), management demanded a quid pro quo. While ready to make wage concessions in the expansive years, corporations wanted a promise of industrial peace on the basis of long-term contracts and the maintenance of management prerogatives. This was part of a more tough-minded strategy, aiming to maintain tight control over the work-place in which new methods of organizing the labour process were being introduced. Management expected union officials to police their own members so that industrial discipline could be maintained. The old militancy of the 1930s had largely been dissipated; one-time leaders had joined the ranks of officialdom or had become conservative. The big unions, including those of the CIO, had become bargaining agents for a largely passive membership looking to the unions to win periodical wage rises and better fringe benefits. Mainstream unionism, though now including the big mass-production industries, in other respects was back where it had been before the great CIO organizing drive had begun.

THE NEW AMERICAN DREAM

Looking back at the progress made in the decade since the end of the war in a mood of self-congratulation, the editors of the business magazine *Fortune* wrote:

> This is not only the world's greatest economic achievement, it is as great a social and cultural achievement. Man-made abundance is making the average man wealthy by the standards of fifty years ago, swiftly eliminating poverty and distress, stamping out disease, prolonging life, undermining useless or obsolete industries, building up useful ones, helping other nations to struggle up the difficult and often disappointing road to efficiency, creating more and better leisure, and changing swiftly and radically the tastes and habits of the people the world over. Nothing, perhaps, has altered the world more in all the history of Western civilisation than rising American productivity has in the last half century. And barring atomic annihilation, nothing is more likely to alter the world so much in the next half century.
>
> (*Fortune*, July 1955)

The celebration of the American dream was never so confident and enthusiastic, supported as it was at this time by undoubted industrial achievements (albeit based often on technology developed elsewhere) and unrivalled levels of production and productivity. With economic performance went a newly-acquired military power and political influence: it seemed to be the American century.

Within a decade or so the celebration was to begin to turn sour. Domestic rumblings were to be heard: on the assembly lines – *Fortune* talked about consumption, not about working conditions – from disgruntled youth, from Blacks and other minorities still disadvantaged, from women (*Fortune* speaks only of 'the average man'). Poverty in America would be 're-discovered' behind the façade of affluence. Market forces did not automatically ensure minimum standards of welfare or of medical care. The United States was seen to lag behind badly in most fields of social welfare. Moreover, access to the good things of American life extolled by *Fortune* depended upon disposable income, of which many deprived people had little: the majority of Blacks, poor farmers, the less skilled, the aged and other victims of the inequalities generated by a market economy. There was little change in the existing inequality in the distribution of property and income. It was chiefly the high level of demand for labour – or the low unemployment rate – which was responsible for the raising of living standards for the better paid (and usually unionized) workers, as well as for the salaried people and self-employed who made up the new middle class. Benefits trickled down to the less skilled and lower paid as a result of the all-round scarcity of labour in these years.

A mass market was necessary if products like motor cars and consumer durables, which required enormous investments of fixed capital, were to be produced profitably. This America had, well ahead of Europe, and would continue to have if a return to the 1930s could be avoided. Undoubtedly the thought that these material things were not only desirable, but also within their grasp, provided an incentive for the masses more powerful than any 'work ethic' based on thrift and hard work. The stress was on the importance of money and thus the need to acquire more of it, by one means or another. That could mean an incentive to work harder and longer; it could also mean hard bargaining through trade union organization. The existence of these incentive goods did not necessarily mean a dulling of class consciousness, though, in the prevailing social and political environment, sectional interests tended to dominate. There was no working-class political alternative in the shape of a Labour Party. Adapting themselves to the climate and to the legal restrictions of Taft-Hartley, the union bureaucracy concentrated on winning wage rises and fringe benefits for their own members. Even the abrasive John L. Lewis of the miners went no further. At most, union leaders supported reforms of the New Deal type expected from the Democratic Party.

What the celebrants of the American century forgot in the 1950s was that the world outside America was changing rapidly. There was not only the threat from the Soviet Union, which, with the launching of Sputnik (1957), was to be seen as scientific and technological as well as military, but also the changes taking place in the other capitalist countries of Europe and Asia and, more widely, in the colonial and semi-colonial world. The rehabilitation of Western Europe, helped by American dollars pumped in by the Marshall Plan and US military aid and spending, opened the way for rapid economic growth, veritable 'economic miracles' as they seemed. In the case of Japan, the reversal of the original Occupation policy cleared the way for the rebuilding of a technologically advanced industry, making that country a strong bulwark against the Soviet Union and China. In the longer run, however, both the West European countries and Japan would become rivals as well as partners. Much of the plant in Japan and West Germany was new and of the latest design since it replaced what had been destroyed, mainly by Allied bombing, during the war. By the 1950s their economies were growing much faster than that of the United States; in part this was a catching-up process as American techniques, production methods, products and forms of management were adopted. The process was helped along in Europe, if not in Japan, by the presence of American branch plants, many of them set up since the war. There was nothing specifically American about the high rates of productivity which so enthused the editors of *Fortune*, no mystery which industry in other countries could not learn. So, in time the other advanced capitalist countries would do as well, or better, even far better in some fields, than their American model and mentor. Some would push faster into new technological fields in the latter part of the twentieth century. In saving capitalism after the war, as it was bound to do, the United States nurtured economic rivals and potentially difficult allies. The lead acquired in the immediate post-war years was soon to be lost as growth rates in the United States began to lag.

Nevertheless, in the 1950s the American economy still seemed to be on top and such changes had not become apparent, even to Europeans. The depression had not come back and the business cycle appeared to have been tamed; the 'new economics' associated with John Maynard Keynes seemed to offer means of preventing any recurrence. The Korean war had been fought without a reduction in civilian income and its ambiguous conclusion had not been followed by a slump. Private investment went confidently ahead, boosting industrial output, with autos in the lead. More than ever the car had become part of the American way of life. The backward and forward linkages of the car industry helped keep large sections of the economy prosperous. The car entered into a complex of expansionary forces operating in early post-war America. After the hiatus of the Depression and men returning from the war, many new families were constituted: hence the high level of house-building and the demand for household goods and durables. The shift to the suburbs, made possible by the car, meant the need for new highways. Rising per capita income fostered the growth of the tertiary sector: services of various types provided by white-collar, salaried people and professionals. Mortgages and loans from banks, easily available consumer credit on favourable terms, helped fuel consumer demand. Industry, meanwhile, was able to supply much of the funds for new investment from its own resources and re-invested profits.

Simultaneously, the government was in the market for military hardware and equipment on a scale hitherto unknown in peacetime. As long as the Cold War persisted, such spending was taken for granted and seldom challenged. It was acceptable to business for good cause. The big manufacturing corporations (and some others like the American Telephone and Telegraph Company) held master contracts for the Defense Department (referred to as the Pentagon, from the shape of its headquarters in Washington). These contracts helped to keep the production lines rolling, providing an additional flow of guaranteed profits from which new investments in civilian or military production could be financed. Technological developments from the military side, financed by government, might fructify in the civilian side of the business. The giants with the prime contracts also acquired power over small sub-contracting firms.

Although the 1950s were generally prosperous, growth was steady rather than outstanding and there were slow-downs and even mild recessions. At times particular markets reached saturation point; consumers had to be attracted with easier credit conditions and, in the case of cars, with model changes, mostly adding superfluous metal. Thus the volume of debt tended to increase as the obverse side of prosperity. The mildness of the recessions were attributed to 'built-in stabilizers', notably the fall in tax receipts and the increase in unemployment and similar payments which followed a falling-off in economic activity. Politicians and public opinion were more ready to countenance budget deficits than they had been before the war, at least in times of recession. With revival, tax receipts were bound to rise and government spending would fall off again. The beauty of the 'built-in stabilizers' was that the government had to do very little. Agriculture was now cushioned from violent price swings by price supports. Arms orders absorbed part of capacity working and the services were kept at a higher level than previously. All these factors seemed to make the economy depression-proof even without an armoury of counter-cyclical measures. Moreover, there seemed to be no special problem of inflation control; price rises were modest even during the Korean war.

To draw a balance sheet of the post-war period up to the end of the 1950s amounts to explaining why the economy managed to grow steadily without renewed depression. Built-in stabilizers are an inadequate explanation; long-term forces of expansion were also asserting themselves. This did not mean, as most economists claimed, that there were no longer any stagnationist tendencies. On the contrary, the underlying forces which had brought about the prolonged depression of the 1930s were merely latent, pushed into the background for the moment by more powerful influences making for expansion.

The war had brought about changes which reached far down into American society. For example, the stagnationist thesis had paid a good deal of attention to the slowing down of population growth in the 1930s. The post-war years saw a reversal of this trend: a baby boom heralded a period of population growth. Total population increased by about ten million between 1939 and 1945; it grew again by over ten million in the next five years, standing at about 151,683,000 in 1950. Average annual growth rates, which were a little over 7 per 1000 in the 1930s, rose to 15.6 per 1000 for the years 1945–50 and to 16.9 per 1000 in the years 1950–5. Not until the late 1970s did the rate of growth fall back to the 1930s level.

A growing population, with the expansion of the lower age groups edging up the age pyramid through school to university or the job market, created new demands and eventually new strains. In the first place, it stimulated demographic investment in the public sector: schools and colleges (a charge for local government), as well as hospitals and health services.. Population growth played a role in the generally high level of private fixed capital investment as well, whether measured in absolute terms or as a percentage of GNP.

American capitalism embarked upon a new cycle of expanded reproduction. Assisted at first by the destruction of values represented by a decade and a half of depression and war, it was financed by the greater liquidity resulting from war-time government spending. The higher level of investment meant the expansion of the means of production sector, which equipped the consumer goods industries with new plant and equipment. In turn, the means of production industries grew to meet their own demand. More advanced technologies were incorporated in the new capital equipment, qualitatively superior to that of the past, and the proportion of such equipment also increased. Technical change could be manifested in the means of production (new machines, automation, shop-floor re-organization) without much change in the product, for example the motor car, which was not fundamentally different from pre-war models. New products were also developed, displacing old ones or entirely different. Some technological developments had been held back by the war (television and FM radio, for example), while others had been promoted by it and could now be adapted to peaceful purposes (jet propulsion, radar, nuclear power). New materials such as nylon and plastics, soon passed into common use. Improved machines and machine tools were introduced; automation and computerization began to make an appearance. These techniques helped maintain or increase productivity in large-scale manufacturing industry. For the time being the United States had an advantage in many of these new fields.

The new phase of expanded reproduction went on steadily through mild recessions instead of exhausting itself after a few years. A major reason for this has already been pointed out: the fact that the road had been cleared for a high rate of new investment by a long period of depression and war. When the corporations had used up their liquid funds from war contracts, and the public no longer held pent-up purchasing power, the momentum continued. The financial means now came from re-invested profits or bank credit, while consumer demand was also buoyed up by a billowing volume of credit. While government military spending fluctuated, it remained at a relatively high level throughout the period, constituting a new element in the post-war situation.

Although the rapid growth of Japan and the revived European economies had some ominous implications for the future, the United States enjoyed immense advantages in the first post-war decade. The GIs had been great merchandizers for American products. They helped create a demand throughout the world for typically American consumer goods: chewing gum, cigarettes, breakfast cereals, convenience foods, nylon stockings and a host of others. They opened the way for American multinationals to move into new markets or to expand their operations where they already existed, whether by buying up local firms or by setting up new branch plants. This process was especially marked in high income countries such as Canada (a rather special case) and Europe, but it was visible in other areas as well, for example, in the colonies of the European countries.

American capital already had a dominant position in some expanding fields, such as petroleum extraction and refining, the distribution of oil and petrol and the production of petro-chemicals. It had an almost impregnable position in the supply of transport aircraft to the world's airlines, especially when the switch over to the jet-liner began. In the booming field of television production, American programme companies assumed the leading role just as Hollywood dominated the market for movies. The size and power of the American economy made it possible to invest strongly while consumption continued to rise, bearing in mind that both processes were financed by growing debt. High levels of employment meant a more regular income for the majority of workers; at least for the white, adult males (the backbone of the unions). They could thus buy more of the homes, autos and consumer durables and achieve a level of consumption closer to that of the middle class.

For the healthy and continuously employed, living standards were rising and were well above those in Britain and Western Europe. These higher living standards were not the result of some conscious design on the part of business or of the rulers of capitalist America. It was not that employers paid high wages so that workers could buy back the goods that they produced, or that there was any policy of high wages. As long as the accumulation and investment of capital continued at a high level, so there would be a strong demand for labour. This was reflected in the wage level, determined by the historical conditions of labour in America, containing a built-in social element – the consumption needs and expectations of the mid-twentieth century American working class – and operating in particular conditions in which workers enjoyed a relatively strong bargaining position. Indeed, in the confrontation with the trade unions over wages, the aim of the employers was to pay the least possible, often preferring to make concessions or fringe benefits which tied the worker to the contract. What they wanted was the maintenance of managerial prerogatives and an agreement with the unions which would give them calculable wage costs for as long as possible.

Average gross hourly earnings rose (in constant 1956 dollars) from \$1.52 in 1946 to \$1.98 in 1956: a steady but not a remarkable increase. Profits rose at a faster rate, so business was well able to afford some concessions. Inequality in the distribution of wealth and income continued as before. Something like one-third of American households received incomes below the Bureau of Labor Statistic's minimum standard. This disadvantaged section included a disproportionate number of Blacks and other minorities. Poverty was not confined to the ghettos and slums of the big cities; it plagued whole regions in Mississippi, Arkansas, West Virginia and parts of Kentucky. In fact, there were two sorts of deprivation which afflicted mid-century America. On the one hand there was the stark poverty of a pre-industrial society, where many people depended upon poor soil agriculture as tenants and sharecroppers. On the other hand, there were the casualties of a highly industrialized and impersonal society: the sick, aged, unemployed and handicapped. Few of their needs were as yet dealt with by the social security system. Both sorts of poverty were aggravated by racial discrimination and segregation. As time went on, of course, people left declining areas and industries; they were mostly of the younger generation and they moved city-wards in search of jobs. Part of this was the northward trek of many black families into the ghettos. At the same time, labour-intensive industries, such as textiles, moved into the South to tap a cheap labour force without the protection of trade unions.

The working class as a whole certainly benefited from the higher overall demand for labour during the 1950s compared with the depression, which was still very much alive in the consciousness of working people. With more regular work, or the prospect of getting another job quickly if they were sacked or moved home, working-class families could afford better homes, perhaps buying on mortgage, and take on instalment commitments. Unionized workers tended to appear as a privileged group, a kind of labour aristocracy, on the strength of the fringe benefits (such as pensions) provided for in the new-style contracts. At the same time, the general social security system (for which the fringe benefits were a substitute) based on the 1935 Act remained rudimentary.

Although many of the women who had entered the labour force during the war returned to the home, typically to have families, the same ones, or younger women, returned to the labour force in large numbers during the 1950s. In 1946 the number of women workers had fallen to 16.84 million compared with a wartime peak of 19.37 million in 1944. By 1955 the figure had risen again to over 20.84 million. Most of the newcomers went not to the assembly lines or the shipyards but into the white-collar jobs newly created by the growth of the tertiary sector: as secretaries, typists and shop assistants – 'women's work'. This meant that many families now had two or more wage-earners, which often made it possible to meet the mortgage payments and assume heavy hire purchase commitments. Working women had to spend part of their income on clothes, accessories and meals as well as transport to and from their work. The combination of paid work with domestic tasks raised the demand for the very appliances and gadgets for which their wages helped to pay. It also boosted the demand for various types of convenience food: frozen foods for the deep freeze, food in cans and packages, instant coffee and soft drinks – the products which now predominated on the shelves of the giant supermarkets.

MILITARY SPENDING

It was an index of the strength of American capitalism in the 1950s that it could increase the output of goods for the civilian market, undertake a massive arms programme, and finance a war and military aid to its allies and satellites. As a proportion of GNP, military expenditure reached a peak in 1953 and fell back again after the end of the fighting in Korea. Military spending on this scale represented a massive public works programme, except that it produced nothing which returned to the cycle of reproduction. It was the one form of government spending which met scarcely any opposition or criticism, so unquestioned was the appeal of 'defence' and the conviction that the Soviet Union represented a threat to the American free enterprise system. The arms bill had to be met by the taxpayer, like any other expense of government, or had to be financed by debt. The disbursement of government funds for military purposes meant lucrative contracts for the major corporations as well as for the many smaller firms which acted as sub-contractors. Government orders provided substantial sections of industry with assured markets, a stable demand and a high rate of profit.

The maintenance of large armed forces also kept down the number of job-seekers. In 1955, after the rundown following the end of the Korean war, there were over 2.93 million on active duty; at the height of the depression, in 1934, there had been less than a quarter of a million in the services, while the unemployed had numbered over 11 million against 2.6 million in 1955. At the same time, military spending created jobs and incomes which might not otherwise have existed, thus creating a demand for the output of firms not necessarily connected directly with military production.

Some forms of military equipment wore out rapidly or became obsolete and had to be replaced, thus ensuring a constant flow of new orders to the arms manufacturers. Technology in fields like aerospace and nuclear weaponry changed all the time; the Pentagon had an insatiable appetite for the latest and best that industry was able to develop. The permanently high level of arms spending brought about a close working relationship between the military and the managers of the big corporations which supplied the weaponry. Described as the 'military-industrial complex' by no less a person than President Dwight Eisenhower (1953–61; Supreme Commander of the Allied Expeditionary Force in the Second World War) who warned against its dangers, it represented a close working relationship between those disposing of government money and the discretionary power to award contracts, and the big corporations which came to depend upon them for a large (sometimes the major) part of their business. The military chiefs wanted whatever was most effective in the shape of lethal hardware, and all the accessories. The corporate elite needed the sheltered market offered by military demand.

To whatever extent arms spending contributed to the high level of activity in the post-war American economy, in the longer run it was far from being an unmixed blessing. Resources devoted to armaments production were not returned to the productive cycle but were entirely unproductive. Research and development on weaponry drew away much of the best scientific talent. Firms with arms contracts might have less incentive to develop new products for the civilian market or to improve their efficiency. Moreover, prolonged arms spending tended to build up inflationary pressures. Meanwhile in Europe (especially West Germany) and in Japan an impressive industrial upsurge was beginning to take place. Firms in these countries, after the destruction and dislocation of the war, were re-equipped with plant and machinery of the latest design while supplies of labour came from displaced persons, refugees, peasants leaving the land and immigrants from less developed areas. The United States (like Britain) had a larger proportion of older equipment – in some industries (though the reputation of American entrepreneurs was that they were ready to renew machinery before it wore out if it seemed profitable to do so). In any case German and Japanese firms became powerful rivals in the technologically most advanced fields. After German re–armament began arms spending remained comparatively modest (about 2.5% of GNP) and insignificant in Japan (under one per cent). The cost of American hegemony and carrying on the Cold War was proving to be burdensome even for the world's most powerful economy. In the long run it meant a serious loss of competitiveness in the manufacturing sector.

CHAPTER 6

Affluence and the Vietnam War: the 1960s

The 1960s form a decisive watershed in the post-war history of American capitalism. America experienced its longest period of uninterrupted expansion, bringing a wave of affluence to large sections of the population. At the same time, poverty was rediscovered as an ugly sore on the prosperous face of the richest country in the world. Legislative programmes were launched to deal with this social anomaly, with uneven success. Keynesian policy came into its own, and was applied with wide support from public opinion and the economics profession. Yet before the decade was out, the brave 'new economics' of the early 1960s had been largely discredited. High military spending became institutionalized as a feature of the business scene, benefiting the large corporations. From 1965 the administration slid rapidly into an all-out commitment to back up the anti-Communist regime in South Vietnam. The surge of war-spending brought the culmination of the boom and prepared the way for its demise. The decade ended with a knot of new problems: endemic inflation, a dollar under pressure, an industrial slowdown and widespread social discontent.

THE KENNEDY–JOHNSON BOOM

Since Roosevelt, or even since Hoover, the presidency has had an important role in determining the economic policy of the state and, through its growing regulatory functions, the course of economic development. The economic history of this period can, therefore, easily become a record of economic policy, which is certainly its best documented aspect. While the policy of the state can obviously not be ignored, some attempt will be made to consider the wider structural changes taking place in business and in other sectors of the economy.

The taking of office by Democrat John F. Kennedy in January 1961, with the promise to 'get America moving', quickly led to a change in economic policy. The youngest ever president, from a wealthy political family, although he was elected with only a slight majority over his rival Richard M. Nixon he soon achieved great popularity especially from those looking for change. In the preceding Eisenhower period the dominant mode was caution and conservatism, leading to the risk of high-level stagnation with an abnormal proportion of unused resources. The Kennedy administration was prepared to increase federal spending and to run a budget deficit if that was necessary to increase investment and speed up the rate of economic growth. It had inherited a recession, which had brought the unemployment rate up to almost seven per cent and this provided the background, first for a number of short-term measures and then for the launching of a Keynesian-type programme which became known as the 'new economics'.

The aim was to use state spending and taxing powers at a level sufficient to ensure that the economy operated at near 'full employment' levels. Deficit spending (that is, an unbalanced budget with expenditure exceeding receipts) would thus make up the gap left by private investment, when it fell short of savings. If investment ran ahead of savings, however, state spending should be reduced to prevent inflation. It was expected that conscious policy would be reinforced by built-in stabilizers; that is to say, recessionary tendencies would be counteracted by lower tax receipts and higher state outgoings on unemployment compensation and social security, while a boom would be moderated by higher tax receipts and by the fall in unemployment payments.

In fact, in the course of 1961 recovery began without much help from the government, and this proved to be the start of a long boom. Once it had begun, therefore, Kennedy and his Keynesian advisers had the task of raising the economy to 'full employment' and keeping it there through fiscal policy. The main weapon in their armoury was a cut in taxation to stimulate investment and spending.

Although regarded with suspicion by many businessmen, who were traditionally Republican, Kennedy was a convinced upholder of private enterprise capitalism. He was persuaded by his advisers that the state should create the best conditions for the accumulation of capital. The first way in which he sought to do this was by the granting of special tax incentives for the renewal of plant and machinery. In fact, a bill to that effect was held up by Congress until October 1962.

The next step in this direction was the call for a major tax cut, taking the risk of a larger budget deficit in order to promote long-term economic growth. The proposal was first made publicly in June 1962, when the economy showed signs of flagging. The aim was to keep unemployment at around four per cent by raising aggregate demand without provoking inflation. A rate of unemployment at this level was calculated to give the highest possible rate of growth without inflation or serious disproportions. The tax cut would probably mean an increase in the budget deficit and thus an increase in the national debt. Both these prospects were alarming to orthodox opinion in political and business circles. Using the argument from the concept of 'built-in stabilizers', the administration claimed that a high level of activity would mean an increase in tax receipts despite a lower rate of tax, while a recession would increase the deficit. The tax cuts, as announced in January 1963, were to benefit individuals and corporations and were part of a reform of the tax system. In the measure's progress through the Senate and Congress where it faced opposition from Southern Democrats as well as Republicans, most of the tax reforms were sacrificed, and the scale of the tax cuts was reduced. The bill became law as the Revenue Act of 1964, after Kennedy's assassination. The economy then surged into a boom with a five per cent growth rate, a fall in unemployment to around four per cent and bumper profits for business. What part of this was attributable to the lower rate of tax is difficult to say. The tax cut amounted to about $13 billion and was expected to stimulate investment and consumption. Tax receipts rose in the following years and the budget deficit was reduced. Monetary policy also took a new turn; the Federal Reserve Board met the expanding credit needs of the economy until the end of 1965.

Despite recovery from the 1960 recession, growth remained sluggish in 1961–2; the economy was running well below its potential as shown by unused capacity and unemployment. Prices and costs remained fairly stable. Accelerated growth began in 1963 and continued for some years, while monetary policy played a passive role. When Lyndon B. Johnson took over the presidency in 1963, he continued the policies of his predecessor, but with a new style. Controlled affluence and political consensus were said to be the aims of the policy of the 'Great Society' which Johnson announced in 1964. The emphasis was on social reform to bring the American welfare state closer to European standards. This would obviously require further measures of state regulation and large-scale expenditure. A necessary complement, therefore, was continued economic growth to generate the required tax revenues. Johnson was re-elected by a large majority in 1964 over the conservative Republican, Barry Goldwater. It could be seen as a mandate for reform.

There was bound to be a time-lag before the different parts of the Great Society programme could be approved and come into effect. Meanwhile Johnson had taken the fateful decision in February 1965 to step up United States military involvement in Vietnam, by bombarding the North. Hitherto the war had been regarded as only a small part of the struggle against world communism which could be settled with only a limited commitment of military resources. This proved to be a serious underestimation of the determination of North Vietnam. By the end of 1965 there were 184,300 American troops in the country and at the height of the war there were over half a million. Costs rose accordingly until escalating military expenditure began to introduce a major destabilizing factor into the economy, even while it fuelled the existing boom.

Civilian consumption had come on strongly during 1963–4, assisted by the prospective tax cut and by the expansion of consumer credit. The latter made possible an increase of almost fifty per cent in the sales of consumer durables between 1961 and 1965. This was partly a consequence of the boom in residential construction in the previous years. Although affected by strikes, car sales also showed a rising trend and were boosted by the availability of credit. The willingness of consumers to go into debt to a greater extent than ever before was certainly now a key factor in sustaining industrial expansion. By 1965, repayments represented over fifteen per cent of disposable income compared with 12.3% in 1960. Manufacturing industry thus benefited from a high level of civilian demand. Investment in technologically more advanced machinery and tighter labour discipline helped raise productivity, while costs were kept down. Higher wages were compensated for by increased productivity; raw material prices, including oil, remained stable or only rose moderately. In a situation very favourable for profits, so that many corporations were able to finance their own investment needs, fresh money could readily be raised from the banks or by stock issues.

By 1965–6 the economy had been running at a high level for five years. In his message to Congress in January 1966, Johnson claimed 'The unprecedented and uninterrupted economic growth of the past five years has clearly demonstrated the contribution that appropriate fiscal action can make to national prosperity'. Aided by the judicious use of tax and expenditure policy, the nation continued to benefit from the longest period of sustained economic growth since the end of the Second World War. He envisaged its continuation and linked it with the Great Society goals.

In fact, shadows were already beginning to appear. Expenditure on the Vietnam war was beginning to make itself felt and the position of the dollar on foreign markets was deteriorating. In December 1965 the Federal Reserve raised the discount rate to 4.5%, despite the President's objection. Johnson had asked for a supplementary appropriation for Vietnam in the summer of 1965. Early the following year he took some measures to limit demand. The budget was now being called upon both to find additional funds for the war and to begin to finance the Great Society measures. War orders were now added to civilian demand and there was an investment boom.

INFLATION AND ITS REPERCUSSIONS

Paradoxically, despite the role of the war in undermining the dollar it was 'a small war' in relation to America's resources. Its total cost amounted to about 14 per cent of GNP in 1970 or about 2 per cent of GNP on a yearly basis. American battle deaths were comparable with one year's loss of life on the roads.

At the same time, and especially in the long term, the effect of the war was profoundly destabilizing. It encountered more opposition than any previous war and it ended in disaster and defeat. The economic consequences were enduring, opening the way for inflation and the currency disorders of the 1970s. If the main aim of economy policy down to 1965 had been to prevent the decline into recession, the new preoccupation was to be how to combat inflation. Although in principle the 'new economics' knew what to do, in practice it was blocked by the political realities, or Johnson's perception of them. Moreover, inflation had a momentum of its own. Once expectations of continuing inflation were established, then workers and trade unions, consumers and businessmen, savers and borrowers adjusted their behaviour accordingly and made inflation more likely. And the methods used to counteract inflation had undesirable side-effects on investment and employment.

Already, at the end of 1965 monetary policy had begun to take over from fiscal policy in an effort to stem inflation, but higher interest rates had their biggest impact on new housing construction. Government expenditure continued at a high level as the war went on. Johnson asked for a tax surcharge first of 6%, then of 10%; the measure was passed and became law on a one-year basis in June 1968. When it became effective in the course of the following year, income-tax payers tended to reduce savings rather than consumption. Business continued to invest at a high rate. Consumer prices rose by over 6% and wholesale prices by 4.8% in 1969.

Moreover, the 1960s had seen a deterioration in the international economic position and the emergence of a balance of payments problem, leading to the weakening of the dollar (see appendix to this chapter. Advocates of the 'new economics' failed to take full account of the international repercussions of the policies they recommended. Although the balance of payments deficit was halved between 1960 and 1966, appearances were deceptive. Still the dominant economy, America's position was deteriorating and when new strains had to be met, following on from the Vietnam war, there was a sharp decline in the standing of the dollar. A major factor was the outflow of capital seeking higher profits abroad in long-term investment and short-term lending to foreign markets where interest rates were higher. American multi nationals were opening up new branch plants or buying up established businesses, especially in Europe. Voluntary guidelines were tried in 1964 in an attempt to stem the outflow. Kennedy was a keen advocate of trade liberalization through the General Agreement on Tariffs and Trade, but this brought a clash of interest with the European countries which feared the invasion of their markets. There was, however, an appreciable reduction in trade barriers between 1964 and 1967.

Lower tariffs may have played some part in the boom of those years and international trade continued to expand. As the lowering of American tariffs became effective, however, rising prices at home and the overvaluation of the dollar contributed to a great rise in imports. The merchandise trade surplus began to decline in 1965 after reaching high levels in the previous years, and did so dramatically in 1968. This indicated what was to be confirmed in future years: in many manufacturing industries American firms were becoming less competitive and now had to face the relentless competition of the revived and modernized industries of Europe and Japan and the low-wage 'newly industrializing countries'. As they read the signs, the managements of the big corporations shifted more of their manufacturing facilities to these areas, thus beginning the long-run 'de-industrialization' of some old manufacturing regions at home.

All the ominous features in the external position were brought to the surface by the inflationary trends, now boosted by the Vietnam war expenditure. The international monetary system, and the central role of the dollar in it, was now under pressure. This system enabled American deficits to be financed with an outflow of dollars which foreign central banks were expected to hold – with inflationary effects on their economies if they were used as a basis for additional note circulation. Unlike a country losing gold under the classic gold standard, the Federal Reserve was under no pressure to contract the note circulation. On the contrary, it financed the deficit by creating fresh money – that is, it bought Treasury bonds. Foreign critics, notably in France, attacked the Bretton Woods system, alleging that it enabled America to export its inflation, buy up foreign industry and continue to run a balance of payments deficit without penalty. Tremors of impending crisis in the world monetary system came with the sterling crisis of 1967, the conversion of dollars into gold by the French and the continued decline in the gold reserves held in Fort Knox. By the time that the crunch came, however, Johnson had left the White House.

FINANCING THE WAR IN VIETNAM

The Vietnam war was not simply an exogenous factor which hit the economy from outside. Involvement in South East Asia (like that in Korea a decade earlier) arose from America's world role as the main force to block the spread of Communism. In any case the war, like the arms programme as a whole, had a dual effect upon the economy. It offered big orders and guaranteed profits to the contractors – that is to say, above all the corporate giants – and thus jobs for many workers; with 8.3 million in war industry unemployment dropped below four per cent during the war. The Vietnam war constituted an outlet for existing military equipment as well as a source of new orders. It resulted in a further build up of the armed forces to around 3.5 million by 1969. Something like full capacity working and full employment were thus achieved, thanks to the war.

Some part of the expansion since 1964 had been attributable to the Kennedy tax cut. In the face of the new drains on federal funds, especially the Vietnam war, and the threat of inflation, there was a strong case for a tax increase in 1966. Military expenditure, which had been falling as a proportion of national income (though not in absolute amount) from 1962 to 1965 then began to rise sharply in late 1965 and through 1966. Owing to the fact that such expenditure only appears in the national accounts when contracts have been fulfilled the real impact of an increase was felt by the economy before it was recorded in the accounts. Contractors received advance payments, raised money from the banks and paid for raw materials and labour, all of which tended to push up prices. Government economists and politicians were slow to realize what was happening and react to it. Meanwhile the escalation of the war in Vietnam pushed up costs much faster than Johnson and his advisers had expected.

Johnson had been returned to office with a big majority in 1964, largely on the promise of reforms, a re-awakening of the hopes of the New Deal era. Like his hero, Roosevelt, before him, Johnson became increasingly preoccupied with the maintenance of America's world position, focused on the struggle for South East Asia. But the war escalated when the economy was already experiencing full employment and was tautly drawn and thus exceptionally vulnerable to inflationary pressures.

The anti-poverty programmes of the Great Society were intended to increase the efficiency of the labour force and to deal with those social problems which were unaffected by economic growth. The first object was to be achieved through raising educational standards and retraining. The second required specific measures targeted to aid the main victims of poverty, said to comprise one-fifth of the population. These were made up of the unskilled and poorly-educated, especially the non-whites, large families, especially those without a male bread-winner, the elderly (half of whom were in poverty) and the poor-soil farmers of under-developed regions. A sense of urgency was added by the riots which erupted in a number of inner-city areas from 1965 onwards.

To a growing extent the war in Vietnam and the war on poverty competed for funds; although Johnson tried at first to accommodate both, in time the needs of the Vietnam war gained priority. This was inevitable given the failure to act promptly by raising taxes as war expenditure soared far beyond all the original estimates. Both the balance of payments problem and the anti-poverty programme were pushed into the background. The belief that the war would be short and relatively inexpensive died hard. The Defence Department under Robert McNamara had made its estimate of costs on the assumption that it would end by 30 June 1967. McNamara and other officials were afraid to admit publicly what the true costs were likely to be. For the rest of Johnson's administration the Defense Department went on spending the billions of dollars that the war was costing in excess of the estimates, e.g. $10 billion in the fiscal year 1967.

While the war became increasingly unpopular and polarized opinion as no issue had done since the 1930s, its financing fed the inflationary spiral. Coming on top of a domestic boom supported by a growing volume of credit, it burst through the barriers erected to deal with milder forms of inflation. Shortages of materials, industrial capacity and labour drove up costs, prices and wages. The old wage-price guidelines were swept away. Meanwhile the swingeing increases in the federal deficit bore witness to the growing cost of the war and the failure to impose tax increases in time.

The war added one more gigantic item of overseas spending to the existing outflow of funds abroad. In particular, it was an addition to the already massive sums which the government was spending on military bases round the world and subsidies to foreign governments to maintain America's world role. There was no way in which the private sector could earn surpluses on foreign transactions to cover these sums. On the contrary, as has been shown, there was a constant outflow of capital in search of a higher rate of profit than could be obtained in the capital-satiated United States. To add to the complexity, the big corporations complacently enjoyed the proceeds from the lush contracts which followed from this military role. Nor should it be forgotten that the constant flow of dollars into the world market provided part of the liquidity necessary for the expansion of foreign trade and the boom conditions which prevailed in the other advanced countries during this period. The better-placed of these countries were able to increase their own reserves, with a strengthening of their currencies, while the competitiveness of their industries improved. While the United States was criticized for the liberties it was able to take because of the dollar's role as a key currency, Americans resented the fact that its main economic competitors, whose industries had been re-built with their help, were not enthusiastic about contributing a larger share of their national product to military purposes. Some of them, indeed, while paying lip service to the need to 'contain Communism', were seeking to extend their trade links with the COMECON countries and mainland China. Foreign central banks were meanwhile using the convertibility of the dollar to turn more of their holdings into gold at the expense of the stocks in Fort Knox.

Thus as the Vietnam war escalated, so the external economic position deteriorated, as indicated by a ballooning trade deficit and the growing unwillingness of foreigners to hold dollars. Since the war came on top of a boom with no slack anywhere in the economy, it generated a runaway inflationary process which reacted back upon the external situation. A stronger government might have been able to take more stringent measures to bring the situation under control, but only by frankly accepting the rules of a war economy. Neither the Johnson administration nor its successor were able to do this. The war became increasingly unpopular, bringing about a social and political upheaval without precedent for decades. The combined result of the failure to defeat the Vietnameses revolution by orthodox military means, and the unwillingness of the American public to give the war whole-hearted support and make further sacrifices, forced a winding-down of the war. But this process proved to be as inept and economically disastrous as the previous escalation.

THE FAILURE OF THE 'NEW ECONOMICS'

By this time the 'new economics' had not so much lost credibility as become irrelevant. Strictly speaking, if Keynes' precepts for running the Second World War had been followed, they might have brought the situation under control, but only at a price which the government, the taxpayers and the American people were not willing to pay. In a sense, foreigners, too, voted against the war by their attitude towards the dollar and to Washington's monetary policy. Meanwhile, the American economy paid the price of involvement in Vietnam in the form of a now grave balance of payments deficit, a severely damaged dollar and insidious inflationary pressure. It was perhaps ironic that by the end of the 1960s it was the policy advocated by the monetarists – one which had not been tried, or only episodically – which retained some respectability. Keynesianism was not yet dead, but it had seen its best days. As for Bretton Woods, the defeat in Vietnam was the start of its undoing until, in 1971, President Richard Nixon drew the logical conclusion – that no amount of massage could maintain the value of the dollar and its convertibility.

Before Nixon drew this conclusion the dollar had gone through a series of crises, seriously undermining confidence in it. In November 1967 a rush into gold began following the devaluation of the pound sterling, reaching its climax in the following March. The central banks off-loaded $3,000 million of gold to speculators and businessmen convinced that a devaluation of the dollar was imminent. Instead, the finance ministers of the leading industrial countries introduced the 'two-tier' gold price. While the price for transactions between central banks remained at the official rate of $35 per fine ounce, it was left to find its own level on the free gold market. Thus the dollar received a temporary reprieve just when the Tet offensive in Vietnam shattered Johnson's hope of winning the war without serious economic complications.

Instead, the President decided not to run for re-election and the way was open for the return of the Republicans in the shape of Richard Nixon in the 1968 elections. This meant that a new team of economic advisers took over in Washington from early 1969, applying new methods to deal with the knotty problems they had inherited from their predecessors. It was a booming, peace-time 'war' economy, operating at full employment levels with strong inflationary pressures, a deteriorating balance of payments position and a shaky dollar just pulled back from the brink. We shall see in the next chapter how the Nixon administration made a fresh attempt, with its 'new economic policy', to change the course of American capitalism, and with what success.

In summary it can be said that the 1960s represented the continuation of the extraordinary wave of prosperity which had begun after the Second World War. This success story convinced many that the kind of problems which had caused the Great Depression of the 1930s had been overcome. The proof seemed to be evident in the ever-increasing growth of production and the high standard of living enjoyed by the majority of the population. With the proclamation of the Great Society, the end of poverty in America appeared to be in sight. Before the decade was out everything had gone sour: society was in turmoil, the dollar was under pressure and new question-marks hung over the future of the economy.

APPENDIX: THE US BALANCE OF PAYMENTS

Changes in the international position of the United States were already discernible in the 1960s as imports climbed upwards and the balance of payments on current account fell off. During the 1970s, merchandise imports rose rapidly, outstripping exports in most years. In several years there was a large balance of trade deficit (imports of merchandise exceeded exports). By the late 1970s imports were regularly exceeding exports, while the balance of payments on current account appeared to have moved into a permanent deficit position.

Table 6.1 summarizes the worsening position:

Table 6.1: US Balance of Payments, 1960–1983 *(in $millions)*

	Merchandise			*Net balance on*
	exports	*imports*	*net*	*current account*
1960	19,650	–14,758	4,892	2,824
1961	20,108	–14,537	5,571	3,822
1962	20,718	–16,260	4,521	3,387
1963	22,272	–17,048	5,224	4,414
1964	25,501	–19,700	6,801	6,825
1965	26,461	–21,510	4,951	5,432
1966	29,310	–25,493	3,817	3,031
1967	30,666	–26,866	3,880	2,583
1968	33,626	–32,991	635	611
1969	36,414	–35,807	607	399
1970	42,469	39,866	2,605	2,331
1971	43,319	45,579	–2,260	–1,433
1972	49,381	55,797	–6,416	–5,795
1973	71,410	70,499	911	7,140
1974	98,306	–103,811	–5,505	1,962
1975	107,088	–98,185	8,903	18,116
1976	114,745	–124,228	–9,483	4,207
1977	120,816	151,907	–31,091	–14,511
1978	142,054	–176,020	–33,966	–15,446
1979	184,473	–212,028	–27,555	–964
1980	224,269	–249,781	–25,512	1,898
1981	237,085	–265,086	–28,001	6,294
1982	211,198	–247,667	–36,469	–9,199
1983	200,257	–261,312	–61,055	–41,563

CHAPTER 7

Structural changes in American capitalism since 1945

The purpose of this chapter is to outline some of the main changes which have taken place in the American economy since the end of the Second World War. In the first part of this period, which corresponded with American world hegemony, the corporations re-established the position which had been undermined by the Great Depression. Now they again seemed capable of providing an affluent society with the good things of life, while maintaining a huge military establishment, much of it in bases overseas. A new symbiosis had apparently been reached between corporate capitalism and the market economy on the one hand, and the interventionist state on the other – legacy of the New Deal and the war economy. For the time being new technologies provided new fields for investment and foreign competition appeared to impose no threat. The American corporation was the model for the rest of the capitalist world.

Measures to meet the Depression had begun to bring the United States into line with other advanced capitalist countries in providing a system of social security to deal with the poor and the aged. This was extended during the Presidency of Lyndon Johnson ('the Great Society') only to be seriously challenged during the 1970s and especially with the advent of Ronald Reagan to the White House.

The legacy of Reaganism hung heavily over his successor, George Bush, when he assumed office in 1989. The existence of a huge budget deficit together with the reduction in the role of government left little scope for dealing with the social and economic problems which also, in part, arose from the policies of his predecessor. Bush's electoral promise not to raise taxes meant that the deficit would have to be dealt with mainly by holding down or reducing government expenditure.

The huge national debt, as well as the pledge not to raise taxes, acted as a barrier to federal spending in any field except defence. Critics claimed that Reagan's essentially short-term view had disarmed the federal government in the face of pressing problems, from the battle against drugs to the disposal of toxic waste. Economy measures had meant a deterioration of the infrastructure, such as roads and bridges. In the face of growing disquiet about the failures of the educational system, federal expenditure and block grants to the states had been drastically reduced. Likewise, the slashing of federal subsidies for public housing aggravated the problem of sub-standard housing and homelessness (said to affect some three million people). Cuts in 'safety net' programmes, health care and research and consumer protection were among the fields in which reduced federal involvement had left behind serious problems for which market forces could provide no answer.

Meanwhile, rising average incomes were increasingly spent on services, while the proportion of income spent on food and manufactured goods tended to decline. Health care, education and the widening functions of government had brought with them a growing army of professionals and service workers. While the number of blue-collar workers tended to decline, the army of white-collar employees grew absolutely and relatively. The importation of foreign manufactured goods increased, some of which represented the growing tendency of American corporations to shift labour-intensive manufactures to branch plants abroad, where labour was cheaper. Changes in markets, in technology and in the localization of industry brought the decline of the old 'smoke-stack' industries which had once been the dynamic centre of American industry. In the face of these trends, some analysts spoke of 'a post-industrial society'.

American leadership of the capitalist world in its adversarial stance towards the Soviet Union and its allies resulted in a permanent high level of arms spending (rising in periods of actual conflict, as during the Vietnam war). A new and close relationship grew up between the defence establishment (symbolically represented by the Pentagon in Washington) and the corporations which supplied the military hardware; the 'military-industrial complex' became a permanent (and threatening) feature of American capitalism.

Finally, something must be said about agriculture, which has long since ceased to be the occupation of the majority of Americans, and by the 1970s employed only about four per cent of the occupied population. That did not prevent Congress, in 1977, from asserting its belief that 'the maintenance of the family farm system is essential to the social well-being of the nation . . .', claiming that the extension of corporate-owned enterprises into farming would be detrimental to the national welfare. Despite this testimony to the strength of the myth of the family farm, subsequent years have seen the remorseless decline in the number of such farms and the strengthening of the hold of agri-businesses in the agricultural sector. At the same time, as a legacy of the New Deal, and what might be called the agrarian myth (the virtues of country living and farm work), agriculture continued to be the most regulated activity. In a sense, the farmers became victims of their success. The technological revolution meant that more and more food could be produced with fewer farmers. The decline in the numbers employed in the agricultural sector was inevitable, but left problems in its wake as well as the ever-present threat of over-production.

CORPORATE STRATEGY

By the 1960s it could be said that American capitalism had reached a certain stability in its structure. Its main strength lay in the mass-production manufacturing industries turning out vehicles, aircraft, machinery, consumer durables and other consumer goods, backed up by the traditional heavy industries, mining, chemicals and energy. These industries had been stimulated by the Second World War, had prospered during the post-war boom and were boosted by new technologies. In the main they were the domain of the big corporations; the typical pattern was oligopolistic, where a small number of large firms controlled the bulk of the output and had market power. These industries were also the main centres of trade union organization, with a relatively well-paid work force whose wages were settled by collective bargaining through periodic contracts. They were located mainly in the urban areas of the North and East, though during and since the war industrialization had spread into parts of the South, and especially to the West coast. This shift continued as the industries based upon new technologies grew in importance, as well as those directly dependent upon government military orders, especially aerospace. The building of new highways, financed by the state, influenced locational patterns and undermined the position of the railways, the first of the industries of the old type to go into decline.

In the earlier part of the century the typical industrial firm generally produced a single product range but by the 1930s many of the larger corporations had diversified into new fields. In some cases the firm was split up into autonomous divisions based on a particular product. These changes reflected the pressure to keep up profit rates. An accompanying trend, related to the frequently oligopolistic market situation, was an increase in selling costs and advertising, the provision of consumer credit and the frequent change of models or types (most obviously in the car industry). Diversification resulted from the saturation of the market for existing products together with the need for outlets for accumulated capital. With new technologies, like those deriving from the silicon chip after the Second World War, a firm might develop new products through a newly-added division.

By the 1950s the corporate giants might have a presence in many and varied fields both in the military and the civilian sectors. Thus, American Telephone and Telegraph, one of the pioneers in the 'talkies', developed new products through laboratory research; the most spectacular result was the transistor (developed 1947–52 and improved upon by companies which bought the licence, such as Texas Instruments). ATT also held major defence contracts.

Another trend in capital accumulation, not entirely novel, but prominent from the late 1950s, was the 'conglomerate', where acquisition of share capital brought together in one organization a diverse cluster of wholly unrelated firms. Examples include Gulf and Western Industries, International Telephone and Telegraph, Litton Industries and Ling-Temco-Vought. They were usually the creation of an ambitious and dynamic entrepreneur such as James Ling of LTV which included firms in electronics, aerospace, meat-packing, chemicals, car-rentals and steel-making. In 1969 LTV fell foul of the anti-trust laws and in 1985 it was declared bankrupt and Ling was in eclipse. The 1980s saw a renewed surge of mergers, take-overs and buy-outs along the same lines. A new feature was that these operations could be financed by borrowing against the assets of the company being taken over through the medium of what became known as 'junk bonds' because of the high risk and high yield involved. One of the most spectacular mergers, in 1985, brought together R. J. Reynolds the tobacco giant with Nabisco, a leading food manufacturer.

The limitations on the absorptive capacity of the home market, and perhaps the existence of tariff walls around foreign markets, encouraged more corporations to go multinational, that is to establish branch plants overseas or buy up foreign firms. The Singer Sewing Machine Co. had come to Britain in the 1890s and Ford opened its first British plant in 1910. Most of the large American corporations have their branch plants in Canada and most manufacturing industry and mining is in American ownership.

After the Second World War substantial holdings were built up in Western Europe, especially in the modern branches which grew rapidly during the boom, as well as in food and beverages. A further growing trend was the moving of manufacturing facilities from the United States (or other advanced countries where US corporations had branch plants) to the low wage, 'newly industrializing' countries. In this case the object was not to supply the limited home market but to use these countries as export platforms from which to supply not only the world market but also the American market. Some of the manufacturing facilities of the corporations in the United States were curtailed or closed down: for example, Singer imported sewing machines from branch plants overseas. An increasing volume of cheap consumer goods, although they might be produced by American firms, were imported from Taiwan, South Korea, Hong Kong, Mexico, the Philippines and other 'developing' countries where labour was cheap. At the same time there was a decline of manufacturing industry in America, which, coupled with the decline of the old heavy industries, contributed to 'deindustrialization'.

Undoubtedly American business had developed management techniques to a high pitch of perfection by the mid-century, acting as a model for foreign rivals and accounting for much of the success that American-owned firms had abroad. Systematic specialization of function, the splitting up of large corporations into semi-autonomous divisions, forward-planning and the use of input-output analysis and data-processing all contributed to the successes of the corporation. At the production level, management insisted upon reinforcing its authority both against the trade unions and against informal workshop organization. Continued mechanization and increasing automation strengthened management's hand by giving it greater control over the flow and pace of the production process. At the same time, increasing numbers of managerial personnel were directly or indirectly concerned with establishing and maintaining control over the labour process. Managerial strategy aimed at integrating the workers into the enterprise, encouraging them to identify their own interests with those of the firm and to pursue individual rather than collective goals. Job descriptions were made more precise, leaving as little initiative as possible to the workers and intensifying the work-load. If possible trade unions were excluded, but where they existed the aim was to make contracts for a period of years to give some stability to labour costs. Assisted by labour-saving technologies, management sought to obtain regular increases in productivity making it possible to produce more with the same or a smaller labour force. Thus the main issue between capital and labour was the intensification of work, the struggle for *relative* surplus value in the Marxist sense, or obtaining maximum output at the lowest labour cost per unit.

The number of production workers in manufacturing industry, which stood at 11.9 million in 1947, had increased by only 2 million by 1979 and their proportion of the labour force in industry had fallen from 83.2% to 67.3%. Although there was some slippage in the rate of growth of productivity, total output of manufacturing industry continued to rise (by about fifty per cent during the 1970s). Despite its relative decline in terms of employment, and the shift into tertiary employment, the manufacturing sector continued to be of basic importance for the American economy and for the high standard of living which this very movement indicated.

The traditional 'proletariat' was concentrated mainly in manufacturing and mining. The old distinction between skilled and semi-skilled workers continued, perhaps in a new guise with the importance of technical knowledge. Unionization of factory workers gave some job protection but the unions were concerned primarily with selling the labour power of their members on the most favourable terms. The segmentation of the labour force on ethnic lines, which in the past had tended to limit the growth of a specific working-class consciousness, especially in the political field, continued to operate. Even with the efforts of management to create a contented labour force, the very conditions of modern industries tended to produce alienation and discontent, though this took an often inchoate form, such as high rates of absenteeism, alcoholism and drug addiction, lack of co-operation, especially on the part of the newer layers of workers, or the occasional wildcat strike.

'THE AFFLUENT SOCIETY'

With the post-war boom the American system once again seemed capable of churning out large quantities of consumer products and offering stable jobs over a long period (virtually from the end of the war until the early 1970s), see Table 7.1 for levels of unemployment between 1950–86. Higher incomes fostered the growth of the service trades. The corporations employed more and more people in administration, sales and advertising. Federal, state and local government offered increasing numbers of jobs. During the 1950s and 1960s something like full employment prevailed, with the annual average generally below

Table 7.1: Unemployment in the United States, 1950–1986 (*per cent, all workers*)

1950	5.2	1969	3.4
1951	3.2	1970	4.8
1952	2.9	1971	5.8
1953	2.8	1972	5.5
1954	5.4	1973	4.8
1955	4.3	1974	5.5
1956	4.0	1975	8.3
1957	4.2	1976	7.6
1958	6.6	1977	6.9
1959	5.3	1978	6.0
1960	5.4	1979	5.8
1961	6.5	1980	7.0
1962	5.4	1981	7.5
1963	5.5	1982	9.5
1964	5.0	1983	9.5
1965	4.4	1984	7.4
1966	3.7	1985	7.2
1967	3.7	1986	7.0
1968	3.5		

Unemployment was at a generally low level in the 1950s and 1960s, with brief rises in recession years. In the 1970s and 1980s it was significantly higher.

5%; in 1969 it came down to 3.4%. Considering that the incidence of unemployment was always greatest among ethnic minorities (especially Blacks), women and youth, it can be said that among adult white males unemployment during the long post-war boom was purely minimal and mainly of a frictional character (changing jobs). No doubt there was greater insecurity (as well as lower pay) for the unskilled, especially in the ballooning service sector. Even so, movement upwards to a better-paid job was within the reach of many as the boom continued. Moreover many women, including married women, returned to the labour force so that many working-class families had two incomes, making it possible to move into better housing with the usual domestic appliances, colour television and at least one car in the garage. In 1984 88% of families had colour television, 87% had a car and 51% more than one. In the Los Angeles area there were more cars than people. The landscape had changed in such a way, with residential areas, business districts, shopping centres, schools and churches separated by such long distances, that a car had become a necessity of life and public transport was skeletal. Practically all households had a gas or electric cooker (and by 1989 more than 83%

had a microwave oven). In 1984 73% had a clothes washer (the rest using the ubiquitious launderette), 37.6% had dishwashers and 36.7% separate freezers.

The mass of the working class, like the middle class, was now immersed in the pursuit of material possessions; consumerism appeared to have taken over. While, with apparent job security and promotion some workers became more conservative, other typically 'middle-class' occupations were depreciated as a result of automation and bureaucratised control. Members of the liberal professions were more likely to be working for a salary, perhaps as an employee of a large corporation. The challenge to the market system appeared to have reached a low ebb by the mid-1960s in the Kennedy-Johnson era. The 'end of ideology' was proclaimed; 'the affluent society' was heralded. Something like a social-political consensus had been realized. The Cold War, and with it a high level of military expenditure (always called for 'defence'), had been institutionalized. The 'new economics' would ensure that there would be no return to the traumatic 1930s-type Depression. The development of social security would deal with the casualties of the market economy and wipe out any poverty not eliminated, in the course of time, by the sheer growth of the economy. Ugly sides of American life, especially racial segregation, would be dealt with through legislative reform and the education of the public.

As events were to show, this consensus was to be undermined in the late 1960s by the Vietnam war and the succession of shocks which followed in the 1970s. In any case, the changes associated with the boom were mainly on the surface, while the boom itself was feeding the forces which were to undermine it. The corporate order remained intact and was reinforced. The degree of inequality in the distribution of wealth and of income remained as great as ever. Historical experience suggests that when capitalism is expanding income inequality tends to increase. This was the case in the 1920s and, after a period during and following the Second World War when the trend was reversed, it began to operate again, especially during the 1980s. The degree of inequality, as well as this trend, is shown in the following table (7.2). The distribution of property is similarly unequal with the richest 0.5% of families increasing their share from 25.4% of total wealth in 1963 to 35.1% in 1983. They did better than the next rich 0.5% whose share slipped back from 7.4% in 1963 to 6.7% in 1983. The next 9% of families dropped from 32.0% of the total in 1963 to 29.9% in 1983.

At the bottom of the heap are those Americans living below the official poverty line (which is stated as a given annual income for

Table 7.2: Income distribution in the United States

US population in quintiles	*Total percent of income received* 1978	1981	1983	*Comparison of 1983 to past percentages*
Top 5 per cent	15.6	15.4	15.8	
Highest fifth	41.5	41.9	42.7	Highest per cent since 1950
Fourth fifth	24.1	24.4	24.4	Highest per cent since 1950
Middle fifth	17.5	17.4	17.1	Lowest per cent since 1947
Second fifth	11.6	11.3	11.1	Lowest per cent on record
Lowest fifth	5.2	5.0	4.7	Lowest per cent since 1961

(US Department of Commerce, *Money Income of Households, Families and Persons in the United States,* 1983, p. 49. Bureau of the Census, and *In These Times,* 22 August–4 September 1984.)

a family of four – in 1987 this was $11,611). On the reckoning made in 1986 there were 32.4 million people in this position, making up 13.6% of the population. This total included many of the aged and single-parent families and a disproportionate number of Blacks and Hispanics. Of the black population 31.1% were below the poverty line, 27.3% of Hispanics and 11 per cent of whites. Although some figures suggest that poverty is declining, largely because of non-money income available to the poor (like food stamps), it is clear that a substantial number of citizens, especially in the ghettos and *barrios* (Hispanic districts) have low living standards. Their plight is compounded by lack of education and skills so that, even when working, they only qualify for the lowest-paid manual and menial jobs. It is no easier than it was in the past for the poor to extricate themselves from their poverty. Most Americans enjoyed living standards which were the envy of people in many poorer countries. By the 1980s those working for a living found that their real incomes were not rising anything like as fast as before. Consumption standards were sustained by an ever-growing volume of debt which, in turn, sustained the demand upon which continued capital accumulation depended. On the other hand, the low savings ratio meant less available for investment. Foreigners were filling the gap.

Characteristically, many of the now indispensable consumer electronics, TVs., VCRs and micro-wave ovens, were imported by the million. The relationship of the American economy to the world market was changing in a way which spelt trouble in the future. Cheap energy and low raw material prices would not last for ever. The growth of government expenditure and the rising costs of the social programme ('defence' was seldom criticized, remaining part of the 'consensus') meant unbalanced budgets, a rising national debt and a menacing tax burden; in due course the backlash came.

THE REGULATED MARKET ECONOMY

The shock of the Depression had resulted in a marked increase in state intervention in the economy. The volume of regulatory legislation increased rapidly, and continued to increase in subsequent decades. Not until Reagan came to office in 1980 was any attempt made to stem the process. In substance the United States had become a regulated capitalism, with the concentrated economic and market power of the corporations on the one side and on the other a state which managed a complex social security system and operated an apparatus of controls which modified the working of the market system. A larger proportion of GNP thus flowed through the budget of the federal, state and local governments, which became big spenders and employers of labour in their own right. Their revenues were derived from income, payroll and indirect taxes mainly, with any gap being made good by borrowing. There was no state sector or attempt at central planning, and nationalization of industry was not a significant political issue. Acceptance of an interventionist state did not mean opposition to capitalism; rather, it was considered that an effectively operating capitalist economy required that some functions be taken out of the market-place and be administered by the state, which was also charged with curbing the free play of market forces when it was in the 'public interest' to do so. The state thus acted not in the interests of particular capitalists or corporations, but as the custodian of the long-term interests of the private property system.

Just as New Deal policies had been unpopular with business, so many businessmen opposed the regulatory policies of the post-war period. They saw in 'big government' a threat to their own interests, opening the way for a rival bureaucracy which would interfere with their decision-making powers. Some ideologues such as Milton Friedman or the Austrian economist Frederick von Hayek identified the extension of governmental powers with creeping socialism, and called for a reversal of the process and a return to a free-market economy. Various organizations like the American Heritage Foundation propagated those ideas. Taxpayers resented paying for the beneficiaries of social security payments. An objective assessment of the overall situation was often lacking, and the fact that 'defence' played a major role in big government was conveniently overlooked.

Certainly interventionist policies produced contradictory results, including the creation of a huge bureaucracy and a multitude of regulations and restrictions penetrating many spheres of social life. The real question is whether the system could have performed as well as it did without regulation. Did the regulatory functions of the state assist in the preservation of capitalist property relations or tend to undermine them? Were they necessary to moderate the operation of market forces, for example by protecting the consumer or preserving the environment, or did they prevent private enterprise from delivering the goods which the public wanted? The divisions around these questions, now central to American politics, are not over a choice between capitalism and some alternative social system, but how best to preserve the existing social relations based upon private ownership of the means of production and market forces. The increasing role of the state has been designed to do that; critics claim that it is undermining the business system rather than strengthening it. The shift to the right, signalled by the election and re-election (1984) of Ronald Reagan, represented a victory for the latter point of view – though how far there can be a winding down of state intervention, or a full-blooded return to market forces, remains dubious.

An examination of Table 7.4 at the end of this chapter shows the extent of regulated capitalism and the historical process whereby it has come into being. Some of the early examples of regulation were intended to deal with monopoly power; others were of a type to be found in most industrially advanced countries. The 1930s saw a proliferation of acts as part of the New Deal. Some, like NRA, had a brief life; others, to do with banking, stock-market dealing, public utilities, specific industries and agriculture have survived. From the early 1960s, there has been an emphasis on consumer protection, the preservation of the environment and safety. No doubt these impose costs on business and are disliked for that reason but there has been, and continues to be, strong support for such measures, reflecting public suspicion of business methods, if not hostility to capitalism as such. Deregulation under Reagan had to proceed cautiously.

TOWARDS A WELFARE STATE?

One of the biggest structural changes, moving away from the untramelled free market, has been the development of the social security system. Dating back to the Social Security Act of 1935, a part of the New Deal, it was greatly extended during the 1960s as a result of the Johnson legislation that was to be the harbinger of 'the Great Society', and grew subsequently by its own momentum. It involved a re-organization and extension of the functions of the Federal government and of state and local governments. The result has been a great increase in the number of public officials and in the proportion of the GNP passing through the federal and other public authority budgets. The provisions of the social security legislation were, in a sense, an admission that the American system was no longer able to provide, through the market, a necessary minimum of income sufficient to secure medical care, education and support in times of sickness, incapacity, unemployment and old age. Belatedly following European models, the state has come to accept such a responsibility, for a variety of reasons. These were partly humanitarian, partly a belief that social reforms were necessary as a matter of political expediency: the alternative being the growth of movements supported by the poor and needy and opposed to capitalism. In such cases it is difficult to know how much to assign to idealism and how much to hard-headed calculation.

By the end of the 1960s the social security system had reached something like a finished form, only to be contested with vigour in the course of the next decade. It included some contributory schemes which provided protection against incapacity, unemployment and old age, the benefits being received in cash. There was also a growth of in-kind payments to those with inadequate incomes, such as medical care (under the Medicare and Medicaid programmes), food stamps (which enabled food to be bought at low prices), free school meals, employment training schemes, grants for education and social services. By 1981 payments in cash and non-cash benefits to people with limited incomes totalled $116,659 million, of which $87,316 million came from the Federal government. Over twenty-four per cent of American families benefited from such programmes. Most of such payments went to what may be called 'the working poor' – the less skilled and less well-educated, who did the less well-paid and most insecure jobs – and included the aged, the handicapped, and the one-parent families in this stratum. For example, over eleven million people received assistance under the Aid to Families with Dependent Children programme.

Table 7.3: Cost of social welfare, 1950–1980

Year:	*Current $s*	*Constant $s*	*Percentage GNP*
1950	23.5 bn	73.6 bn	8.2
1960	52.3	129.9	10.3
1970	145.9	281.9	14.7
1980	493.4	492.2	18.7

(Statistical Abstract of the United States, 1984.)

The result of the extension of social security entitlements to those below the poverty line and to sections of the working poor was to establish something like a minimum standard, below which no American was supposed to fall. They also provided a 'social wage' to supplement what could be earned by the sale of labour power or to provide income when the recipient could not work owing to age, ill-health or the fact that no jobs were available. The labour force, as a whole, established such entitlements through contributory schemes which also added a 'social wage' element into the total income received by the working class.

Critics claimed that the social security system weakened incentives, undermined the work ethic and encouraged voluntary unemployment. On the other hand it could be claimed that, taken as whole, the effect was to maintain and improve the health, physical fitness, adaptability, education and training of the present and future work force, from which employers stood to gain. In other words it could be seen as an investment in human capital, providing necessary services not supplied through the market and sustaining demand in periods of cyclical recession.

Interventionist measures were costly, involving higher taxation to finance the large increase in public spending involved, and employed large numbers of people in federal, state and local government. The cost of social welfare services rose, as shown in Table 7.3. Social security and expenditure on human resources generally help to account for the growth in the federal budget. Standing at ten per cent of GNP in 1940 (during the war period it rose to over forty-two per cent) it was double that by 1960 and by 1980 it was over twenty-two per cent, with a tendency to rise. Correspondingly, receipts rose, but not fast enough to match the continuous upward movement of expenditure. Budget deficits became a regular feature of public finance and increased sharply in the 1980s. By 1980 the federal government had 2,875,872 people in paid civilian employment; full-time, white-collar civilian employees numbered 1,985,000 in the same year (though the numbers have fallen subsequently, or so it appears).

As far as the costs of welfare are concerned they were, in part, a transfer of income from one section to another, or within the working class itself. Federal, state and local governments administered those transfers rather than appropriating revenue and using it wastefully as some asserted. Additional employment in government offices was necessary to carry out the administrative tasks, more or less efficiently. Indeed, much of the increased employment came in state and local government and it was at this level that the interventionist regime had most effect. Thus, in 1977 federal civilian employment accounted for 1.87% of the civilian labour force, while state and local governments accounted for 5.54%. It is mainly at this level, then, that there has been a growth of 'bureaucracy'.

THE MILITARY-INDUSTRIAL COMPLEX

While social welfare reforms have come in for strong criticism from the resurgent right in American politics in the past decade or so because of their expense, the size of the 'bureaucracy' needed to administer them, and their allegedly harmful effects on labour discipline, another form of government spending enjoys wide support. The Cold War consensus has institutionalized a high level of military (always described as 'defence') expenditure which, in economic terms, has been unproductive. Such expenditure covers a variety of categories including pay of military personnel, maintenance, procurement, research and development in weaponry, and bases overseas. Federal budget outlays are often cited as a proportion of GNP. Here the percentage rose when the country was at war (in Korea and Vietnam), and fell in periods of relative *détente* in the Cold War. On the average, for the 1960s defence spending stood at 8.7% of GNP, falling to 6.1% in the 1970s, rising again during the Reagan presidency. In constant dollars, however, the *amount* of military spending has not changed very much over the years, with a slightly ascending curve from the late 1970s.

To take 1980 as a fairly typical year, the military accounted for 23.6% of federal expenditure and 5.3% of GNP. In that year the armed forces consisted of 2,102,000 active personnel, of whom 287,000 were of officer rank. This compares with about 300,000 in the peace-time forces before 1939. Over half a million members of the armed forces were stationed overseas. In addition, the Department of

Defense (the Pentagon) employed over 3 million people and another 5.95 million were employed in 'defense oriented industries'. Amongst other military material, they produced $7,000 million worth of aircraft and engines, and over $18,000 million of missiles, space vehicles and associated hardware.

Thus in 1980 the jobs of eighteen million people in the armed forces, in government and in industry depended upon the existing level of arms expenditure. The prime contracts made by military procurement officers have gone to the large private corporations; America's industrial giants, ever since 1940, have made part of their profits from the supply of weaponry and other material to the Pentagon and its foreign allies. These contracts have given the Pentagon the power to determine the structure of some of the most technologically advanced industries: aerospace, electronics and nuclear energy. On the other hand, while the military have disbursed government funds, the profits have been made by the corporations. The partnership between the Pentagon and the corporations, described as the military-industrial complex, has been one in which the material and financial gains have ended up with the corporations. Retired military officers join the boards of the prime contractors, acting as advisers and helping to ensure that their firm secures the biggest possible share of government 'defence' spending. It is safe to say that they have been more interested in these posts as a means of personal enrichment than in using the military-industrial complex to gain political power. However, a military officer, like Oliver North, involved in the Irangate scandal (supplying arms to Iran and the Nicaraguan Contra rebels) could achieve enormous popularity which conceivably could be exploited for political purposes.

While in the business arena, even under conditions of oligopoly, competition leads to a drive to reduce costs in order to increase profits, military contracts have been notorious for their lack of cost control. The Pentagon has financed cost overruns on a lavish scale, especially where new equipment has been involved. The general basis for contracts provides for costs plus a profit, and is not subject to the discipline of the market.

While it would not be true to see armaments expenditure as the major factor in the post-war boom, the figures cited above suggest that it was a stabilizing and sustaining factor throughout, both by creating secure and well-paid jobs and by opening up a market for industrial capacity which might otherwise have been unused. Moreover, the spending on military hardware had the peculiarity that the products supplied did not have to be sold on the market, and they constantly wore out or became obsolete. That did not prevent it keeping up the rate of profit on capital invested in the contracting corporations. Such profits could be used to finance outlays in those departments of the firms devoted to civilian production, with perhaps some technological spin-off as well.

Various calculations have been made about the possible effects of scaling down military spending; while it is not inconceivable that such a reconversion be carried out, it would require considerable upheaval over a period of time and probably government intervention to deal with the unemployment and dislocation of industrial plants and whole communities likely to result. Powerful lobbying could be expected. It is not implausible, therefore, to assume that the general level of unemployment and excess capacity would have been markedly higher than that actually recorded; that arms spending, in short, has counteracted 'stagnationist' tendencies in the American economy.

However, the problem does not end there. Arms spending also had a destabilizing effect on the economy during this period. Firstly there was the contribution which it made to the federal budget, at some periods amounting to over forty per cent of all spending, coming down to around twenty-five per cent in most years since the end of the Vietnam war. It also contributed to 'big government' by the size of the civilian labour force required to administer the military programme. Military spending thus contributed to the financial problems of the time, being, by its very nature, inflationary (Fig. 7.1).

Assuming that the members of the armed forces and the civilians employed by the Defense Department could have been employed elsewhere, it has been a subtraction from national output (always excused on the basis of the threat from the Soviet Union, and the imperative claims of national security). There have been frequent complaints by members of the Administration that other members of NATO, and Japan (presumably living under America's nuclear umbrella on the cheap) could increase the proportion of their national income going to the military sector. The implication is not only that the United States bears too large a part of the arms burden but that, as a consequence, its industry has been lagging behind in advanced technologies. In other words, the opportunity cost of high military expenditure has been a falling behind in some key industries and the taking over of the domestic market in some high-tech industries by foreign rivals.

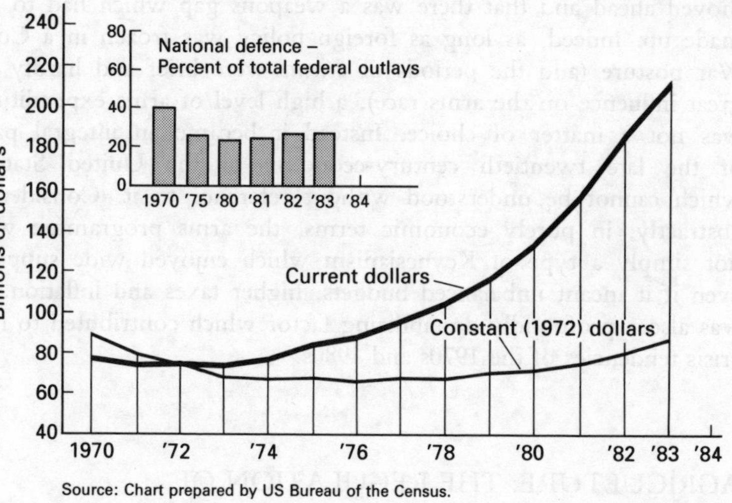

Fig. 7.1: Federal Budget outlays for National Defence: 1970–1983

In this case a contradiction had emerged between the adherence to the free market and the interests of the United States. Both military security and the technological capacity of industry seem to be under threat. Particular industries, such as footwear and ball bearings, have succeeded in ensuring that Pentagon contracts should go to domestic firms. More significant, perhaps, is that the Pentagon has financed numerous research projects in the high-tech field by private firms threatened by foreign competition. These examples do not constitute a coherent policy. Although some industries may benefit, the fact that seventy per cent of government-financed scientific and technological research goes on military projects suggests that many highly skilled people, such as research scientists, who could be making a contribution to national wealth, are engaged on the development of weaponry. Moreover, much military spending has been overseas, supporting half a million servicemen in bases scattered throughout the world. This has undoubtedly contributed to the balance of payments problem showing itself in the 1970s, amongst other ways, in a sharp reduction in investment abroad. Part of the price has thus been a weak dollar and reduced international economic influence.

The Cold War consensus meant that the appropriations of the Pentagon were virtually immune from criticism. Kennedy in the early 1960s and Reagan in the late 1970s campaigned for an increase in arms expenditure, on the grounds that the Soviet Union had moved ahead and that there was a weapons gap which had to be made up. Indeed, as long as foreign policy was frozen in a Cold War posture (and the periods of *détente* were brief and hardly of great influence on the arms race), a high level of arms expenditure was not a matter of choice. Instead it became an integral part of the late twentieth century-economy of the United States, which cannot be understood without reference to it. Considered abstractly, in purely economic terms, the arms programme was not simply a type of Keynesianism which enjoyed wide support even if it meant unbalanced budgets, higher taxes and inflation. It was also a profoundly destabilizing factor which contributed to the crisis tendencies of the 1970s and 1980s.

AGRICULTURE: THE REGULATION OF MARKET FORCES

The relative decline of agriculture, once the backbone of the economy and the source of the livelihood of a majority of the population, has been one of the most spectacular changes of the late nineteenth and early twentieth century, a process which accelerated after the Second World War.

In 1945 agriculture employed one in five of the labour force; by the 1970s this was down to below four per cent. This drastic reduction took place despite an array of government regulations intended to assist farmers, based upon the policies of the New Deal. The relative decline of agriculture had been going on since the mid-nineteenth century and was a necessary accompaniment of industrialization. It reflected the shift of manpower and resources from less to more productive uses, together with a spectacular increase in the productivity of agriculture itself.

Mechanization of harvesting and many other operations which had previously required manual labour, together with the application of chemicals to cultivation, notably fertilizers, pesticides and herbicides, have brought about the 'industrialization' of agriculture itself. While commercial farms have become highly specialized, many of the farmer's inputs have to be purchased off the farm. Inevitably this has meant that farming has become more capital-intensive. Heavy investment in machinery and other equipment means economies of scale: the average farm size has steadily increased. Smaller, less capitalized farms have either gone out of business or have survived only because the farmer and his family held off-farm jobs to supplement family income. While in some areas large, corporately owned farms came into existence, most farms (even those having a corporate form) continued to be run as family enterprises. Despite the steady movement out of agriculture, the myth of the family farm, upon which New Deal policies had been based, continued to have some vitality.

The strength of the family farm, which made it unbeatable in the nineteenth and well into the twentieth century, lay in the willingness of the farmer to work hard for a return on his labour below that which he might have obtained in an alternative occupation, and, more especially, his ability to use family ties and loyalty to use the labour of his wife and children on terms which would have been unacceptable had they been working for an employer. In bad times the family would simply retrench, tightening their belts in an effort to keep the farm going. These factors gave the family farm a sharp competitive edge over any alternative involving the use of hired labour. Large-scale farming, on the other hand, has had to depend upon low-wage migratory labour and recent, and often illegal, immigrants. Nevertheless, inexorably the financially less viable family farms have been squeezed out by the operation of market forces over which they have no control. The effect of government intervention has probably been to spread this process over a longer period of time, not to arrest it. This has not prevented government intervention from being blamed for problems arising from the operation of market forces.

The concept of the family farm goes back to Jeffersonian times: the ideal of a nation of small, self-reliant producers, based on the family and leading a healthy and wholesome rural life. It was counterposed to the city with its anonymous masses, its slums, poverty and crime. The family farm was part reality, part legend. It never meant in practice a self-sufficient producer with only limited ties to the market – historically this had long been superseded. Rather was it a small business, orientated towards the market but employing little or no hired labour from outside the family. Even in the 1980s most of the surviving farmers fitted such a concept, although the optimum size of such farms and the amount of capital required to operate successfully has considerably increased. The farmer is thus tied into the market and the urban-based business system in many ways. He has to purchase vital inputs from machinery-makers and giant chemical corporations. He may need loans and other forms of credit to finance these inputs. He depends upon food-processors or agri-businesses for the sale of his output, or he may be cultivating his land on contract to an agri-business (which accounted for thirty per cent of farm output by 1980).

Besides diverging in many ways from the idealized family farm of the past, present-day farming is carried on within the context of a mass of regulations deriving from the New Deal period, which makes it the most regulated sector of the economy. Government intervention in the 1930s was devised to deal with an overproduction crisis which resulted in a fall in prices and a catastrophic fall in farm incomes. No doubt without intervention to buy up surpluses and subsidize a cut in production many farmers would have become destitute and have been forced to leave the land and join the millions of jobless in the cities. Framed as an emergency programme, the package of interventionist measures, beginning with the Agricultural Adjustment Act of 1933, had some justification. In any case, President Roosevelt and others heard the sound of the farmers' marching feet, and considered that stricken farmers would need help if they were not to revolt. This sentiment was a corollary to the potent family farm myth. But legislation then, and later, was based upon the premise of helping farmers to stay on the land, not easing them off it into alternative employments which were just not available at that time, although they were later.

Then came the Second World War which, like the First, created a voracious demand for everything the American farmer could produce. Just when the new technologies were bringing a revolution to the farm, the bogey of over-production disappeared. For some time after the war there was a buoyant demand for American food and raw material exports. As the world economy revived and countries became better able to meet their own needs, the old problems came back, intensified by the continuous improvement in productivity. Thus, while in the 1950s and 1960s industry and other branches of the economy enjoyed a long wave of prosperity, agriculture was once again grappling with the familiar problem of over-production. Mounting surpluses threatened to drive down prices and push more and more farmers off the land. In fact that is exactly what happened, despite the continuance of price supports and subsidies. The forces of the market had not been abrogated, they simply operated less blindly than they might otherwise have done. By a process of slow attrition farmers did leave the land in increasing numbers, and those who remained often turned to other work to maintain their incomes. The ratio of capital and land to labour for successful farming continued to rise, forcing out more and more of the smaller, marginal farmers. With the help of price supports and subsidies, however, medium and large-sized farms enjoyed a fitful prosperity according to market trends.

The number of farms, which had peaked at 6.8 million in 1935 was down to a little over 2 million by the mid-1980s and still declining. By the latter date the average farm size was well over 400 acres, up from 155 acres at the earlier date. Between 1950 and 1984 productivity had risen five-fold, and the labour force had been cut by 75%. Many smaller farms had ceased to be viable units capable of supporting a family and their owners and family members were also engaged in off-farm work. To increase output, farmers were pouring more and more fertilizers and other chemicals on to their land. The fall in farm labour requirements reflects the fact that many jobs previously done by farmers and farm workers were now performed off the land, and their contribution to output thus falls under the heading of industry or services. Concentration of production in the larger units was a perceptible trend. Very large farms seem to have been the optimum only in some branches of production, such as the production of fruit and vegetables in California and Florida by great agri-businesses. In the case of cereals and other crops, medium-sized farms appear to have been the most successful. But although conserving a family structure, they required heavy capitalization to enable full use to be made of the improved farming technologies. The application of these methods, however, tended to aggravate the problem of over-production, which steadfastly refused to go away. With the adoption of the corporate form by family-owned units, the growth in scale, the growth of agri-business and contract-farming, the family-farm system was in a state of transformation during the 1980s. Over 50% of total farm sales came from the 30% of medium and large farms, heavily committed to investment and vulnerable to adverse price movements.

Farmers were obviously sensitive both to the prices of their inputs and domestic needs and to the prices which they received for their products. During the 1950s through to the late 1960s most branches of agriculture experienced something like a price-scissors: inflationary price rises in inputs on the one side, low or falling prices for agricultural products on the other. This relative decline as reflected in farmers' incomes provoked the movement from the land which took place during that period. Family members were attracted into off-farm jobs or obliged to take them to avoid poverty. Many left farming altogether for city jobs and the attractions of city life, especially potent for the younger generations. Many black share-croppers migrated northwards, while many white farmers and farm-hands from the rural South moved into the industrial cities of the region. This movement began during the Second World War on a growing scale and continued after it.

The farm policies initiated in the 1930s continued throughout this period with varying degrees of emphasis and effectiveness. There was really a congeries of policies, never brought together into a single coherent whole. Their underlying purpose was to pay farmers to restrict production and to reduce the amount of land they cultivated. Although designed to sustain the family farm, these policies eventually had the effect of encouraging the larger farmers, able to apply the more capital-intensive methods required to make use of technological advances, while family farmers decreased in number. Only the myth of the family farm retained its durability.

During the immediate post-war years world-wide food shortages ensured a market for American farm products, whether sold at current prices or disposed of as part of foreign aid programmes. For a while, then, over-production ceased to be a problem, or was on a lesser scale. But this period was short-lived and by the mid-1950s the old problems were re-asserting themselves. New advances in technology, especially the use of artificial fertilizers and other chemical products, reinforced the trend towards over-production. More and more could be produced with ever shrinking labour inputs. The farmers fell back once again upon state support. The Agricultural Adjustment Act was revised in 1949 and remained the basis of farm policy for the next forty years (and more, since no alternative is in sight). In short, the government undertook to take surpluses off the market in one way or another, thus subsidizing agriculture at the expense of the consumer (who paid higher prices) and the taxpayer. For certain of the main crops a target price was fixed by the government, which then lent the amount each farmer would expect to receive at that price with their harvest as collateral. If the market price exceeded the target, farmers could pay off their debt and keep the difference. If it did not, then the farmers kept the loan money, leaving the government with the responsibility of storing and disposing of the surplus.

Various means were found for doing that. One was Public Law 480 (Food for Peace), which made it possible to supply food to poor countries with food shortages as outright gifts or on a long-term, easy payment system. This made it possible to use food as a political weapon. Favoured regimes could be supported through these food subsidies (which obviated the need for agrarian reforms), while those pursuing a policy of which Washington disapproved would not receive food aid or might be deprived of it if they failed to maintain such a policy. Another way of disposing of surpluses was to distribute them free, or below market price, to America's own poor. This could be done by handing over commodities to certain categories of people. The main way of dealing with the surpluses at home came with the Food Stamp Act passed in 1964, at a time when America's own poor had been 'discovered' amid the prevailing affluence. Those entitled by low incomes could buy stamps at a price below their face value, which could then be used to buy commodities in the stores. The very poor were issued with free stamps. By the 1980s over twenty-two million Americans benefited from food stamps at a cost of over $13 billion. As a means to aid the needy the food stamp programme remains controversial, especially since the abolition of the purchase requirement in 1977. It is one way among others of mopping up commodity surpluses.

Meanwhile, the dependence of American farmers upon overseas demand remained. When it slackened off, surpluses piled up; when it increased, they disappeared and prices rose, farmers again experiencing what invariably proved to be a transient prosperity. In the early 1970s and especially from 1972 with large Soviet grain purchases, the surplus problem seemed to be on the way to resolution, paradoxically, as a result of the agricultural weaknesses of America's Cold War adversary. Later, China also appeared in the market as a purchaser of US grain. American farmers were also adjusting their production to changing world demand, notably for animal feeding stuffs; soybeans became an important export crop, largely used for animal feed in Europe. Food proved to be a double-edged weapon; when the Carter administration cut off grain exports to the Soviet Union after the invasion of Afghanistan in 1980, mid-West farmers lost an important source of income.

When agriculture became prosperous, as was the case in the early 1970s, farmers were tempted to buy more land and to go into debt – which could lead to trouble when prices fell again. The attempt made by the Nixon administration in 1973 to take government out of agriculture and give market forces greater scope proved to be short-lived. Production had been increased under the spur of higher prices, the new target figures proved to be too high and surpluses re-appeared. In the Food and Agriculture Act of 1977, the structure of price supports continued, with loans on crops withheld from the market and subsidies for wheat and corn producers who reduced their acreage. The trend towards larger farms was now well established and farm policy actually contributed to it. The larger farm has always benefited from guaranteed prices and subsidies for land not cultivated more than the smaller farm, yet farm policy was usually defended on the grounds that it assisted the family farmer.

Even the Reagan administration, although ideologically committed to the free operation of market forces, was not able to carry out a fundamental change in agricultural policy. Doubtless, if the government withdrew its interventionist measures agricultural surpluses would drive down prices. The already existing trend for the smaller, less efficient farmers to leave agriculture would be accelerated. Without some way of helping these farmers over their financial difficulties and assisting those under retirement age to re-cycle into urban occupations, the effect would be considerable social upheaval in some areas and political losses for the party responsible for the return to the market.

The inexorable decline in the number of farmers and the concentration of agricultural production into a smaller number of large units showed, if belatedly, that agriculture was subject to the same laws as industry. It was the reverse side of the technological revolution which developments in farm machinery and in chemistry had brought to the tilling of the land and the raising of livestock. Most agricultural products found their way to the consumer via highly capitalized processing plants and supermarket chains. The busy housewife, perhaps also a member of the work force, wanted a uniform, standardized, quality product at the lowest price. With its great variety of climatic and soil conditions and a highly developed marketing and distributive system, American agriculture was able to meet this demand and more, and have a surplus available for export, where it was not a positive embarrassment. At the same time, a minority of consumers were becoming aware of the possible dangers from food grown with the help of massive doses of fertilizers, treated with pesticides and preservatives and meat from animals treated with hormones and other chemicals. The increasing emphasis on health, as well as on preservation of the environment and the ecological balance, could yet bring about changes in agricultural practice. 'Organic' foods are already being sold at premium prices, tempting some farmers to return to more traditional methods.

Table 7.4 Federal Economic Regulatory Statutes, 1887–1976

Year	*Law*	*Function*
1887	Interstate Commerce Act	Establishes ICC to regulate price and entry in rail and related water transportation
1890	Sherman Act	Prohibits joint action to restrain trade, monopoly, and monopolizing
1906	Hepburn Act	Extends ICC regulation to pipeline rates
1906	Food and Drugs Act	Establishes FDA to regulate adulteration and misbranding of foods and drugs
1910	Mann-Elkins Act	Extends ICC regulation to telephone, telegraph, cable
1914	Clayton Act	Prohibits anticompetitive mergers, price discrimination, and business practices
1914	Federal Trade Commission	Establishes FTC to enforce Clayton Act and police unfair trade practices
1916	Shipping Act	Establishes Federal Maritime Commission to regulate water transportation
1918	Export Trade Act	Authorizes 'Webb-Pomerene' exporters' cartels
1920	Transportation Act	Extends ICC authority to set minimum prices
1920	Water Power Act	Establishes FPC to regulate power projects
1921	Packers and Stockyards Act	Establishes Packer and Stockyards Administration to regulate practices in livestock markets
1922	Grain Futures Act	Establishes regulation for future trading in grain
1922	Capper-Volstead Act	Exempts cartels of agricultural producers from antitrust
1927	Federal Radio Act	Establishes Federal Radio Commission to control use of radio frequencies
1931	Davis-Bacon Act	Requires federal construction projects to pay prevailing wages
1932	Norris-LaGuardia Act	Establishes legality of unionization and collective bargaining
1933	National Industrial Recovery Act (declared unconstitutional, 1935)	Establishes NIRA to cartelize industry and regulate wages and hours of labor
1933	Agricultural Adjustment Act (declared unconstitutional, 1936)	Establishes production controls and price supports for farm products
1933	Securities Act	Regulates public offering of new securities
1934	Securities Exchange Act	Establishes SEC to administer

Table 7.4 Cont.

Year	*Law*	*Function*
		Securities Act and to regulate trading on securities exchanges
1934	Communications Act	Establishes FCC to administer communications regulation
1934	Fishery Cooperative Marketing Act	Exempts cartels of fishermen from antitrust
1935	Public Utility Act	Extends FPC control to all interstate electricity and required deconcentration of utilities
1935	Motor Carriers Act	Extends ICC regulation to trucking
1935	Banking Act	Establishes FDIC to insure and regulate banks
1935	National Labor Relations Act	Establishes NLRB to regulate unfair labor practices and requires collective bargaining
1936	Robinson-Patman Act	Amends Clayton Act to prohibit price differences
1936	Merchant Marine Act	Authorizes Federal Maritime Commission to subsidize shipbuilding and ship operation
1936	Commodity Exchange Act	Establishes Commodity Exchange Authority to regulate futures trading in agricultural commodities
1937	Miller-Tydings Act	Authorizes state resale price-maintenance contracts in interstate commerce
1937	Bituminous Coal Act	Establishes the Bituminous Coal Commission to set minimum prices for coal
1938	Civil Aeronautics Act	Establishes CAB to regulate entry and price and to subsidize interstate air carriers
1938	Natural Gas Act	Extends FPC regulation to transmission and resale price of natural gas
1938	Fair Labor Standards Act	Regulates minimum wages and maximum hours for labor
1938	Wheeler-Lea Act	Amends FTC Act to prohibit deceptive acts and practices
1938	Food, Drugs, Cosmetics Act	Extends regulatory authority of FDA
1938	Agricultural Adjustment Act	Reformulates regulation of farm prices and production to avoid Supreme Court objections

Table 7.4 Cont.

Year	*Law*	*Function*
1940	Transportation Act	Extends ICC regulation to inland water carriers
1942	Small Business Mobilization Act	Authorizes War Production Board to grant exemptions from antitrust
1945	McCarran Act	Exempts state-regulated insurance firms from antitrust
1946	Atomic Energy Act	Establishes AEC to regulate nuclear power production
1947	Taft-Hartley Act	Prohibits unfair union practices
1948	Sugar Act	Establishes quotas on imports and production of sugar
1948	Reed-Bulwinkle Act	Exempts cartel prices approved by ICC from antitrust
1950	Cellar-Kefauver Act	Amends Clayton Act to prohibit anticompetitive mergers by acquiring assets
1950	Defense Production Act	Authorizes the president to exempt industries from antitrust for defense purposes
1953	Small Business Act	Establishes SBA to administer subsidized loans to small business
1954	Atomic Energy Act	Extends AEC regulation of nuclear power
1958	Transportation Act	Authorizes ICC to disregard effect of a regulated rate on other modes of transportation
1959	Landrum-Griffin Act	Prohibits unfair union practices
1962	Food and Drug Amendments	Extends FDA control of testing and marketing drugs
1962	Air Pollution Control Act	Establishes air pollution standards
1964	Civil Rights Act	Establishes Equal Employment Opportunity Commission to regulate job discrimination
1965	Water Quality Act	Requires state standards on pollution
1966	Fair Packaging and Labeling Act	Sets required information on product labels
1966	Child Protection Act	Prohibits sale of hazardous toys
1966	Bank Merger Act	Requires banks to notify regulators of intention to merge
1966	Traffic Safety Act	Establishes National Highway Safety Administration to set standards for autos
1967	Agricultural Fair Practices Act	Prohibits unfair practices by farm-products handlers

Table 7.4 Cont.

Year	*Law*	*Function*
1967	Flammable Fabrics Act	Extends control of fabrics standards
1968	Truth-in-Lending Act	Specifies information on terms of credit transactions
1969	National Environment Policy Act	Requires environmental impact statement for projects
1970	Amendment to Banking Act	Regulates credit cards
1970	Economic Stabilization Act	Authorizes general price controls
1970	Securities Investors Protection Act	Establishes insurance for brokers accounts
1970	Occupational Safety and Health Act	Establishes OSHA to set and enforce safety standards for employment
1970	National Air Quality Act	Establishes EPA to administer pollution standards
1972	Consumer Products Safety Act	Establishes Consumer Products Safety Commission to set standards and to prohibit hazardous products
1972	Noise Pollution and Control Act	Sets limits on noise of products
1974	Federal Energy Administration Act	Establishes FEA authority to require conservation of energy
1974	Employee Retirement Income Security Act	Establishes terms of firm pension plans
1974	Commodity Futures Trading Act	Establishes CFTC and extends the regulation of futures trading
1975	Consumer Goods Pricing Act	Repeals Miller-Tydings Act
1975	Magnuson-Moss Act	Sets terms and wording for product warranties
1976	Antitrust Improvements Act	Amends antitrust laws to require firms to notify FTC of intent to merge

Sources: Commerce Clearing House 1977; Wilcox 1960; Wilcox and Shepherd 1975; Weidenbaum 1977.

(Table 7.4 derived from Cox, Charles C., 'Monopoly explanations of the Great Depression and Public Policies towards Business' in Brunner, Karl (Ed.), *The Great Depression Revisited* (Boston, 1981), pp. 185–8.)

CHAPTER 8

The troubled economy: the 1970s and beyond

The 1970s proved to be the most troubled decade since the end of the Second World War. The long post-war expansion turned into the new phenomenon of 'stagflation' (stagnation with rising prices). Inflation began to spiral out of control. Whatever other factors may have contributed to inflation, and there were several, any chance of keeping it under control was wrecked by President Lyndon Johnson's unwillingness to raise taxes in order to pay for the war in Vietnam, a war which proved to be longer, tougher and more expensive than he, or anyone else, had expected.

The dollar had already ceased to be a scarce currency. American spending overseas for military and other purposes, and the export of capital, notably by the multinationals, had undermined the stability of the dollar and made its devaluation a relevant issue. The revived economies of Western Europe and Japan, which had been restored with American aid, had now become formidable competitors in the home market as well as in the markets of the world. Their new found strength began to erode American hegemony, apparently established for all time after the Second World War. At home, the techniques of economic management and fine tuning adopted after the war under Keynesian influence now appeared to be inadequate and irrelevant in dealing with persistent inflation, and, indeed, could be held to be partially responsible for it. Domestically and internationally, policy was in the melting pot.

In the international field, prosperity had concealed the weakening of the dollar and the coming challenge to American hegemony. The countries sustained by the United States in the early post-war years for political as much as economic reasons – they were needed allies in the Cold War – now became rivals as industrial producers. In the 1950s and 1960s they had, with the exception of Britain, experienced high rates of growth and a much higher rate of investment than the United States. Their interests no longer coincided at every point with those of Washington. They no longer needed US aid but they did need markets and investment fields; they resented the privileged position which the dollar had acquired as a result of the Bretton Woods agreement, while their own currencies were getting stronger every year. From the standpoint of Washington, countries like West Germany and Japan were no longer pulling their weight in the military 'defence of the free world' but were more interested in building up their own international commercial and financial position, leaving the US to bear the arms burden. The dollar, which had begun its post-war history as a strong and scarce currency, was now in abundant supply as a result of the ability of the Federal Reserve Board to create new credit to finance American overseas outlays. Whether they liked it or not, foreign central banks had to accept large quantities of newly-created dollars, while a new phenomenon, the Eurodollar market, appeared. It consisted of dollars deposited with banks outside the United States which could be used for loans to corporations or governments and permitted a great increase in the volume of international credit available. It grew swiftly from the late 1950s, fed in part by large US balance of payment deficits. American banks participated in the Eurodollar market (which ceased to be purely European) because they could thus evade banking restrictions at home. The huge build up of 'off-shore' dollars contributed to the explosion of international lending, the beginning of the debt crisis of the late 1970s and early 1980s.

Significant changes were taking place in the relative economic rankings of the major industrial countries. West Germany and Japan had rapidly built up powerful and dynamic economies, with great industries based upon new and advanced technologies. To avoid a crisis of over-production and maintain the profitability of their capital investments, these countries, as well as the 'newly-industrializing countries' of Asia, had to have markets. The biggest and most lucrative market was that of the United States. At the same time, American private capital had moved abroad on a considerable scale, establishing branch plants in many countries or buying up local businesses, and was playing an increasingly important role in overseas financial markets. The cost of the Vietnam war, added to that of other military commitments, strained American resources and undermined the dollar. It was evident that, while remaining the premier country of world capitalism – mainly because of its military-strategic role – it no longer held the dominating position among its allies that it had at the time of the Marshall Plan and the foundation of NATO (1949). Yet the United States, with its world-wide military bases, was inextricably involved in international questions from Central America to the Persian Gulf, from Berlin to Kabul. Events in the 1970s were to underline the point.

Besides involving the country in a long, costly and ultimately unpopular war, the Johnson administration had also, through its Great Society programmes, increased federal spending. It thus needed either to raise more revenue by taxation or to accept larger budget deficits, covered by borrowing. The boom of the 1960s had built up irrepressible inflationary pressures which existing techniques of economic management, applied Keynesianism, were unable to subdue. However, this boom was not simply based upon inflation. It represented, in fact, a process of expanded reproduction in which accumulation and investment were going ahead both in producer goods and consumer goods industries, especially the former. This expansion was supported also by the high level of military expenditure now customary, though that had been falling as a proportion of GNP until the full effect of the Vietnam war began to be felt. Military expenditure was the most inflationary type of government spending, since it pumped money into the economy without a corresponding increase in the output of goods and services. Expenditure overseas also aggravated pressure on the dollar.

During the long post-war boom the basic industries like steel and heavy engineering continued to grow, as did the great mass-production industries in the consumer goods sector. Unemployment was low (especially for adult, white males), living standards were rising and labour was in a strong position to win wage increases. To finance continued expansion, industry and consumers borrowed heavily, as did the government. By the late 1960s, despite signs of relative decline in America's international position and the strains on the dollar, continued expansion with only minor interruptions seemed to lie ahead.

These appearances were deceptive. The forces which had fuelled the boom were working themselves out and it became more difficult to maintain the rate of profit. Inflationary forces were building up as the Vietnam war dragged on, though it did not have the same effect as a total war. It did, however, contribute to a taut labour market; it helped boost business profits, especially of those firms having arms contracts, mainly the giant corporations; it came at a time when increased government expenditures for 'the Great Society' were coming on-stream. In the typically oligopolistic market situation, the corporations were able to pass on higher costs to their customers, including the government. Inflation reduced the real burden of fixed charges and encouraged more investment as demand continued to grow. These domestic trends tended to weaken the dollar internationally, and thus its role in the Bretton Woods system. The contradictions involved in maintaining the parity of the dollar while grappling with inflationary pressures at home became more acute.

ENTER RICHARD NIXON

When President Richard Nixon took office early in 1969 he was confronted with all the problems ensuing from the war, including its growing unpopularity at home. At first he took a gamble on escalating the war, with intervention by American forces in Cambodia. When that failed and inflation continued, he changed his tactic, looking for some way of winding down the war and checking inflation. This meant imposing restrictive monetary and fiscal policies: a conventional remedy but one which stifled growth and produced all the symptoms of recession. During 1970 GNP fell slightly; unemployment rose, but inflation remained at an average rate of 5.5% (then considered a high level). When the war finally began to be de-escalated, new defence orders were cut, helping to damp down inflationary pressures. From a political point of view, Nixon knew that the association of his presidency with recession was not a good omen for re-election. Consequently, he looked around for an alternative 'game plan' which finally took shape as the 'New Economic Policy' of 1971.

The new policy was unveiled in his speech, which was to become famous, made on 15 August 1971; in some ways it represented the end of the post-war era and a new departure for US international economic policy. The centrepiece of what was seen as 'the Nixon shock' by outsiders was the unilateral winding up of the 1944 Bretton Woods agreement between America and its allies, upon which the world monetary system had been based, ending the convertibility of the dollar for gold.

Ever since 1934, when President Roosevelt is said to have stuck a pin into a list of numbers, the dollar had been convertible into gold at the rate of $35 per fine ounce. The system of fixed exchange rates established by the International Monetary Fund set up at Bretton Woods had as its basis a convertible dollar as the key currency at that rate. Nixon had effectively ended the system at a blow, presumably in the interests of American finance, leaving other countries to work out what they would do and how they would respond.

Time was to show that, if in a diminished way, the dollar would conserve its position as an international money and thus retain a privileged position in relation to other currencies. The other leading industrial countries had an interest in preventing a return to the kind of competitive exchange depreciation which had been so destructive of monetary stability in the 1930s. Hence the Smithsonian agreement at the end of 1971 under which the major Western countries agreed to a devaluation of the dollar. Negotiations in 1972 and 1973 provided for further devaluations of the dollar and the adjustment of exchange rates. Their success was short lived; the exchange rate of the dollar would be left to market forces tempered by the interventions of central banks: the beginning of what was known as the 'dirty float'. The essential change was that two pillars of the Bretton Woods system had gone: the convertibility of the dollar and fixed exchange rates.

To deal with pressing domestic economic problems, Nixon's 'New Economic Policy' imposed mandatory wage and price controls (which he had previously said he would never accept), beginning with a ninety-day freeze. This was a complete reversal of a policy which had been re-affirmed as recently as his Economic Report to Congress in February 1971. Nixon was quoted as saying that 'we are all Keynesians now'; convert or not, his new policy was extraordinary for a Republican president. The measure can be seen as an emergency attempt to forestall a wage explosion, mollifying the unions with the promise of price stability.

Machinery was set up to administer the new controls, programmed to go through four phases, moving towards a return to free markets in the final one. Some success was recorded in holding down inflation in the first two phases, but during 1973 prices began to bound upwards and continued to do so until controls ended in April 1974. Nixon's package included other measures to stimulate the economy, notably fiscal incentives and a temporary ten per cent surcharge on dutiable imports. The latter requires a word of explanation. In the post-war period the United States had been a strong supporter of the General Agreement on Tariffs and Trade, dropping its traditional protectionist stance. By this time lower tariffs had resulted in increased imports of manufactured goods from America's industrial competitors, as well as from developing countries beginning to establish their own industries. While some of these countries began to accumulate dollar balances from their trade surpluses, they did not necessarily buy more

American products. This was the beginning of a new relationship between the United States and the world market which was to be the source of many problems and much friction for the rest of the century. Already, in his speech, Nixon complained that the United States was fighting with its hands tied behind its back and called on its trading partners to accept a greater share of its defence burden. This was another theme which was to be repeated over the years to little effect.

Other stimulants to the economy announced by Nixon included a seven per cent investment tax credit for business; consumers were gratified with the repeal of excise taxes on motor vehicles and a higher personal allowance for federal income tax purposes. Altogether these measures helped to stimulate a boom which, as a bonus for Nixon, saw his re-election in 1972. As it turned out, the upturn hardly survived the election. In the course of 1973, while growth continued, serious problems were brewing up below the surface.

The Nixon administration had not been able to master the inflation inherited from its predecessor, despite the palliatives of the 'New Economic Policy'. The world-wide repercussions of American inflation and the shock of dollar devaluation came back into the United States, first of all by a rise in the price of imports. Meanwhile, world demand for various foodstuffs and raw materials began to outstrip supply; some spectacular price increases took place. Worse was to come. At the time of the war between Israel and Egypt at the end of 1973, Arab oil-producers proclaimed a boycott of those countries, including the United States, which supported Israel. This was followed by a fourfold increase imposed by the Organization of Petroleum Exporting Countries (OPEC). The energy crisis had arrived. Oil and petrol began to be in short supply, driving up their prices, and thus affecting the price of practically everything else.

The ending of wage and price controls, which had held back rises, was followed by renewed inflationary pressures. Combined with the ostensibly 'exogenous' supply-side shocks, notably higher primary products prices coming from outside and the exhaustion of long-term factors making for growth, the stage was set for the deepest recession since the 1930s. The long period of post-war expansion had at last come to an end; American and world capitalism entered a new phase of turbulence which, amongst other things, threw economic policy and economics as a theory into a state of flux.

Various strands can be traced in the weaving of the ragged texture which made up the new period (the period of the *post* post-war boom). Firstly, over the long term, the high rates of investment during the booming 1960s, prolonged by Nixon's interventionist policies from 1971, had built up massive capacity which could only be used fully given continued new investment and the steady growth of consumer demand. But as the boom flagged, capacity became excessive, the rate of profit was being pressed down by the weight of existing embodied capital, which likewise discouraged more investment in industry. In the past, the normal accompaniment of such a market situation would have been lower prices, as firms tried to keep their market shares and get some return on capital, as well as a downward pressure on incomes. In the 1970s this just did not happen; instead, inflation continued unabated or even became more acute, despite symptoms of stagnation in the economy as a whole: a falling rate of profit, excess capacity and sluggish or no growth. Hence the new phenomenon of 'stagflation' (rising prices with low capacity operation and unemployment) which, besides causing problems of theoretical explanation, revealed the inadequacy of the Keynesian prescriptions which even a conservative like Nixon had espoused.

Meanwhile the Watergate scandal which had disclosed widespread corruption in the Administration disposed of Nixon, who was replaced by Gerald Ford, a more orthodox Republican. The economy continued to plummet downwards through 1974 and 1975 before there was any sign of recovery. The term 'crisis' now came into wide use to describe the condition of the economy. Indeed, it could be claimed that the US economy entered a long drawn-out crisis of a kind which endured right through to the late 1980s and perhaps beyond.

Unemployment rose markedly in 1975, reaching about nine per cent by May of that year; a high level by post-war standards. Inflation peaked late in 1974 and then came down to five per cent in the following year; also high by post-war standards (though it would later seem modest). Business confidence fell to a low ebb, as evidenced by the reduction of stocks of goods and the reluctance to embark on new investment, evident from 1973. When something like recovery began, it was significant that the economy failed to attain its previous rates of growth, levels of investment or productivity gains. Stagflation had not been conquered. Ideas about what constituted full employment and the tolerable level of inflation were being revised upwards.

Severe as the recession had been – and it is worth emphasizing that it was a worldwide phenomenon – it failed to reach the depth of the Great Depression of the 1930s, the spectre of which had not gone away. It was bad enough to re-awaken fears that a slump as severe and as long was no longer as unthinkable as had generally been assumed by economists, businessmen and politicians. Although bearing a family resemblance to previous recessions, that of 1974–5 differed from them in one salient respect: there was no deflation, instead, the dollar continued to lose purchasing power and prices continued to rise. The clearing of ground for recovery by a downward revaluation of assets and the lowering of costs, thus restoring the profitability of capital, did not happen in the classic manner. What did happen from about this time was that plants that proved unprofitable in the recession did not re-open in the boom: 'de-industrialization' had begun. In response to the declining rate of profit at home, corporations sought higher profits by transferring manufacturing facilities to low-wage countries. Real investment increased by only twenty-five per cent in the 1970s compared with forty per cent in the previous decade. It was the end of the period of growth and expansion inaugurated after the Second World War.

On a world scale, too, the recession of 1974–5 was a turning-point in economic history. Those countries which had enjoyed 'economic miracles' now saw their growth slowed to a snail's pace. Unemployment on a mass scale afflicted the West European countries. Japan and the Asian industrializing countries stepped up their efforts to expand their share of the world market to avert a similar slow-down which would have shattered their growth and export-orientated economies. Growth became much more uneven between countries, and between regions and sectors in the same country, including the United States. The old 'smoke-stack' industries went into decline; new high-tech industries like those in the well-publicized Silicon Valley near San Francisco began to boom. Not unemployment, but what to do about continued inflation, became the major preoccupation of economic policy. The choice seemed to be stark: accept some inflation as the price of expansion and adapt business and accounting practices accordingly, or pursue a firm deflationary policy even if that meant accepting a higher level of unemployment than had been customary since the Second World War. The latter policy would require a reduction in spending, both public and private; the model was that of West Germany. While some economists and policy-makers accepted some inflation as inevitable if the economy were to avoid tumbling into the abyss of runaway deflation, others feared the consequences of inflation and saw it as a barrier to a full and healthy recovery.

The monetarist school (its best-known representative being Professor Milton Friedman of the University of Chicago), which held the latter view, had gained in stature and influence as a result of the perceived failure of Keynesian policies (as they were described) both before and after 1971. It saw the key to stability in the control of the money supply – exercised by the Federal Reserve Board, not by the Treasury – which should be increased in harmony with the overall growth rate. The monetarists also advocated the dismantling of much of the apparatus of government regulation and intervention which had grown up since the New Deal and a return, as far as possible, to the free market. Monetarists and other advocates of a return to market forces rapidly gained ground.

The actual government response to the economic problem of 'stagflation' during the Ford administration was entirely pragmatic. After he took office in August 1974, following Nixon's disgrace, the President pronounced inflation to be public enemy number one. The slogan was 'Whip Inflation Now', abbreviated as WIN. A major weapon against inflation was seen to be reduction in federal government expenditure, but as the recession deepened, the Ford administration had to re-adjust its sights and began calling for tax reductions. In March 1975 a law was passed which included a rebate on 1974 taxes, a temporary reduction in personal income tax and a $50 payment to needy recipients of social security relief. The tax cuts may have assisted the slow recovery which began as consumption revived and there was some re-building of stocks. Meanwhile, in the light of the steep rise in fuel prices, the administration groped for an energy policy. Decontrol was rejected by Congress in favour of a gradual removal of controls. In January 1976, Ford proposed further tax cuts, to be matched by additional reductions in federal expenditure. Fear of inflation, and growing budget deficits, inhibited a more expansionary policy and, on the whole, recovery was left to the operation of market forces without any clear-cut action by the administration. Throughout this period inflation tended to be identified with excess demand, rather than cost-push factors, though the main pressure on prices was coming from the supply side: the steeply increased cost of fuel and of certain primary products. Producers, of course, benefited, including many American farmers, who had a temporary bonanza from soaring world food prices, and domestic oil-producers in Texas and elsewhere.

OIL AND INFLATION

The 'Nixon shock' of 1971, followed by the first 'oil shock' of 1974–5, were landmarks in the deepening crisis of US capitalism, but they were its symptoms, not its causes. The latter were to be found in factors such as excess capacity, over-production and the foreign industrial challenge which had brought the post-war boom to an end. They were accompanied by unexpected and untoward changes in the international position of the United States, coupled with structural changes in the world market and the new turbulence they produced in capital and foreign exchange markets. The problems were exacerbated by the lack of politically coherent leadership in the aftermath of the Watergate scandal, continued through the Ford (1974–6) and the Carter (1976–80) administrations.

After the ending of dollar convertibility and successive devaluations in the 1970s, it might have been expected that the dollar would be ousted from its predominant position in the world monetary system. But that was not to be so. The devaluation of the dollar gave export industries a reprieve, actually doubling the ratio of exports to GNP, and enabled profits to be maintained.

When the dollar threatened to fall too far, the Fed raised interest rates, attracting foreign capital into the US. Before long the hugely inflated earnings of the oil-rich countries found their way on to the New York money market, thus encouraging the banks to extend their lending in other directions, notably to the developing countries of Latin America and Asia – a trend which stored up problems for the future. The mid-1970s also saw a great build-up of the eurocurrency market as a source of funds for the internationalization of capital. The fact was that the dollar was able to retain, or even consolidate, its dominant role in the world market, where three-quarters of international trade and capital movements continued to be transacted in dollars. Consequently, creditor countries continued to hold dollar balances and the Federal Reserve Board retained the prerogative of creating new money to meet American payments overseas, while providing an indispensable flow of credit into the world market as a whole. Export-orientated countries were able to increase their penetration of the US market, as indebted developing countries also grew and increased their demand for imports.

An American balance of trade and payments deficit became a virtual necessity if the world monetary system were not to collapse or a general crisis freeze-up the whole world economy. No longer underpinned by gold, there was a danger that the dollar would gyrate uncontrollably, thus the need for high interest rates, which became contagious. These high rates were necessary to attract money to New York, or to keep it there, in order to finance the twin deficits. The disadvantage was that high rates slowed some kinds of investment (e.g. industrial modernization) and encouraged a search for high and quick returns.

Still more funds were attracted into the American money market, pushing up paper gains and favouring a proliferation of financial transactions which had little or no relationship to production. Pushing paper around was becoming more lucrative than long-term investment in production; whole sections of industry went into decline or closed down in the following years as capital sought to counteract the falling rate of profit.

Hence the phenomenon of 'de-industrialization' which began to afflict the so-called 'smoke-stack' industries in the traditional centres. Import penetration increased; growth rates remained low; productivity failed to grow at the accustomed rates. At the same time, since the 'Great Society' reforms of the 1960s, social welfare costs made up a growing proportion of federal budgetary expenditure, partly financed by borrowing. The reaction from Keynesianism was coupled with growing criticism of this expenditure and the budget deficits for which allegedly it was responsible. The theory was advanced that government spending 'crowded out' private investment, while the trend towards a ('European-style') welfare state attracted increasing resistance from the Republican right as well as from the free-marketeers.

Inflation continued through the 1970s; untamed by the Ford administration, it survived to plague the Democratic administration of Jimmy Carter which followed it. In 1979 the price of oil doubled, following the revolution in Iran. Continuous inflation had, of course, been reducing the real cost of petroleum since 1975 and economies were being realized in its use. Despite earlier forebodings, the richer countries had been able to absorb the higher prices with little difficulty and even the slowdown in 1974–5 could be mainly attributed to other factors. Higher prices had stimulated the search for other reserves worldwide, encouraging investment in high-cost fields such as those of Alaska and the North Sea, in which US corporations had a dominant position. This helped to keep up the rate of return on capital. Taken together, economies in the use of energy, the shift to other sources of oil, and the general slow-down in world economic growth eventually brought the era of high prices to an end, at least temporarily. But the lowering of prices, which OPEC had to accept, caused almost as much upset in the 1980s as the increases of the previous decade had done. Indebted oil-producers could no longer pay their debts, and fewer funds were available to lend to developing countries, thus aggravating the international debt problem.

In the short run, however, the two oil shocks were felt across a wide range of consumer expenditure in the United States. In turn, investment was temporarily choked off from such fields as motor vehicles, civil aviation and thermally-generated electric power. Externally, however, it meant new riches for the oil-producers; as already noted, much of the oil wealth, foreign or American, was recycled via US banks, much of it to developing countries of dubious credit-worthiness. The strong, oil-consuming, industrial countries intensified their export drive, targeting particularly the American consumer market and aggravating the balance of payments deficit. Domestic supplies of oil continued to fall behind demand; imports of crude oil rose from twelve per cent of consumption in 1970 to thirty-seven per cent in 1980.

THE ROLE OF THE 'FED'

The series of new problems which plagued American capitalism began in the 1960s under the Democrat, Lyndon Johnson, continued under the Republican administrations of Richard Nixon and Gerald Ford and their successors, the Democrat Jimmy Carter and the Republican Ronald Reagan. The changes in the political complexion of the administration or the personality of the president, had less influence on the course of events than either their supporters, or their critics, variously claimed. A potent factor was the policy of the Federal Reserve Board, that semi-autonomous body charged with controlling the money supply, and custodian of the long-term well-being of the American business system. A powerful personality, like that of Benjamin Strong in the 1920s, could leave his mark on policy as chairman of the board. In 1979 the Carter administration appointed to the post a professional economist, Paul Volcker, who had already played a crucial role in the dismantling of the Bretton Woods system in the early 1970s. Under Volcker, who remained in office until 1987, a momentous change in policy took place.

It should be pointed out that the control of the money and credit supply by a public institution like the Fed, working closely with the Treasury, constitutes a most effective form of intervention by the state. It possesses a position of central importance in regulating the level of domestic activity and determining the exchange value of the dollar. It exercises these powers in 'the national interest', as perceived by the administration and as influenced by the leading figures in the Fed itself; in practice this becomes a euphemism for the needs of corporate business and the big banks. The weakening influence of Keynesianism and the rise of monetarism (emphasizing the monetary stock) and supply-side economics (concerned with factors influencing production costs) were reflected in the advice given by government economists and the policy of the Fed itself. At the same time there was growing aversion to state intervention and deficit-financing in political and business circles.

The Volcker policy was based upon the principle of aiming at more control by the Fed over bank reserves to reach targeted money supply figures, rather than depending upon interest rate changes; this meant, in effect, an adaptation to monetarist theory. The object in 1979 was to control inflation and to indicate to business that the Fed was determined upon a tough policy; it was a kind of psychological shock. It was also aimed at checking the decline of the dollar on the foreign exchanges, thus halting the fall in the value of US investments abroad. On the other hand, this strengthening of the dollar (its overvaluation, in other words) made exports from the US more expensive and cheapened the manufacturing imports which were flooding into the market from Japan and other export-orientated countries. The maintenance of the international role of the dollar and the dampening down of inflation exacted a price, paid in the recession of 1980–2 in the jobs and incomes of millions, many of whom had voted for Carter. There was little consolation for them in the fact that the policy switch in late 1979 enabled the United States to continue to play a pivotal role in the world market as a purveyor and receiver of international liquidity (capital and credit flows), which paralleled the international operations of the multi-national corporations and the big banks.

Ever deeper involvement in complex international transactions, in the age of the computer, enhanced the economy's susceptibilities to external shocks. It required more active intervention abroad and a pugnacious international policy to uphold the dollar's world role. To an even greater measure than in the past, foreign problems became, or threatened to become, American problems.

A NEW PHASE OF CAPITALISM?

The outward signs that American capitalism had entered a new phase in its history in the 1970s were various. They included: a higher average rate of inflation and unemployment at all phases of the business cycle; a lower rate of new capital formation, especially in industry; the falling-off in the growth of productivity compared with the past record; the decline of the smoke-stack industries; increased penetration of the home market by foreign manufacturers; a chronic balance of payments deficit, and a growth in the national debt. American performance showed up as especially mediocre, even in high-tech industries, compared with that of other major industrial countries, notably Japan and West Germany. The sheer size of the American market, with its varied resources and high per capita income, still supported super-power status (and a huge arms budget), but its hegemony was no longer undisputed, at any rate in the economic sphere.

Significant changes in the structure of American capitalism were becoming more prominent in the 1970s. The idea that labour leaders would become 'new men of power' (the title of a book by C. Wright Mills) had turned out to be an illusion. Membership of labour unions fell from a high of thirty-four per cent to less than twenty per cent in this period and was to go even lower in the next decade. Traditionally, unions had been strongest in heavy industry, like coal and steel, and in the mass-production industries. These were the most affected by technological change and foreign competition. The contraction of these industries or their transfer by the multi-national corporations to other countries were hard blows for the unions. Militants of an earlier period had mellowed or retired. Wage and salary incomes increased more slowly in real terms. Employers took advantage of the slack labour market to drive hard bargains; some unions made concessions to save jobs and pension rights. Anti-union corporations became tougher, employing well-paid 'industrial consultants' to rid their plants of union organizers or members.

Expectations of a continuous improvement in living standards, compared with their parents, were no longer being realized for large numbers of American workers. The response of many families to inflation or lower real wages was to have two family incomes. Female labour-force participation rose to unprecedented levels, with feminism and the desire of younger women to have more independence obviously playing a role as well. Most of these women went into the tertiary sector where wages were often low; a minority went into low-paying factory jobs. Despite pleas for equal rights, women suffered from wage discrimination (less pay than men for the same work), and job discrimination (exclusion from some jobs on account of their sex).

There was a deterioration of job security, especially for women, the young and unskilled, Blacks and some other ethnic minorities. There was an increase in part-time and temporary work. Job insecurity was coupled, for perhaps a fifth of the labour force, with lack of any protection in case of sickness. Many families had learned to maintain their living standards by going into debt via instalment buying and the ubiquitous credit card or charge card. This helps to explain why consumer spending held up so well through periods of inflation or recession. Borrowing by business firms and by governments, state and federal, also increased. The United States was deservedly described as a 'debt economy' by the magazine, *Business Week* in 1974. Continued economic growth seemed to depend upon a huge and growing volume of debt. Repayments and interest absorbed a larger share of income. All levels and sections of the economy became more susceptible to interest rate changes.

Behind many of these phenomena was the exhaustion of the factors which had promoted the long post-war phase of prosperity. The great industries which had equipped other industries with machinery, plant and equipment were now in decline. They had excess capacity and their equipment could no longer be maintained at the same level of technological efficiency as before because of the squeeze on profits. Capital goods industries and consumer durables ceased to be the growth points as they had been previously. Markets no longer grew so rapidly as before and, in some cases, had reached saturation point. The impact upon capital goods industries was especially critical. Slow growth or stagnation resulting from these changes were compounded by changes in taste, new technologies and increased, low-cost, imports.

Highly protectionist in the past, the United States was now committed to trade liberalization under the terms of the General Agreement on Tariffs and Trade. Free trade suited the needs of a dominant economy, as it had done in Britain's case in the nineteenth century. With the revival of Western Europe and Japan and the spread of industry to new low-cost areas, the home market was exposed to import penetration on an unprecedented scale. Rival foreign industries had been expanded and re-equipped, were highly competitive in price and quality and drove hard to expand their exports in order to amortize heavy investment in plant and machinery (mostly newer and more up-to-date than that in use in the US). Newly-industrializing countries, with low wage costs, were penetrating the market with cheap consumer goods, such as clothing and footware. The electronic age also brought on to the market a whole new range of consumer products, such as colour television, stereo equipment and tape recorders, often highly labour-intensive. American-owned MNCs were often in the forefront of this process, closing down manufacturing facilities in the US and establishing branch plants overseas, and making agreements with foreign entrepreneurs to sell back finished goods to the home market. Foreign firms, especially those from Japan, established a strong position in such fields as cameras, electronics and cars. To some extent, then, a global re-distribution of industry and a new international division of labour were taking place, sometimes at the behest of the American MNCs, sometimes to the disadvantage of American firms.

Old-style industries began to stagnate, slow-down or decline as their markets shrank and profitability fell. The traditional industrial areas, mainly in the north east, formerly booming areas whose prosperity had been built on the old 'smoke-stack' industries – iron and steel, coal-mining, engineering, vehicles, rubber and consumer durables – went into decline. These areas became known as 'rust-bowls', abandoned steel-mills, gaunt and empty factories and disused railroad track composing a lugubrious landscape. In these regions many jobs disappeared; whole communities found that their economic basis had caved in. Capital hastily moved out in search of more profitable investments in other areas and activities, perhaps abroad.

'De-industrialization' was the term coined to describe this process. In the new world of industrial rivalry, failure to renovate and modernize older industries rapidly led to plant becoming out-dated while replacing it became increasingly expensive. In some fields the technological leadership passed to foreign firms, or they took advantage of lower costs to gain a bigger market share at the expense of their American rivals. Once the process took hold it tended to gain momentum. In the prevailing ideological atmosphere of reverence for market forces, the tendency was to allow matters to take their course. After all, one of the founders of modern economics, the Englishman Alfred Marshall, had likened the industrial structure to a forest in which some trees were growing to maturity while others declined and died. There was obviously some truth in this: but while the old trees were dying, were the new ones appearing fast enough to maintain the forest?

Even in twentieth-century America there were limits to the tolerance of market forces when they threatened the stability of the system as a whole. In some case, then, the Federal government did intervene to shore up tottering banks or support ailing firms. The most notable case was the salvaging of the bankrupt Chrysler Corporation, one of the big three auto-makers, with a government guaranteed loan of $1.5 billion in 1980. A dynamic executive, Lee Iacocca, formerly president of the rival Ford Company, was brought in to revive the firm, which had been handicapped by antiquated plant and uninspiring models.

His task was to restore profitability as quickly as possible. The method employed was to cut its labour force in half while closing sixteen of its fifty-two plants. Iacocca's success, for which he was handsomely rewarded, was shown by the fact that in 1984 profits amounted to $2.4 billion, though it was not a single-handed triumph – workers made big sacrifices.

The point is that the Carter administration could not allow a giant firm which directly employed 111,000 people, and indirectly many more on sub-contracting and marketing, to go out of business. It was the very size of Chrysler, and the immense impact which its total collapse would have had, which forced the administration's hand. As it was, only about half the jobs were saved and the unions had to make big concessions. No doubt, too, the example of Chrysler, together with growing Japanese competition, impelled the other car-makers to speed up their re-organization, slimming down their labour force, wringing concessions out of the unions, and introducing more attractive models. For a number of years, in the late 1970s and early 1980s, they had difficulty in making profits and avoiding losses. The car industry had ceased to be an engine of growth for the whole economy. Its renewed ability to make profits came not from a big increase in demand, but rather from rationalization, a tougher labour policy, new production strategies and the introduction of new 'international' models. The US corporations entered into agreements with their Japanese rivals to import or assemble cars. They also diversified their interests, which included weapons, space contracts and aviation. Magazine and television commercials proclaiming 'Watch the Fords Go By' featured satellites, not Mustangs.

A similar government bail-out occurred during the Reagan administration when a major bank, the Continental Illinois Bank and Trust Co., was faced with bankruptcy in 1984 following a classic run on the bank by institutional investors and depositors. The bank's troubles arose from the fact that it had lent over $1 billion to another bank, Penn Square Bank of Oklahoma City, which had collapsed in 1982. The Federal Reserve Board organized a consortium of other banks to save the Continental Illinois from collapse. There was a steady rate of failure among smaller banks, and savings and loans associations, which mainly lent in the form of mortgages, but without such official aid; (though depositors were protected by the deposit insurance schemes – FDIC, FDSLC – set up in the 1930s). A costly government bail out was organized for the latter in 1989.

Rescue operations of these types were determined by pragmatic considerations and political expediency in defiance of free-market dogmas, but only because of the scale of the firms concerned. The slow erosion of the older industries evoked no response from government. The mid-1970s recession, and the long-run trends to which the economy was subject affected a number of industries which had performed well during the post-war boom. They included such industries as aircraft production – though US manufacturers retained a virtual world monopoly of long-haul jet-liners – machine tools and heavy machinery. The fortunes of the agricultural-machinery producers (who had once led the world) depended upon the state of farming in the United States and the vagaries of foreign demand. Fresh capital and entrepreneurship were going rather into the glamour industries based upon new technologies, especially electronics and the new marvel it had spawned, the computer. California's 'Silicon Valley' became world famous and a must on the itinerary of visiting business tourists, much as Detroit had once been.

The new developments opened up by the silicon chip were seized upon by American multinationals such as IBM, as well as by a swarm of newcomers, of which a few became giants in their turn. In such a field as the computer, international competition was intense and firms were constantly searching for ways of cutting costs. One favoured way was to transfer labour-intensive operations to low-wage countries (Hong-Kong, Singapore, Taiwan and South Korea were favourites) or to seek out cheap labour supplies at home, from recent immigrants, or across the border in Mexico. The MNCs were able to co-ordinate their operations on a world scale so that goods bearing American brand names might well be manufactured, wholly or in part, abroad.

In the American arena there was a constant re-location of manufacturing industry, mainly away from the old northern industrial areas to new areas in the South or South-West, specifically the attractive 'sun belt' (notably Southern California, Texas and Florida), where, at least at first, land was plentiful and there were supplies of cheap, mainly Hispanic, labour. The high-tech industries were able to attract highly skilled and trained personnel from other states and from abroad; proximity to high-grade research facilities attracted scientists. But some older areas also grew on the basis of the diffusion of new technologies and high-tech military contracts, as was the case in Massachusetts, with a number of first-class universities.

Since public discussions tended to be focused on failures and problems, the false impression may be given that the whole of American industry was in decline and beleaguered by more efficient foreign competitors. Disquiet about productivity concerned its rate of growth; in absolute terms it was high, and in some sectors well above the level in foreign industries. Even in Japan two men might be necessary where one would do the job in the United States. The Russian worker produced between a third and a half of that of his American counterpart. There were, moreover, important 'sheltered' industries which had little or nothing to fear from foreign competition, at least for the time being. This might be because American firms enjoyed a competitive lead based on technology, availability of raw materials, possession of a skilled labour force, and so on. Such 'sheltered' industries were often made up of smaller or medium-sized enterprises, rather than giant corporations, perhaps still under family control. The vastness of the geographical area meant that such firms might enjoy the protection of distance and transport costs and thus have a strong foothold in a local or regional market. There were fields like agri-business and food-processing in which there was little direct foreign competition, though foreign capital might establish itself by buying out American-owned firms. The same thing could be said about such commodities as toilet goods and pharmaceuticals – some underpinned by foreign capital but mainly manufactured in the United States. The case of the food processors is interesting. Dominated by a few larger firms, based on brand names, packaging and advertising, they had established a world market for their products, mainly in the period since the Second World War. This was so much the case that it would be difficult, in Western Europe and other parts of the world, to go round a supermarket without buying American brands: detergents, soap, tooth-paste, canned and processed foods, soft drinks and over-the-counter remedies. These brands have become household names all over the world, though the products themselves might not have been made in the United States. They show the pervasive influence of American models on consumption patterns.

In some manufacturing industries however, American firms had lost, or were losing, the relative advantages they once possessed as large-scale producers of standardized items. This applied to capital goods as well as consumer goods industries. There was a tendency to continue to use old equipment while foreign competitors were starting up with state-of-the-art machinery and machine tools, and re-investing a high proportion of their profits. For the first time, in some major fields such as steel and engineering, American firms were falling behind their foreign competitors. Some would be closed down in the end, some might be taken over and modernized by foreign capital. An increasing proportion of sophisticated machinery and machine-tools was being imported from West Germany, Japan and other countries. At the sharp cutting edge of new technology, foreign rivals were often to be found. Some products, such as colour television and VCRs virtually ceased to be made in the US. The markets for clothing and footwear ware flooded with cheap imports.

The *American Challenge* (the title of a best-selling book of the 1960s), when the United States was still the world leader and model in technology and management techniques, was now superseded by the challenge *to* America, especially from Japan, but also from Europe. Government agencies played a greater role in strategic economic planning and in bending economic forces to serve national goals than was the case in the United States. No such strategy appeared in the United States; indeed, ideological commitment to market forces became stronger. In any event, the United States became more intricately related to the world market than ever before; as a consequence, competitive weaknesses were being revealed more starkly. The MNCs might be doing well, but there was a disconcerting growth in the trade deficit which was to loom ever larger in the 1980s. The big corporations were looking after their profitability by developing their overseas operations and tapping new sources of cheap labour. The old-style tendency towards vertical and horizontal combination – determined by production needs, the main way in which great concentrations of economic power had been built up in the past – had, to a large extent, been superseded. The return on capital could no longer be greatly enhanced by absorbing competitors in the same line of business or by extending control over inputs or the markets for a given range of products. In any case, in many industries oligopoly ruled; they were dominated by a small number of large firms. Further combination would arouse the populist hostility to 'monopoly' which was deeply rooted in some sections of public opinion and might fall foul of anti-trust legislation. In any case, it might not be profitable.

By the late 1970s, and even more in the following decade, take-overs and mergers dominated the capital market, while Wall Street prices began their apparently irresistible climb (the famous 'bull market' similar to that of the 1920s). The result was two-fold. On the one hand there was a movement away from the traditional set-up where a corporation produced a single product range to one in which it brought together a group of not necessarily related firms into a great conglomerate. Examples include Gulf and Western, International Telephone and Telegraph, Litton Industries and Ling-Temco-Vought. Mergers, buy-outs and take-overs became increasingly frequent during the 1980s with the formation of new giants. Thus the tobacco firm R.J. Reynolds linked up with the food giant Nabisco and Philip Morris merged with General Foods. A corporation such as ITT owns a chain of hotels, a publishing house, bakeries, an insurance business and a manufacturer of garden products. These components can be readily sold-off and new ones acquired. Thus, for a time, RJR-Nabisco owned the fast-food chain, Kentucky Fried Chicken and Canada Dry which came with the purchase of a brewery; it sold them off, but still retains such firms as Del Monte, canners of fruit, much of it produced in its own plantations in various parts of the world.

On the other hand, the mergers and take-overs involved in this process generated a great deal of stock market business, offering enormous profits to investment bankers, brokerage firms and wealthy speculators. The aim was now to deploy liquid funds towards the buying and selling of stock to realize the maximum capital gains. Even more than before the economy could be seen as the by-product of the operations of a casino (as Keynes had said). The various component firms of the corporate giants were bought and sold by rival financial groups. Foreign capital was attracted by the lure of the rapid appreciation of stock, vastly in excess of the real value of the assets represented, globalizing the whole process. Firms were bought up in order that they could be broken up and part of their assets sold off to pay for the take-over. 'Corporate raiders' appeared on the scene whose speciality it was to buy a block of shares in a company and then offer to buy enough from other shareholders to give them control, in which case they would re-organize the firm, perhaps selling off part of it. If they failed, their raid would have pushed up prices, enabling them to sell their holding at a handsome profit nevertheless. Successful raiders included oil tycoon T. Boone Pickens, Sid Bass who took over Texaco, Irwin L. Jacobs who obtained control of ITT and Saul Steinberg who acquired Disney Productions. Sometimes the raiders were forestalled by 'white knights' acceptable to the existing management and able to offer the shareholders better terms.

These operations enabled huge fortunes to be built up in record time and the successful take-over artists enjoyed something of the same reputation as the 'robber barons' of an earlier era, both through their business methods and their often lavish life styles. But the possibilities of rapid enrichment were also an invitation to greed and dishonesty. By using information not generally available to other traders, insiders could make millions of dollars in a single transaction. In some notable cases insiders overstepped the fine line between the permissible and the illegal business practice and paid the penalty. The most notorious case was that of Ivan Boesky, one of the wealthiest speculators with connections in London as well as New York. He paid $100 million in penalties as well as serving a gaol sentence and banishment from stock trading for life, in 1986.

A feature of the take-overs and mergers of the past decade is that they have given rise to new methods of financing, notably the 'junk bond'. Bonds of this sort offer little security but carry a high rate of interest compared with other investments. Put into circulation by little-known firms or expressly to finance take-overs, the high yield may attract money managers of institutions such as pension funds as well as the individual speculator. The lead in the junk bond market was taken by the investment bankers Drexel Burnham Lambert and their financial wizard Michael R. Milken. Gross earnings of the firm were estimated at over $1 billion and Milkin's income in 1987 was $550 million. In the course of the investigations into his wrongdoings Boesky implicated Milkin in similar practices and in 1989 he was indicted on 98 Federal charges ranging from fraud to racketeering. Early in 1990 Drexels filed for bankruptcy. Some have seen in Milkin a brilliant entrepreneur who has helped to re-vitalize American capitalism, others see in him a cheat who lied and bribed himself to great wealth. The Boeskys and Milkens are, in any case, a sign of the times. While their greed may have accelerated the pace of capital accumulation, it also showed that the way to get richer faster in present-day America is by 'paper entrepreneurship', 'pushing paper around', rather than through building up a manufacturing firm. Some of the best talents in American business management have been attracted by these activities, sanctioned as they are by the prevailing ideology. Many a 'yuppy' (young, upwardly-mobile people) set out with the ambition of making a million dollars by his thirtieth birthday.

Meanwhile, at a deeper level, the physiognomy of American business has been constantly changing. The staid, family-type business with a single product line, like Campbell's Soups, has almost become a thing of the past, at least in the major industries. There are raiders ready to pounce should the family owners decide to give up control. The result would be an ending of the paternalistic relationships with the labour force and a drive to push up earnings. The more general pattern is of firms which are bought and sold, merged and separated for purely financial reasons often without the employees knowing what was going on.

One result of the merger mania is that firms have become overloaded with debt whether they have been taken over or in order to buy off corporate raiders. Since creditors have priority over shareholders this may mean greater vulnerability to shocks in the future when competition for markets is likely to become more intense.

FOREIGN COMPETITION

In those sections of industry dominated by three or four giant corporations profits appeared to be calculable and guaranteed as long as demand was sustained. Increased costs were simply passed along to consumers (as during the inflation of the 1970s) or counteracted by re-organization and greater mechanization of production lines to increase productivity. Successive developments in the organization of the labour process and continuous improvements in technology had this as their aim. At one time American industrial productivity had led the world and continuous gains were virtually taken for granted. The slowing down of productivity growth in the 1970s was another sign of the sea-change in the position of American industry; it was, in many fields, being pushed into second or third place, notably by Japanese and West German firms. The main reason seems to have been the failings of management. While productivity continued to be high by world standards, the significant change was that foreign industries were not only catching up with, but also outstripping, US productivity levels. Probably, however, in a well-established and already highly productive industry there was bound to be less scope for year-to-year gains than in one more recently established.

American business, like Britain's at an earlier period, was now tending to suffer from the disadvantages of having been first in the field. (It was symptomatic that about this time some American economists and economic historians began to display increased interest in the causes of Britain's economic decline.) One of the problems of Chrysler, and the other car manufacturers, was that they had many out-of-date plants and too much antiquated machinery compared with the newly equipped Japanese firms. There was also such a thing as diminishing returns. Continued high productivity gains required constant improvements in equipment and in the organization of the labour process. Many of the gains from the latter, based on time-and-motion study and intensive supervision, had probably been exhausted. There were signs that new recruits put up more resistance to the tempo of work demanded than their predecessors. Some employers gave more attention to eradicating unionism, while American firms emulated some of the practices of their Japanese rivals (such as the arrival of components 'just in time').

It was becoming evident, also, that future productivity gains would depend, even more than in the past, on an up-dating of technology, thus making necessary huge investments in new plant and machinery incorporating automation, computerization and robotization. Foreign firms, by the 1970s, were often more ready to take such steps than their American counterparts. Advanced technology enabled foreign products to compete with American manufactured goods on grounds of quality as well as price. Thus Japanese car-makers used their relatively high unit profits to update their methods of production, rather than increase dividends or lower prices. While the giant corporations could respond to competition from imports by moving their labour-intensive processes to low-wage areas, this resort was not so readily available to the smaller and medium-sized firms. Pressure for protectionist measures came largely from such sources.

Meanwhile, many types of manufacturing virtually disappeared during the 1970s, especially in clothing, footwear and consumer electronics. In the new international division of labour which was taking shape, the comparative advantage of American production lay in certain types of high technology as well as those lines which still had cost advantages over foreign rivals in catering for the huge internal market. In some traditional fields loss of industrial leadership was accepted with equanimity, since they were no longer regarded as profitable, or were being re-organized abroad by American-owned MNCs. Some compensation could be found in the international service sector; however, even in banking, finance and insurance foreign competition was growing.

'POST-INDUSTRIAL' SOCIETY

The American economy rode out the shocks of the 1970s without sliding into a major depression, but with a distinct change of pace. Policy responses to the new challenges were mainly pragmatic, though with a growing tendency to leave market forces to work themselves out and less confidence in 'fine tuning' of the Keynesian type. Government spending nevertheless remained as a sustaining force during the Carter administration and throughout the Reagan era. Military spending was sacrosanct and continued to play a cushioning role, while drawing upon scarce resources such as scientific manpower (and contributing to inflation and the balance of payments problem). The growing influence of monetarism was reflected in the new emphasis given to monetary policy in the struggle against inflation during the Carter administration by the Federal Reserve Board. At the same time, a higher level of unemployment was accepted as inevitable. From one perspective it may be claimed that capitalism in America displayed exceptional resilience in the face of what was a global crisis in the decade of the 1970s. The giant multi-national corporations were able to extend their activities on a world scale, protected by the military power of the United States and the activities of the CIA as well as the State Department. Policies were aimed at making the world safe for capitalism and keeping the United States in front. The stage was set by the continuing Cold War (though it blew hot and cold), by the policy of supporting those governments considered to be friendly and undermining those hostile to US aims.

The MNCs continued, meanwhile, to direct manufacturing facilities, research and development to those areas in which they could be carried on most profitably. Thus plants were closed down in the US, little attempt was made to modernize out-of-date plant, while new facilities were opened in low-wage countries where regulations concerning safety, health and pollution were less severe than in the United States (hence such disasters as that of the Union Carbide plant in Bophal, India in December 1984). The growing influx of imported manufactured goods recorded in the balance of trade came in part from wholly or partially American-owned factories operating abroad. These off-shore facilities were export platforms for reaching the world market and a major way of combating the pressure on the rate of profit of the MNCs. Balance of trade figures showing a deficit in trade in manufactures concealed the fact that the ramifications of American capitalism were world-wide. About a quarter of the workers employed by American firms in manufacturing industry were to be found in foreign countries and they accounted for perhaps one-third of total 'American' production. Thus imports from Taiwan or Hong Kong might mean profits for American corporations.

While employment in manufacturing industry remained fairly stable during the 1970s at around the twenty million mark, it formed a diminishing proportion of the total labour force. The growth in employment thus came essentially from the ever-growing tertiary sector. One consequence of this was that the decline in the influence of trade unions continued. The most highly organized plants were those which were being closed down. Unemployment and fear of further plant closures weakened the bargaining power of the unions. A new feature of collective bargaining was that some unions were prepared to accept cuts in real wages and less favourable contracts in order to keep factories in production. By the end of the 1970s, membership comprised only about twenty per cent of the total labour force. Only in parts of the public sector did unionism seem to show much vigour. The time when union leaders were household names had passed, while only union corruption and racketeering achieved much publicity. The position of labour, as a whole, was less favourable than it had been just after the Second World War; for large numbers of workers real wages had stabilized or begun to fall. A political consequence was the weakening of the ties between organized labour and the Democratic Party.

The relatively small proportion of the labour force occupied in agriculture and manufacturing industry fostered the theory that American capitalism had experienced a fundamental change: it was becoming a 'post-industrial' society, dominated by the tertiary sector. The 'tertiary' sector itself is a catch-all category, which includes all those occupations and paid activities not directly related to production. It includes the highly skilled, highly trained and well-rewarded professionals, such as doctors, lawyers, managers, business executives and the like, as well as the enormous army of service workers of diverse kinds to be found in the United States, low-skilled, unskilled and often poorly paid. Of course it is true that, as the income of a market economy rises, its members will spend a declining proportion of their incomes on food and basic necessities and more on 'conventional necessities', luxuries and semi-luxuries with a high personal service component, in accordance with the well-known Engel's law (Engel was a nineteenth-century German statistician). The growth of the tertiary sector was a sign of increasing wealth, but also indicated great social inequality in the sense that large numbers of American workers, especially women, young people and ethnic minorities had no alternative but to take low paid, manual, menial service jobs.

In any case, the term 'post-industrial society' is highly ambiguous. The ability of the American economy to support such a large proportion of 'non-productive' people was only possible because of the huge productivity gains which had been made in the twentieth century both in manufacturing industry and in agriculture. It could be argued, then, that a strong, healthy industrial (and agricultural) base was necessary to support the service sector. Industry had not been relegated to the past. Many service activities were linked to agriculture (e.g. crop-spraying, or the dissemination of information about crops or markets) or to industry (research, accounting, management, and so on). The argument that the United States had nothing to fear from the continued decline of industry and could shift to a service economy was misleading. The decline of industry would drag many service activities down with it and weaken the base for the existence of service jobs on a large scale. It was (and is) the enormous productive capacity of the primary and secondary sectors, and the size of the surplus produced there in tangible form, which made possible service sector growth.

However, there were many (and the view was expressed by President Reagan) who thought that services could become increasingly important while industry declined. The idea was that the United States would dispense services based upon science, technology and information to the rest of the world, leaving other countries to produce television sets, video recorders, cars and consumer goods. It encouraged complacency in the face of the real problems facing the economy. Moreover, while countries like Japan showed no sign of slackening their drive for industrial supremacy in key fields, the international market for services was becoming increasingly competitive and the predominance of American firms could by no means be taken for granted. This was not the transition to a new stage of capitalism, but the working out of the logic of an existing stage, not excluding some features which were storing up trouble for the future: the weakening of the industrial base and vulnerability to foreign competition.

CHAPTER 9

The Reagan Era: the 1980s

The Reagan administration which took over in 1980 consciously intended to reverse the economic policies of its predecessors and bring to an end the historical consensus which had existed since the Second World War. Against the drift toward a broader role for government in maintaining employment and providing greater security for its citizens, it posed the return to free market forces. It sought, therefore, to diminish the role and the cost of government, making possible tax reductions with a balanced budget. It wanted the state out of the economic arena as far as possible; but it also wanted a strong state to defend property and the social order, and to fight crime. Law and order were prominent among the aims of the conservative right, which provided philosophical support for the new administration. At the same time there had to be an increase in the military preparedness of the United States, which had allegedly slipped back, in the face of the 'evil empire' presumably bent on world domination. Increased military expenditure was therefore justified, but other forms of government spending had to be cut, including the social programmes dating from the 'Great Society'. If market forces were given free rein, the economy would expand: there would be more jobs and less poverty as a result of the famous 'trickle down effect'. Although it was not clear to many of those who voted Republican, the Reagan policies, if carried out, would benefit the rich and the burden of reduced government expenditure would be mainly felt by the poor. In fact, the years of the Reagan administrations showed a definite increase in income inequality. Further, it sought, with some success, to reduce the power of the labour unions; the defeat of the air-traffic controllers in 1982 was intended as an object lesson for the labour movement as a whole.

The period of the Reagan presidency thus deserves to be considered as a turning point in post-war American economic and social history. Perspective will be required before its full significance can be measured. Its consequences are likely to endure, perhaps into the twenty-first century. Some attempt will be made to see how far it achieved its aims, and also to explain its paradoxes.

Not only did it fail to do some things which it set out to do, but in some cases the end results were very different from what had been intended. This is evident in the series of budget deficits and the huge increase in the national debt which took place under Reagan, in the equally if not more ominous balance of payments deficits, and in other signs of economic failure. While armaments expenditure was increased, there was an historic change in the relationship between Washington and Moscow, unlike anything which could have been expected from the President's earlier attitude towards the Soviet Union. At home, despite some cuts and a measure of deregulation, the role of government in the economy was not changed fundamentally from what it had been before. It is true that the administration generally eschewed economic management of the Keynesian type, though it might be argued that the series of large budget deficits, partly a result of increased military expenditure coupled with tax cuts, represented a kind of shame-faced Keynesianism which enabled the administration to boast about the long period of uninterrupted expansion which followed the ending of the recession in 1982.

It cannot be said that on the economic level the Reagan administration went out in blaze of glory. Not only were there as many unsolved problems as before, but there was a general air of pessimism, much talk of America's 'decline' or loss of hegemony. The confidence of the early post-war period had been dissipated; it was almost as though the approaching *fin de siècle* was expected to be a twilight era of American greatness, as it had been for Britain a century before.

THE PARADOXES OF REAGANISM

The most obvious observation about the Reagan years, 1981–8, is that the dominant economic trends of the previous period continued to assert themselves. In the closing decades of the twentieth century the United States appeared as a crippled giant, slowly losing the hegemonic role established in the Second World War. It could no longer claim technological or industrial leadership in an increasingly competitive world economy. The other advanced industrial countries were catching up with, and beginning to outstrip, American levels of productivity. The rise of the new, high-tech industries had only partially compensated for the decline of the old-style manufacturing sector. The United States had become a net importer of manufactured goods, and was increasingly dependent upon imported supplies of petroleum and vital raw materials. The changed relationship to the world market showed up in the annual balance of payments deficit. The days when the dollar held sway on the international exchanges were long past. Within an amazingly short period, the United States had been transformed from the leading international creditor to the biggest debtor.

Nevertheless, Washington retained its self-imposed world role as principal protagonist of the Western bloc in the Cold War. This meant not only the maintenance of a large army, navy and air-force, equipped with the most efficient means of destruction and half a million military personnel in bases all over the world, but also the financing of foreign governments and rebel forces in accordance with Washington's perception of the interests of the United States. As American economic power waned, there was a growing contradiction between its military-strategic pretensions and the means for their implementation. In the determination of policy a major, if not dominant, role appeared to be played by the 'military-industrial complex'. Under Reagan, more than ever before, the defence establishment was the *noli me tangere* of the political system. Indeed, one of Reagan's triumphs, in the eyes of his supporters, was the rapid military build-up which took place in his first term, especially of bombers and missiles. It was so central to policy that the economic costs were played down, although both the budget deficit and the trade deficit which yawned so wide in the 1980s were aggravated, if not caused, by the heavy costs of the military build-up, including, later, expenditure on 'Star Wars' (the Stategic Defense Initiative). It can also be argued that 'military Keynesianism', as some called it, stimulated the economy and helped to avoid recession.

The Reagan administration took over an economy weakened and battered by the shocks of the previous decade. It began its term inauspiciously with a plunge into recession, for which it was not directly responsible. The Fed had initiated a deflationary policy under Carter, but the new policy-makers saw an opportunity to control inflation as a preparation for the launching of its own programme. The climb out of recession, beginning in 1982, may be said to have ensured Reagan's re-election in 1984. More surprising was the continuance of moderate expansion and the absence of recession through to the end of his second term, apparently unaffected by the spectacular end of the long Wall Street bull market which had driven up share prices for several years, in October 1987.

The Reagan administration presented itself as breaking away from the consensus politics of the post-war era (based on Keynesian economic policy and government financed social security) with the intention of setting the economy on a new path and stopping the drift towards welfare-statism. The diagnosis of the state of the nation was made succinctly by the President himself: government was not the solution but the problem. The new medicine was to be the return to a free-market economy, notably by dismantling much of the regulatory apparatus in which American capitalism had been cocooned since the Great Depression. This was the essence of what was soon called 'Reaganomics'.

In fact, the policies of the administration and the theories upon which they were based owed little to the President himself and were an eclectic hotch-potch. Deregulation and privatization were goals to which all the disparate supporters of a Republican president could subscribe. They appealed to the leaders of corporate business, many sections of which, paradoxically enough, depended upon government contracts. Millions of people making up 'middle America' felt themselves overtaxed and over-regulated to support welfare-dodgers, and the inflated bureaucracy and politicians of Washington. Battered by inflation, victims of structural change, bewildered by the growth in crime, drug abuse and the so-called 'sexual revolution' (casual sex, pornography, abortion, homosexuality) as well as the Aids epidemic; they made up a right-wing, populist groundswell which gave Reaganism its mass base. Convinced of the menace of Communism, it supported the military and was fervently nationalist.

THE THEORETICAL BASIS OF REAGANOMICS

Reaganism also found intellectual arguments and support from a large section of the economics profession and those who gave theoretical expression to the concerns of corporate business. The most notable characteristic was the turn away from the prevailing orthodoxy of the post-war period. The new problems thrown up during the 1970s had demonstrated, it seemed, the ineffectiveness of the policies of fine-tuning and economic management derived from the American version of Keynesianism (which had originally been designed for a different situation, in another country). Practised by successive administrations (it was the Republican Richard Nixon who proclaimed 'we are all Keynesians now'), as well as by the Fed, it had held up well during the long post-war upturn, when recessions were mild and short-lived and inflation was moderate, and achieved the status of a new orthodoxy. Keynesians were prepared to see the state in the driving seat, using accelerator and brakes to keep the economy on a steady course. They were part of a broader trend in American politics of acceptance of more state intervention to correct what were seen as the injustices or unfairness of a market economy, which reached its peak in President Johnson's 'Great Society' of the 1960s.

For a time, economic management and welfare reforms, cemented by pride in American achievement and an anti-Communist ideology (disastrously expressed in the Vietnam war by the same president who championed the 'Great Society'), seemed to be an integral part of the 'affluent society'. As the economic climate changed in the 1970s, an earlier form of neo-classical economics came into its own again. Keynesianism, far from being a cure, seemed to be part of the disease, contributing to inflation and unable to provide remedies for 'stagflation'. The root of the trouble was seen in deficit spending, though in fairness to the Keynesians they had all along been conscious of the inflationary dangers of deficit spending and did not prescribe it for every situation.

The fall of Keynesianism, in its American version, was even more sudden than its rise. New doctors rushed forward to save the patient, headed by the monetarists of the Chicago school, closely followed by other variants of neo-classical economics, notably the 'supplysiders' and the 'rational expectations' school. They had in common derivation from pre-Keynesian orthodoxy and unlimited faith in the virtues of the free market. Almost relegated to the lunatic fringe, they now came back in triumph, armed with all the righteous fervour of those representing the forces of light over those of darkness. Economists who had perhaps been earlier bewitched by the Keynesian heresy now rejoined the fold with the enthusiasm of new converts. To the chaos of the real world of the 'mixed economy', with its futile if not harmful government controls, it offered the awesome harmony of free market forces and the invisible hand of Adam Smith, the second centenary of whose great work fell in 1976.

The intellectual fascination of free market forces, individual enterprise and pursuit of material success which had made America great, was not to be underestimated. It was part of the mythology of American capitalism, with a wide appeal. Intellectual fascination with the harmonious working of market forces in the abstract is one thing; to substitute it in practice for the hybrid procedures of the 'mixed economy' is another. For several decades the drift of policy had been towards modifying and curtailing the free operation of market forces. Advocates of the free market would thus have to propose a sweeping agenda of counter-reform: nothing less than a programme of intervention to restore the market to its full and proper place by legislating out of existence the formidable body of regulation and intervention built up since the New Deal. Government *was* the problem, Reagan announced; but what government had done only government could undo. This meant going through the complex legislative procedure of the American governmental system. Whatever the President and his administration might have wanted to do, they had to contend with Congress, representing a multitude of the most diverse vested interests, and having a Democratic majority. Thus, unlike Margaret Thatcher in Britain, with a large Conservative majority in parliament, President Reagan could not proceed to translate his programme into action. Reaganism faced the hostility of Congress to much of his programme, as well as the inertia of the status quo.

On his side Reagan had the support of three main streams of political and economic thinking. The core of the Republican Party was made up of conservative businessmen and corporate executives, who provided the large amounts of money needed to finance electoral campaigns, and an army of middle-class voters, not necessarily affluent but fearful of change. More pragmatic than ideological in their politics, their adherence to the free market, free enterprise and economic individualism was a visceral reaction rather than a thought-out ideology. In the 1930s their counterparts had been hostile to the New Deal, and successive instalments of government intervention were made in the teeth of their opposition. On the other hand, they might clamour for government aid if their own interests were at stake. They were strongly nationalist and anti-Communist, identifying their interests with those of the nation at large, and fervent supporters of the Cold War and thus of heavy government expenditure on armaments, the one form of government expenditure that was still not queried. As a corollary of their belief in market forces, Republican rank-and-filers were strong supporters of a reduced role for the state and lower taxation.

Supply-siders made up an active, opinion-forming minority which gave traditional Republicanism a more positive and ideological content. They had a map of how they thought the economy worked and a plan to change the map to reflect market forces. For them, the way to salvation lay in reducing the share of national income going to the federal and other governments, leaving taxpayers with more to spend as they chose. The popularizers of supply-side economics claimed that cuts in tax rates – which they said should be large – would not necessarily lead to a corresponding fall in tax receipts. The incentive effects which they hoped would result from lower tax rates would raise incomes and thus the amount of tax. The fact that the tax cuts they were asking for would benefit the higher income brackets most and add to inequality in income distribution did not embarrass them at all. The increased savings expected to result from lower taxation of the rich would result in more investment and thus create more jobs and wages. At the same time, as its name implies, supply-side economics set out to oppose the Keynesian emphasis on aggregate demand and its manipulation as the centrepiece of economic policy. Instead, they claimed to operate on supply, which was seen as coming from the private sector; reduced taxation was giving back to the taxpayer what was his rightful due, to do what he liked with his own. It was assumed that the private sector was productive and that the state took away, and used unproductively, privately created wealth. Supply-side economics, in its simplistic versions, could have a wide appeal. It was a particular route back to the complete sway of market forces, offering instant improvement in the economic situation via tax cuts (providing they were on a sufficiently large scale). Although to the chagrin of some supply-siders the Reagan administration did not apply supply-side remedies in their maximalist form, its policies included tax cuts which benefited large tax-payers most. The evidence suggests that the increased income did not find its way into new investment, but went rather into conspicuous consumption and stock market speculation.

The monetarist school, sometimes referred to as 'the Chicago school' because leading figures came from the university, made up the third element in the Reagan coalition. It owed its emergence from relative academic obscurity to the object of public debate to the inflationary pressures of the 1970s and the persistence of its guru, Milton Friedman. The wider public was looking for an explanation of the high rate of inflation and of stagflation (the combination of inflation with slow growth and unemployment). Where Keynesians appeared to falter, the monetarists entered to fill the gap, again with a simple theory which could appeal to a wider public outside the lecture-room or the learned journal. The basic wisdom of the monetarists was summed up in the quantity theory of money familiar to every economics student (just as the supply-siders had gone back to a more dubious theorem, Say's Law). The monetarists claimed that changes in the money supply were the key to economic fluctuations. This led to more discussion about what constitutes money and the identification of different sorts of money, M1, M2 etc. Control over the money supply in the United States resided with the Federal Reserve Board and was exercised through open market operations and the interest rate. Once the Fed used its power 'responsibly', it could end inflation and avert major recession. There was thus no need for macro-economic management of the Keynesian type, which gave exorbitant powers to the government and curtailed or distorted the free operation of market forces. The monetarists assumed that capitalism was a perfectly healthy system, providing no impediments to the operation of market forces were imposed. It was intervention, or wrong policies, which produced such disasters as the Great Depression. Control over the money supply was an unavoidable type of intervention, but it should be operated to ensure steady economic growth without inflation or depression. As for the the existing body of regulation and interventionist legislation, it was all a great mistake; the aim should be to get rid of it and restore to the individual his 'freedom to choose', the title of the Friedmans' best-selling book which can be seen as one of the trail-blazers for the acceptance of Reaganomics.

Mention should also be made of the 'rational expectations' school which was based on a more esoteric theory, or bunch of theories, with little influence outside academe. It also grew out of the apparent failure of Keynesianism to explain the events of the 1970s. It sought to explain the ways in which individual economic behaviour reacted to price and other fluctuations, such as prolonged inflation. It also represented a return to older types of economic analysis, concerned more with individual behaviour than with the working of the economy as a whole.

THE NEW LANDSCAPE OF THE 1980s ECONOMY

The economic troubles of the 1970s were not solely the result of conjunctional factors, such as the two oil shocks or the inflationary back-wash of the Vietnam war. They also reflected long-term changes of a durable character in the structure of US capitalism and its relationship to the world market, changes which were widely taken to be symptomatic of weakness or decline. They could also be seen as the reflection of a long-standing crisis, a resurgence of the stagnationary forces which had surfaced in the 1930s and had then been apparently overcome by the Second World War and the upturn which had followed it. In any case, the whole capitalist world had been afflicted with a slow-down in growth and the first major depression since the 1930s in 1974. It appeared that the long-term forces of expansion which had predominated in the 1950s and 1960s had finally exhausted themselves.

As the leading capitalist power, all the new problems of slow-down and inflation, the break-up of the world monetary system, the resurgence of Western Europe and Japan and the rise of newly industrializing countries, were drawn into, and found their sharpest expression in, the United States. The Reagan administration, therefore, was not only trying to impose an alternative way of dealing with the old problems of inflation or the business cycle, but by its actions it contributed to the even more intractable long-term problems which had been building up for two decades or more. Indeed, it was not the solution but part of the problem.

The driving forces for structural change were to be found in the working out of the objective laws of capitalism, which were more powerful than any administration. Reaganism assumed that the economy was essentially sound and healthy, it just needed a different medicine from that prescribed by the conventional (Keynesian) doctors. In going after what it saw as the main sickness – high taxation and government spending – it created unforeseen side-effects. Some of these were passed on to its successors. But while the Reagan administration hailed its 'successes', notably the slowing down of inflation to more acceptable levels without heavy unemployment, and a lower rate of taxation, the underlying, long-term problems palpably worsened; hence the plethora of books and articles predicting America's decline, at least without a radical effort to reverse the trend. While the Reaganites claimed that the economy had been turned around, the prophets of doom had never been more vocal or captured so much attention. Every point which the administration made in its favour could be countered by referring to a series of symptoms suggesting that the deeper, underlying problems had not been seriously addressed.

Leaving aside here some of the structural changes which have already been considered in Chapter 7, notably the role of the military-industrial complex, the relative decline of agriculture and the growth of welfare statism, a number of other major trends can be listed.

Firstly, there has been a fundamental change in the international economic position of the United States: from undisputed leader to one of a number of contestants, at least in the industrial field. As, in the immediate past, political power has gone with industrial might, this calls into question the military-strategic role which it assumed after the Second World War. The country may have been overreaching itself, assuming burdens which are becoming economically excessive. The more conciliatory attitude towards the Soviet Union in the closing years of the Reagan administration may be a reflection of this. Subsequently the pace of change in the Soviet Union and Eastern Europe has been so rapid and spectacular that the old adversarial postures have become outmoded. Although the Bush administration appears to have been taken unawares it will be bound to undertake a major re-evaluation of economic as well as military policy which could result in a winding down of the current level of arms expenditure.

Secondly, there is the decline of manufacturing industry and the disappearance altogether of some industries from the United States ('de-industrialization'). The country has thus become a net importer of manufactured goods. Many capital goods and machine-tools are no longer made in the US. High-tech industry has only partly compensated for the run-down of the 'smoke-stack' industries, and is also under increasing competitive pressure. The importation of manufactured goods has contributed to the chronic balance of payments problem and America's conversion from the leading creditor country to the major international debtor.

Thirdly, there is the increasing importance of the tertiary sector and the claim that this represents a shift towards a 'post-industrial society', leading to further increases in per capita income and the realization of the American dream. How far this process can go without becoming malignant is the question which must be asked, when most of the new jobs being created are in low-paid, low-skill service activities.

Fourthly, there is the growth of 'paper entrepreneurship', where pushing around paper titles to wealth has greatly surpassed the solving of technical problems of production and marketing as the object of business skills. A continuous succession of mergers and take-overs takes place on a purely financial basis. At one moment a corporation will diversify by acquiring a firm in an industry which may be quite remote from that of the parent firm. At another moment it may divest itself of one of its subordinate units to make a handsome profit. Financial strategy, knowing when and what to sell, is more lucrative than investing in new plant. Finance capital has taken over; when pecuniary concerns have priority and thrust technical superiority into a lower place, loss of leadership becomes almost inevitable. British industrial history since the late nineteenth century is strewn with such examples.

Although the United States remains the largest and most powerful economy in the world, its power to shape the course of world events is dwindling. More often, American policy has to contend with, and adjust itself to, situations created by the decisions of foreign governments, businesses and banks. The circuit of exchange of American capital is now more profoundly world-wide than was the case in the past. Its investments follow the course of profitability, wherever it may lead. Its products cease to be specifically American but may contain bits and pieces from many countries and be assembled wherever it is most profitable to do so. A kind of internationalization of production is made possible by air freight, cheap sea transport and modern electronic communications systems: manufacturing operations have become footloose. Changes in relative prices may lead to their transfer from one country to another more rapidly than they could be moved from one town to another in the past.

The internationalization of the corporations means that the accumulation of capital and the income flows they generate have untoward effects on the domestic economy. They export from their branch plants to world markets and to the United States as well. This trade either does not figure in the balance of payments of the US, or does so as a deficit item. Much of the MNCs' capital is held abroad, leaving them with some discretion as to where the final profit will be declared. While such operations may be highly advantageous for shareholders, the result may be fewer jobs for American workers and an adverse balance of payments, apparently weakening the American economy. The process does not stop with activities of American multinational corporations. Foreign-owned industry has substantially increased its share of the American market. The most successful exporters, such as Japan, South Korea and Taiwan, have built up large trade surpluses with the United States. The spectacular growth of the Japanese economy, in particular, poses new problems. Japanese firms have used their profits to build branch plants in the United States, while Japanese earnings have flowed into investments of many kinds, including real estate and government securities. Economically, therefore, Japan has become a formidable rival; one which depends for its prosperity upon the US market but which has only a limited demand for American-made products and has successfully restricted American direct investment in Japan. The purposeful drive likely to make Japan the leading capitalist power in the twenty-first century is regarded with mixed feelings. Although so far (1989) Japanese holdings in the United States are only about half those of British investors they generate anxiety and opposition in some quarters: a clear nationalist response. This is aggravated by the reluctance of Japan to open its own gates to more American trade and investment. At the same time many welcome the stimulus to local economies which Japanese investment brings. Joint enterprises between American and Japanese firms have become increasingly common so while for some the latter arerivals, for others they are valuable partners, bringing new technology and forms of organization as well as capital. The question is whether anything short of discriminatory protection against Japanese products (which already exists in the case of cars particularly) can stop Japan pushing the United States into second place in the capitalist world: a prospect which foreigners can contemplate with more equanimity than Americans.

American consumers have displayed an apparently insatiable demand for cheap imports, whether made by American firms operating in low-wage countries overseas or by Japanese and other foreign-owned enterprises. At the same time, goods manufactured in the US have encountered stiff competition in overseas markets. If American brands survive in the world market, it is often because the goods concerned are made wholly or in part in one of the low-wage, export-platform countries, mainly in Asia. The competition is not confined to cheap consumer goods. Foreign competition has been highly effective in quality consumer goods (such as luxury cars, cameras and motor-cycles) and in capital goods, such as machinery and machine-tools. When, in 1988, a lower dollar gave a fillip to exports, some manufacturers imported foreign machinery to fulfil their orders because the types they wanted were no longer made in the US. Foreigners also extended their competitive edge into high-tech fields. Indeed, once almost any innovation had been developed in the United States the chances were high that its mass production would be transferred overseas wholly or in part. This could be done, of course, by an American-owned multinational corporation, or by a foreign competitor.

National frontiers are seemingly losing their relevance as US capital is accumulated abroad as well as at home, and as foreign corporations depend upon the US for their markets and re-invest their profits in that country. A new international division of labour has grown up between the high-income countries, like the United States, and the newly industrializing, low-income countries. At the same time, an international division of labour between the advanced countries themselves has taken shape as manufacturers sought to reduce costs and maximize profits. There are few items in which American manufacturers held a clear advantage. Although the three major American manufacturers equip most other countries (outside the Soviet bloc) with jet-liners, even here there is a growing foreign-made element in their construction, just as there is in many American-built cars.

There were obvious contradictions in the American position. While, on the one hand, American capital operated worldwide and foreign capital had almost a free field in the American market, national interests remained paramount in the sense that government policy was designed in the interest of American capital and especially the big corporations. But policy developed along pragmatic lines without there necessarily being consistency on the part of different departments of state. There was not sufficient confidence in market forces to let them operate freely wheresoever they might lead, especially in the international field.

Clearly, by the 1970s the United States had lost the economic hegemony it had enjoyed in the early post-war period. It now had to face not only its antagonists in the Cold War as in that period, but also the resurgent losers in the Second World War, Japan and West Germany, both of whom had powerful expanding economies and strong currencies. Washington could not impose its will on Bonn (or on the European Economic Community of which it was the leader) or on Tokyo. The mark and the yen were able to do more than look the dollar in the face; its value internationally was determined by the exchanges in Tokyo and Frankfurt. Indeed, to the extent that the United States became ever more deeply involved in a cosmopolitan business system, its sovereignty was impaired. However, in the triangular relationship with Japan and Western Europe, the US was still the stronger party, though that strength was constantly being undermined. The huge American market and the great opportunities it appeared to offer for profitable investment, acted as a magnet for foreign capital. This capital flow financed the deficits. Above all, the military-strategic role of the United States, with its massive nuclear armoury, was uncontested.

America's allies showed a singular reluctance to increase the scale of their military spending, despite goading from Washington. Some saw in the superior economic performance of these countries an indication of the benefits of not spending heavily on armaments, while the United States was tying up scarce resources (such as scientific manpower) in arms production and paying out large sums to maintain military bases, airfields and harbours all over the world. In order to be a military super-power it was necessary to have a super-economy or to impose sacrifices on consumers. The United States had been accustomed to having both guns and butter because of the enormous productive capacity of its economy. The Reagan administration, by stepping up military spending in the early 1980s, had shown the new problems associated with the arms race. It failed to administer deep enough cuts in other spending programmes; it was steadfastly opposed to increased taxation and thus it had to accept monster budget deficits which undermined confidence and 'crowded out' private investment. Meanwhile foreigners, or at least those who mattered in the financial capitals of the world, saw these deficits as a sign of American weakness. Nevertheless, European and Japanese capital became increasingly active in the United States. Foreign-owned banks were set up, or foreign capital took over existing banks. Foreign investors were attracted by portfolio investments, especially US government securities (income to foreign holders was no longer taxed at source) or by the speculative gains to be made on the Stock Exchange, at least before the end of the bull market in October 1987. Foreign promoters were also active in the real estate market. In fact there seemed to foreigners, especially the Japanese, to be many advantages in re-investing their earnings in the United States. They were attracted by its political and social stability and by the lack of restrictions on capital movements as well as the many choices available to the investor compared with other countries. Hence the Belgian dentist or the Swiss doctor might see purchase of US stocks and bonds as a safe and remunerative investment. Foreigners were also, no doubt, under the influence of the American legend: that the United States was a land of boundless opportunity and unlimited expansion; whether such a judgement was justified remains to be seen. Certainly the Reagan administration claimed that the growth of foreign investment in the United States was a vote of confidence in the future of the American free enterprise system. Included in this was the growth of foreign ownership of the expanding national debt of the 1980s, which was frequently held against this administration.

The cosmopolitanization of capital, a major trend in this period, can be seen as an inevitable consequence of the free operation of market forces. In the last analysis, the free market does not recognize national frontiers or nationality as such. The invisible hand, if left to operate freely, makes no distinction on national lines, whereas the intrusion of a visible hand, whether of the state or of the corporate leadership, distorts, if it does not destroy, the free operation of the laws of the market. The result then is more like national capitalism than free enterprise – a situation in which national economic interests are in some way imposed upon market forces.

A conflict between market forces and national interests thus arises in the course of the internationalization of capital such as that which has taken place in the past twenty-five years or so. Some countries have avowedly adopted a national strategy for peaceful economic conquests while American administrations have operated on the assumption that there is a natural harmony of interests between the free operation of market forces and the power and welfare of the United States. In fact, most of the free-marketeers are implicitly, if not explicitly, highly nationalist in their ideas and aims. The fact that their discourse proceeded within the framework of the national emergency known as the Cold War, made this perhaps inevitable. American economists and strategists together uphold the virtues of 'the best economic system in the world', based on the free market and private enterprise and decry the faulty and failing rival system based on state intervention and planning. The economic breakdown in Poland and Hungary and the turn to the market in the Soviet Union, as well as in Eastern Europe, is greeted by them as a confirmation of their position. Policy in practice suggested that national interests took precedent over the logic of market forces; even Adam Smith had declared that defence was more important than opulence. American diplomacy has been deployed to open up markets and safeguard the interests of investors overseas. Those regimes which offered free scope for American MNCs were favoured; those which prevented or restricted their operations were opposed, and their governments were, in some cases, subverted. Free trade had its limits; in practice there were restrictions on the imports of Japanese cars (a gentlemen's agreement) as well as on textiles. Moreover, as part of the Cold War there were strict limits on the export to the Soviet Union and Eastern Europe of goods which might improve their military capability. Economic and military aid to friendly foreign countries (such as Israel or Pakistan) continued to be of central importance in maintaining the world position of the United States. Food could be used as a weapon to influence the policy of less developed countries faced with serious shortages. Manipulation of dollar exchange rates could also have a protectionist function: a depreciated dollar could, as in 1986–8 be used to stem imports and boost exports. So, if free trade inspired American relations with the outside world, it did so with many modifications made to the advantage of American business. In practice, it was more a weapon in trade war than a case of maximizing the comparative advantage of all participants in the international division of labour. What was best for the US was assumed to be best for the world. Even free marketeers argued with a (perhaps unrecognized) nationalist bias.

While American spokesmen engaged in free trade rhetoric and criticized the trade restrictions of other countries, the US market was not as open as appeared. The import of Japanese cars was limited by agreement, so were textile imports from developing countries while, on health grounds, various restrictions were imposed on the import of agricultural products. In fact part of American foreign trade was conducted through bilateral bargaining with trading partners. The mounting trade deficit and the effect of foreign competition on particular industries reinforced the threat of a protectionist backlash. Pressure from agricultural interests resulted in subsidized food exports, not only to developing countries (as under Public Law 480 and other programmes) but also to others. The Export-Import Bank provided valuable credits, loan guarantees and other advantages amounting to a sizeable government subsidy to exporting firms; 65 per cent of the Bank's credits go to eighteen companies. These forms of trade restriction and financial support for exporters were maintained and even stepped up during the Reagan period; in one way or another by 1988 about 24 per cent of imports were subject to restriction against 12 per cent in 1980. Despite the Reagan administration's free trade rhetoric, therefore, there was much surreptitious protectionism.

Meanwhile the import bill continued to rise and the trade deficit grew. However, much foreign trade was in fact conducted between American multinationals and their overseas branches (something like 40 per cent, in fact). The United States was already in a state of veiled trade war both with Japan and the Asian industrializing countries and with the West European countries making up the European Community. While some sectors of industry have remained ahead, or at least 'competitive' (a term not easy to define), others have already gone under or are facing increasingly acute competition. Some corporations, including the auto-makers, have entered into forms of partnership with their Japanese rivals. The possibility remains of an all-out trade war if the assault on the American market continues.

DOMESTIC POLICY IN THE REAGAN ERA

The Reagan administration inherited the worst post-war economic down-turn from its predecessors. It allowed the recession to mature; positive counter-cyclical action was against its philosophy. It welcomed the opportunity to squeeze inflation out of the economy supporting the Fed's policy of high interest rates, although this meant high unemployment and stagnation. From the end of 1982 there was a mild but prolonged upturn which lasted through to the end of Reagan's second term. During that time inflation came down and remained modest by the standards of the 1970s, but there was still a relentless decline in the purchasing power of the dollar. Likewise, unemployment came down to lower levels; by 1987–8 it was below six per cent. The administration claimed this long period of 'expansion' as an achievement of its policies. It was on more difficult ground when critics pointed to the large budget deficits and the yawning balance-of-payments gap. Were they also to be considered products of Reaganomics?

Although in the short term the Reagan administration was associated with this 'expansion' – the economy had basically moved onto a low-level plateau – it had not overcome the long-term problems besetting it, of which the deficits were the most overt sign. The shock of the 19 October 1987 Stock Exchange crash was weathered without the widely expected recession. Although it may have been precipitated by the raising of interest rates in the preceding weeks, prompt action by the Fed, by increasing the supply of credit, almost certainly limited the fall-out from the spectacular collapse of Wall Street prices, though at the price of storing up problems elsewhere. However, the same display of willingness by the Fed to open wide the flow of credit arrested the 'mini-crash' which hit the market almost exactly two years later, on 13 October 1989. In an important way the crash of October 1987 was a turning point. It indicated a deep anxiety in business circles about the future prospects of the economy, a recognition that the long-term problems had not been solved simply because stock market prices had been pushed to an all-time high and paper fortunes had been made in the bull market. There was an immediate, bi-partisan rallying on the issue of the budget deficit, which was seen to undermine foreign confidence in the United States. Other underlying factors of crisis revealed since the early 1970s can be enumerated as follows: profitability remained low, especially in manufacturing where foreign competition was acute; new investment was well below that in other countries, meaning that much plant and machinery was obsolescent; productivity growth continued to lag; overall growth was slow, despite the absence of recession. Reaganomics did not directly address these questions since the adoption of a positive policy would have amounted to interference with market forces. The question arises, then, of whether what it did, or did not do, alleviated or aggravated these crisis factors. Subsidiary to that is whether the administration achieved its own goals or not: could the invisible hand grope its way out of the crisis?

Reaganism traced the problems of US capitalism to an excess of government regulation and intervention. To dismantle this structure would take time. The first immediate step was to reduce taxation while moving towards a balanced budget, and to direct more resources into the arms build-up begun under Carter. The centrepiece of its policy in its first year was the Economic Recovery and Tax Act. This incorporated a policy of tax reduction and reform which lowered individual tax rates and increased allowances for the depreciation of assets. It was assumed, in accordance with supply-side doctrine, that these tax cuts, especially beneficial to the wealthy, would stimulate investment and growth without a great loss in revenue. In view of the failure to control spending, the tax cut only contributed to the budget deficits of the Reagan years. Wealthy tax-payers seem to have used their windfalls for conspicuous consumption (such as expensive foreign cars) or for stock exchange speculation rather than productive investment.

Meanwhile, the administration counted upon high interest rates, determined by the Federal Reserve, to combat inflation. This policy, however, contributed to an over-valued dollar which, until 1986–7, discouraged American exporters while sucking in cheap imports. High interest rates, accompanied by rising Stock Exchange prices, attracted foreign capital into the country and encouraged foreigners to leave their export earnings to benefit from the high yields. This helped to finance the rapidly growing Federal debt.

The Reagan administration set out to reduce overall government expenditure while considerably increasing expenditure on the military. The argument was that the United States was falling behind the Soviet Union in military preparedness and that existing weapons systems were obsolete and had to be replaced, whatever the cost. After coming down in constant dollar values until about 1974, federal budget outlays for 'defence' remained fairly constant until 1980, but the proportion of the gross national product fell to below five per cent. This was said to threaten America's leadership role, especially in dealing with Soviet activities in 'Third World' countries. However, the biggest increases went into bombers, missiles and military research (later, the Strategic Defense Initiative).

In accordance with declared policy, total outlays on national defence (including veterans) rose as shown in Table 9.1. Defence expenditure

Table 9.1: Outlay on national defence, 1980–1987
(figures shown in constant $bn, 1982)

1980	164.0
1981	171.4
1982	185.3
1983	201.3
1984	211.5
1985	228.7
1986	242.1
1987 (est.)	242.6

(Statistical Abstract of the United States, 1988)

rose from 22.7% to 27.8% of all federal outlays and from 5% to 6.4% of GNP. Military research and development funded by the Federal government rose from $14.9 billion to $40.3 billion in 1987. The budget deficit would have been more manageable without the *increase* in military expenditure over the Reagan years.

According to the Reaganites, other forms of government expenditure were excessive and getting out of hand. They targeted especially the Social Security system and sought to reverse the trend towards what they saw as a European-style welfare state. However, a substantial part of social security programmes, notably retirement pensions and Medicare, were regarded as an indispensable 'safety net' which could not be cut. In fact, they benefited many middle-class retirees that the Administration did not want to antagonize. The most vulnerable programs turned out to be those, such as Food Stamps and Aid to Families with Dependent Children, which most benefited the poor. Thus the main victims of the early cuts were the poor and very poor. Other cuts followed from a failure of expenditure to keep pace with inflation. As time went on, some of these cuts were restored (e.g. AFDC). The main factor in moderating the cuts was that Reagan had to face a hostile Congress, which refused to accept his policies. On balance, therefore, there was no dramatic change in social policy of the kind which had been presaged when the Reagan administration took office. The expansion of social programmes to meet growing needs of the urban poor and disadvantaged minorities, however, did come to an abrupt halt and Reagan supporters had not abandoned their goals.

The increase in military spending, together with the tax cuts and the failure to reduce other forms of federal expenditure on the hoped-for scale, inevitably resulted in large budget deficits. Thus there was the paradox of an administration which had come to power intending to balance the budget (and doctrinally opposed to deficit-spending) actually running up huge budget deficits which could not even be explained by the existence of a recession in the economy. The budget deficit thus became a major preoccupation from 1982.

The re-election of Ronald Reagan in 1984 clearly owed a great deal to the improvement in the economy which had taken place since 1980 as well as to the astonishing popularity of the former movie star. The exchange value of the dollar remained high and the decline in manufacturing industry continued. The banks were launched on a lending spree directed at the so-called developing countries. When these countries found it impossible to pay off their debts, the banks were landed with a large volume of non-performing loans. The easy lending policy abroad and the continued growth of debt on the part of the government, the corporations, and the consumer at home assisted the long but not spectacular expansion of the 1980s. Some relief was also obtained from the fall in oil prices, as far as consumers were concerned, though domestic producers suffered, notably in Texas, which had a taste of boom and bust.

Concern at the growth of the budget deficit led to the passage of the Gramm-Rudman-Hollings Balanced Budget Act 1985, providing for automatic spending cuts until the budget was brought into balance in 1991. There is doubt about whether such a scheme is workable; much will depend upon the complexion of the current administration and the mood of Congress. The deficit has been a useful scarecrow for the administration in warning off Congress from expensive domestic programmes. On the other hand, the renewed movement towards *détente* which got under way in the final stages of Reagan's term of office may make it more difficult to justify high levels of expenditure for the military establishment.

Overall, the Reagan administration left a mass of contradictions in economic policy, its record being one of 'muddling through' rather than applying a determined and consistent policy of the kind which might have been expected. The President and his advisors had, in the end, moved circumspectly and pragmatically, carrying out a policy which resembled more closely mainstream Republicanism than an exercise in applying the theories of the monetarists or supply-siders. It also meant, in practice, leaving more discretionary power in the hands of the Fed, that is to say, Paul Volcker, whose aim was to squeeze inflation out of the economy. Whether this result was worth the dramatic side-effects – an over-valued dollar, a yawning trade deficit, the transformation of the country from a creditor to a debtor and the run down of the old, smoke-stack industries in the mid-West and elsewhere – remains to be seen. Of course, neither budgetary policy or the Volcker tight-money strategy operated in a vacuum. Other factors were involved, and in some cases may have been dominant – such as lack of competitiveness, managerial weaknesses, falling productivity growth and the fall in profit rates – but neither Reagan nor Volcker strengthened the American economy in the long run and may have contributed to its relative decline. In perspective the argument about the budget deficit may seem to have been much ado about nothing. The balance of payments deficit is a different matter; it reflects the weaknesses and vulnerability of the US economy and the failure of the Reagan administration to face up to them.

The fact that the 1980–2 recession was followed by an unbroken if mild 'expansion' through to the end of the Reagan administration did not signify that the economy had found new forces of strength, that a new phase of productive investment had begun. Instead the expansion was kept going largely by consumption and by the growth of debt. The other side of the balance of payments deficit was the accumulation of dollar holdings by foreigners. In effect, then, expenditure on consumption, investment and 'defence' exceeded the earnings of the American economy. The difference was made good by an inflow of foreign capital, amounting to something like 3.5% of GNP. Meanwhile, foreigners acquired a lien on future production. Apart from direct investment by foreign firms, the inflow of foreign capital did not result in an increase in the productive capacity of the American economy. Much went into buying stocks and bonds or acquiring real estate. It indicated the competitive superiority of foreign industries.

Although the possibility existed of a loss of economic sovereignty, the United States was not in the same category as Brazil or Mexico. Its great resources, huge market and high per capita income made it a unique case. Sales in the US market were valuable, indeed indispensable, for the great export economies which had been built up during the post-war expansion, assisted by American capital. Moreover, American individuals and corporations held large investments throughout the world. The American capital market was a major source of funds for developing countries, and others. The military-strategic role of the United States remained decisive, though it contributed to the deficit. There was no doubt that the growing foreign debt increased the vulnerability of the economy to outside shocks, at the same time that events in America would have profound consequences for its trading partners. The most obvious disaster for

America's creditors was anything which reduced America's capacity to buy their exports, such as a protectionist back-lash – of which there were many symptoms – or a recession.

As increased concern was expressed about growing indebtedness, the obvious response was to urge that foreign earnings should be increased, whether from exports of goods or the sale of services to foreigners. The fall in the exchange value of the dollar from 1986 to 1988 was intended to assist this purpose by making imports more expensive and cheapening American goods and services to foreign buyers. However, the run-down of American manufacturing industry in the preceding years of the overvalued dollar made it difficult to expand exports, at least in the short-run. It was not clear whether foreigners would be impressed by American goods when compared with those coming from the other advanced industrial countries, in which much more investment and modernization had taken place in the preceding years. To expand capacity American firms often had to purchase machinery and machine-tools no longer made at home – a sign of the loss of technological leadership and a reversal of the situation which had prevailed only a decade or two earlier. Even in fields like banking, finance, communications and business services the challenge to American leadership, if not always successful as yet, was becoming more formidable. Other countries were facing the same imperatives: a drive for markets and investment fields to maintain the rate of profit. In conditions of intensifying trade war even the administration, with its alleged adherence to free trade, was tempted into protectionist measures of its own, while attacking those of Japan and other countries.

Most of those who deplored the decline in America's world position claimed that the country had been living beyond its means. Indeed Americans as a whole – excluding disadvantaged sections or those in particular occupations or regions afflicted with industrial run-down – had been able to avoid austerity measures of the kind operating in some other countries. Through the Reagan era both inflation and unemployment were brought down to modest levels. Will the next stage in American economic history be an age of austerity, in which consumption levels are held down or actually reduced? If such proves to be the case, the closing decade of the twentieth century may see the end of the American dream of continuous material improvement and advancement. While it would be convenient if economic problems could be solved in this way, it is difficult to see how it could be done without social and political turmoil of a kind which the United States has rarely witnessed.

Unless current trends can be reversed, or brought under control, within the next few years American capitalism may be at the epicentre of a world-wide crisis. The ability of the American market to absorb imports from other advanced industrial countries as well as from newly industrializing and developing countries, and the willingness of foreigners to hold increasing amounts of dollar assets are vital for the operation of world capitalism. A cut-back in American imports could well spark a world recession. A breakdown of foreign confidence in the dollar could result in a mass withdrawal of foreign funds and a Wall Street crash which would make 19 October 1987 seem like a mild adjustment. The vulnerability of the American economy is now greater than at any time. What is more, the size of the existing national debt means that deficit-financing cannot be depended upon to lift the economy out of a depression.

Table 9.2: The US economy: the Reagan Record, 1980–1988
($ billions)

(a) *Federal Budget*	*1980*	*1988*
Receipts	517	910
Expenditure	519	1,065
Deficit	–74	–155
Trade balance	–25	–137
Balance of payments	+2	–132
Balance of foreign debt	+2	–500
Federal debt	914	2,500
Servicing debt	52.6	151.7
(b) *Investment*		
% of GNP	18.6	18.7
(c) *Consumption*		
% of GNP	80.2	83.8

(from *Le Monde Diplomatique*, March 1989)

EPILOGUE

Into the 21st Century: an end to American hegemony?

Despite a long period without recession, the mood in the 1980s was hardly one of unqualified optimism. Discussion of American 'decline' was widespread. For a period after 1945 the United States held an historically unique position both as the dominant military power in the world and the economic and technological leader. Even in the 1980s the United States remained the most powerful nation on earth, the only true 'superpower', but that unique position of 'hegemony', as some liked to call it, had in some versions been lost, in others was under threat.

The empire without frontiers still held together and claimed prerogatives not open to other states. It could occupy Grenada, bomb Libya, remove Panama's ruler, support regimes, however repugnant, which it favoured, and undermine and subvert those which it disliked. It was a main source of capital for developing countries and the most influential voice in international organizations. The United States had not given up its claim to world leadership and the disintegration of the Soviet bloc and the difficulties of China enhanced its position. Neither Japan nor West Germany could contest this role. At the same time, there was evident a relative decline in the economic sphere. The United States was no longer the world leader in industry. Many commodities formerly produced at home were now being imported and in new fields such as consumer electronics the market was dominated by imports. The trade deficit and the growth of net debt with the outside world apparently confirmed the picture of economic decline.

By the 1980s there had been a sensational decline in the old basic industries such as steel, engineering, machinery and machine tools. In manufacturing industry as a whole productivity was growing less rapidly than before or in comparison with foreign rivals. On the whole, however, the industries which had disappeared or were contracting, or which had never obtained a foothold, were labour-intensive or less profitable than alternative investments. Frequently, foreign firms were making the technological break-throughs or turning out goods which compared favourably in quality and reliability with the American product. But many imports came from the branch plants of American corporations which had moved their manufacturing facilities overseas to take advantage of lower wages and other costs.

Those countries which represented the most serious industrial challenge, West Germany, Japan and the four Asian 'little tigers' South Korea, Hong Kong, Taiwan and Singapore, depended to a significant extent upon the American market for their success. The United States had become a net importer of manufactured goods, but it was still a wealthy country. Its high-income consumers were buying more manufactured imports, and an increasing array of services which, by their nature, were mainly supplied domestically. These high incomes were made possible by accumulated assets, private and public, inherited from the past, great natural wealth and financial and commercial supremacy. The huge, and homogeneous, home market made possible great economies of scale. Some economists even claimed that a strong manufacturing sector was no longer necessary for a prosperous economy. However, there are many linkages between industry and services, many of the latter being purchased by the former, to suggest that there is a level below which manufacturing industry cannot fall without impairing the creation of wealth and the maintenance of levels of employment in the economy as a whole. The prophets of doom were generally suggesting that this limit was being reached. Whether this is true or not, the centre of profit-taking has shifted markedly from industrial capital to the financial markets; it is in the latter that high incomes and rapid fortunes can be made. Again it may be asked whether this represents the shift to a more advanced type of capitalism, or a sign of decadence, as pushing paper around becomes more lucrative than producing goods.

The decline of the American economy is a relative, not an absolute decline, at any rate so far. Other countries have grown more swiftly and have been more successful in raising income levels and carving out a larger share of the international trade in manufactured goods. The United States remains, of course, a great exporter of agricultural products. Where would Europe be without American soybeans or Japan without American beef and other products? The Soviet Union and China depend upon American grain exports. The American economy has continued to grow, if only slowly, but it is the *relative* position which suggests decline and the comparison with Japan, above all, which reveals American weakness.

Perhaps symbolic is the inroad which Japanese cars have made into the American market, a share actually held back by inter-governmental agreement. Japanese successes appear to have been at American expense, with Japanese trade surpluses seeking re-investment in the United States in branch plants, government bonds, portfolio investment and real estate. With memories of Pearl Harbour, many Americans watch anxiously as the Japanese push ahead with their peaceful conquests, suggesting that Japanese and American interests are fundamentally opposed. Japanese firms appear to have met every challenge – higher oil prices, world recession, rising wages, a lower dollar – with a resourcefulness seldom found in American business leadership today. The methods used to keep Japan ahead are then blamed for being unfair or even hostile. Of course, while giving allegiance to free market forces, Japanese policy-makers have been ready to disregard them when national economic interests have been at stake. The strongest expressions of Japan-phobia call for a policy of 'containment' before America loses its leadership, at least in the Pacific basin, and Japan builds a still more powerful position in the American economy itself. They fear that a Japanese-led trading bloc could further damage American interests. While the Japanese may be condemned for unfair trading practices, it is not unknown for American negotiators to throw their weight around in international conferences on trade and finance. A form of trade war with Japan undoubtedly exists, but the two countries are also closely bound together: Japan needs the American market if industry is not to run into an over-production crisis. American corporations have operated on the basis that if you cannot beat them, join them. A car with a Chrysler badge may have been put together in Thailand with parts from plants in Japan and Korea owned by Mitsubishi.

What this shows is that the American economy operates in a very different international environment from that of the past. Today it has to share industrial and technological leadership with other countries. At the same time, its adversarial relationship with the Soviet Union and its allies continues to provide the basis for the power of the military-industrial complex. There has been no winding down of American military power, with all that means for the economy, at least so far. The changes in the Soviet Union under Mikhail Gorbachev and the way they are interpreted in Washington may, in the future, result in a significant reduction in military spending. While releasing industrial capacity and manpower it does not in itself ensure that, through market forces alone, alternative uses can be found for them.

Future administrations will have to face the challenge of Japan and the growing economic muscle of the European Community. How they will respond is a matter for speculation. It is certain that the United States will not give up its position without a fight, and that it may well resort to the methods it condemns when used by others in order to do so. It would be unwise, in any event, to underrate the power and potential of American capitalism in the closing years of the twentieth century and to assume that it is declining into a twilight era.

Meanwhile there are pressing problems arising both from the structural changes noted at various points in this work or inherited from the Reagan era. As far as the latter are concerned, the most important problems are the budget deficit and the huge increase in public indebtedness, together with a deteriorating foreign trade position exemplified by the trade and payments deficits. The principal, and intended, result of the Reaganite policies was a reduction in the role of government. Although, because of the opposition of a Democratic Congress, the reduction in government expenditure was checked, that still means that the federal government has less power, and funds, than it might have had, to deal with pressing social problems such as inner-city decay, the decline of educational standards, criminality and drug traffic, and the deterioration of much of the infrastructure vital for economic health (such as bridges, highways, sewerage and water systems, public transport). Reagan's successor, George Bush, though reportedly more pragmatic than doctrinaire, was elected with a promise not to raise taxes, which, if held to for a full presidential term, could seriously limit federal action in these fields.

In retrospect, the Reagan policy of hands off the market may be seen as a policy of drift in the face of a deteriorating situation. Reagan remedies have not been strikingly successful in arresting industrial decline or facing the Japanese challenge. More than 15 million jobs created between 1980 and 1989 have mainly been for low wages in the service sector. Manufacturing employment lost 882,000 workers, but the rate of job loss had slowed down. While many civilian programmes were cut (with adverse social effects probable in the long term), military expenditure rose to new peace-time heights. Reaganomics had important side-effects which were unforeseen, such as the huge budget deficits, and largely benefited the wealthy at the expense of the poor, without jacking up investment levels to the extent expected.

The continued growth of the economy, especially after the October, 1987 stock market crash, has depended crucially upon the growth of debt. Borrowing by the government, business and consumers alike, despite high rates of interest, has made possible the avoidance of recession (the achievement of which gave rise to the most self-congratulation on the part of the President and his supporters). This credit-supported expansion, always threatened with runaway inflation, has enabled the service sector to grow inordinately, and has sucked in foreign imports, leading to a large balance of payments deficit. Domestic investment has continued to fall below that of foreign competitors. Even when the dollar was falling (in 1988) the stimulus to exports was modest. The Reagan administration, falling back on the theory that America was becoming a 'post-industrial society', took a complacent view of the continued decline in industrial competitivity. Nothing like an industrial strategy emerged, only renewed professions of faith in market forces.

At first sight, paradoxically, foreigners have seen an advantage in investing and re-investing their dollar earnings in the capital and money markets. Not so surprising when all sectors of the economy were crying out for credit and the returns were higher than in other markets. America offered a huge range of investment possibilities for the outsider without having to take an active economic role. Foreign money helped fuel the bull market before (and since) October 1987, and helps finance the enormous budget deficit. At the same time, with no visible challenge to capitalism, political stability and weak trade unions, the United States appeared to be the safest haven.

Where there is debt there are obviously creditors. Wealthy Americans have been lending to their less affluent compatriots as well as to business and the government, at the same time as there has been an inflow of foreign funds seeking safety and high returns. A conflict of interest can arise between debtors and creditors. Especially significant is the fact that corporations are more dependent upon loans for long-term finance than in the past. Take-overs and mergers may lead to firms having to carry a high volume of debt, interest on which has to be met whatever the level of profits. As for households, there is a limit to the amount of debt which can be supported; in a recession defaults and re-possessions will grow. Even in a period of 'prosperity', many farmers and small businessmen have been forced into bankruptcy through their inability to meet high interest payments.

America's foreign debt seems bound to grow unless drastic measures are taken to reduce the trade deficit, with a consequent risk of some loss of economic sovereignty. The external position is complicated by the continued international role of the dollar and the flow of payments and capital into and out of the United States. The maintenance of its world position means not only maintaining garrisons and bases throughout the world, with over 500,000 service personnel overseas, but also subsidizing foreign governments, training their forces and supplying arms. While the dollar has been oscillating (for instance, falling in 1987–8, then climbing back until it was generally regarded as being 'overvalued'), there is a danger that its role in international trade and finance will be undermined. Can a country with an unstable, or 'weak', currency aspire to world leadership, whatever its other assets? The volume of foreign capital in government securities as well as the private sector is potentially de-stabilizing should there be a run on the dollar. In any case, an increasing proportion of dividends and profits generated in the United States will be collected by foreign firms, individuals and institutions. But, at the same time, American multinationals and commercial banks have become increasingly involved in foreign countries.

These phenomena are part of the 'globalization' of the economy characteristic of the most recent phase of capitalist development. President Reagan saw the inflow of foreign capital as a vote of confidence in America. Much foreign investment, however, is in the nature of 'hot money', which could quickly be withdrawn as a result of crisis or upheaval in some other part of the world or a collapse of confidence in the dollar for some reason, the most likely being a Wall Street crash. Although the economy successfully navigated the October 1987 crash without a recession, that was in large part due to a speedy response by central banks in increasing the credit and money supply, thus aggravating inflationary pressures. The same remedy checked the mini-crash of October 1989: but many experts consider that in the present state of the market another crash is possible at any time. Increasing involvement with the world economy, and the challenge from Japan and other trade rivals, makes the United States more vulnerable to external shocks than at any previous time in its history.

In late twentieth-century America a certain form of capitalism, described in this book, reached its climax. After a century of unexampled growth which had made it the most powerful nation on earth it was being overtaken by other countries and had to face the consequences of the loss of industrial and technological leadership. In the past Americans had become used to a substantial improvement in living standards during their lifetime, of the possibility of moving up the social scale by educational qualification or success in business. Children expected to live better than their parents and to see their own children improve on it further. There were always those left by the wayside, but the elimination of poverty seemed only a matter of time.

These certitudes have lost much of their appeal; the prospect of continuous material improvement is dimmer than it has ever been. The majority of Americans enjoy what is, by world standards, a high and privileged level of real income; in all probability it has reached a peak and for many the coming decades may see some decline.

Meanwhile, the relative, if not absolute, decline of the United States as a world power is likely to continue with the irresistible rise of Japan and the growth of a German-led Europe. Optimists may see the process as being a mutation rather than a failure, a climb down from a transitory and ultimately untenable position of hegemony. The problem of the 1990s and the prospect for the twenty-first century is much more one of adaptation to world trends which are outside the control of Washington. Whether this will be accepted as the inscrutable will of unchecked market forces to which obeisance must be paid or whether policy-makers will intervene to attempt to check and reverse them remains to be seen. After all, many of those who talk about 'decline' propose policies to arrest or reverse it.

Select bibliography

This bibliography consists of books used or consulted and likely to be of interest to the student. They straddle a wide diversity of views about the causes of the economic growth of the United States and the nature of its current problems.

Ackerman, Frank. *Hazardous To Our Health: Economic Policies in the 1980s*. Boston: South End Press, 1984.

Aglietta, Michel. *A Theory of Capitalist Regulation: the U.S. Experience*. London: New Left Books, 1979.

Belton, Bertrand and Jorge Niosi. *The Decline of the American Economy*. Montreal and New York: Black Rose Books, 1988.

Blinder, Alan S. *Economic Policy and the Great Stagflation*. New York: Academic Press, 1979.

Bluestone, Barry and Bennett Harrison. *The Deindustrialization of America*. New York: Basic Books, 1982.

Boorstein, Edward. *What's Ahead? The U.S. Economy*. New York: International Publishers, 1984.

Boskin, Michael J. *Reagan and the Economy*. San Francisco: Institute for Contemporary Studies Press, 1987.

Boswell, Terry and Albert Bergesen (eds). *America's Changing Role in the World-System*. New York: Praeger, 1987.

Bowles, Samuel, David M. Gordon and Thomas E. Weisskopf. *Beyond the Waste Land*. London: Verso, 1984.

Bruckey, Stuart. *The Wealth of the Nation*. New York: Harper & Row, 1988.

Brunner, Karl (ed.). *The Great Depression Revisited*. Boston: Martinus Nijhoff Publishing, 1981.

Cagan, Philip et al. *Economic Policy and Inflation in the Sixties*. Washington: American Enterprise Institute, 1972.
Calleo, David. *The Imperious Economy*. Cambridge, Mass.: Harvard University Press, 1982.
Castagna, Anthony S. *United States National Economic Policy, 1917–1985*. New York: Praeger, 1987.
Castells, Manuel. *The Economic Crisis and American Society*. Oxford: Basil Blackwell, 1980.
Chandler, Alfred D. *The Visible Hand: The Managerial Revolution in American Business*. Cambridge, Mass.: Harvard University Press, 1977.
Chandler, Lester V. *America's Greatest Depression*. New York: Harper & Row, 1970.
Clark, David. *Post-industrial America*. London: Methuen, 1985.
Cochran, Thomas C. *Business in American Life*. New York: McGraw-Hill, 1972.
Corey, Lewis. *The Decline of American Capitalism*. London: John Lane, the Bodley Head, 1935.
Davis, Mike. *Prisoners of the American Dream*. London: Verso, 1987.
Degan, Robert A. *The American Monetary System*. Lexington, Mass.: Lexington Books, 1987.
Denison, Edward F. *Trends in American Economic Growth, 1929–1982*. Washington: The Brookings Institution, 1985.
Dethloff, Henry C. *Americans and Free Enterprise*. Englewood Cliffs, New Jersey: Prentice-Hall, 1979.
Dibacc, Thomas. *Made in the U.S.A.* New York: Harper & Row, 1987.
Dobson, John M. *A History of American Enterprise*. Englewood Cliffs, New Jersey: Prentice-Hall, 1988.
Dowd, Douglas F. *The Twisted Dream: Capitalist Development in the United States Since 1776*. Cambridge, Mass.: Winthrop, 1974.
Duignan, Peter and Alan Rabushka (eds). *The United States in the 1980s*. London, Croom Helm, 1980.
Eckstein, Otto. *The Great Recession*. Amsterdam: North Holland Publishing Co., 1978.
Edwards, Richard. *Contested Terrain. The Transformation of the Workplace in the Twentieth Century*. London: Heinemann, 1979.
Fearon, Peter. *The Origins and Nature of the Great Slump, 1929–32*. London: Macmillan, 1979.
Fearon, Peter. *War, Prosperity & Depression. The U.S. Economy 1917–45*. London: Philip Alan, 1986.

Foster, John Bellamy. *The Theory of Monopoly Capitalism. An Elaboration of Marxian Political Economy*. New York: Monthly Review Press, 1986.

Foster, John Bellamy and Henryk Szlajfer (eds). *The Faltering Economy. The Problem of Accumulation Under Monopoly Capitalism*. New York: Monthly Review Press, 1984.

Friedman, Milton and Anna Jacobson Schwartz, *The Great Contraction*. Princeton: Princeton University Press, 1965.

Galambos, Louis and Joseph Pratt. *The Rise of the Corporate Commonwealth*. New York: Basic Books, 1988.

Galbraith, John Kenneth. *The Great Crash 1929*. London; Hamish Hamilton, 1952.

Galbraith, John Kenneth, *The New Industrial State*. London: Hamish Hamilton, 1971.

George, Peter. *The Emergence of Industrial America*. Albany, New York: State University of New York Press, 1982.

Gordon, David M. Richard Edwards and Michael Reich. *Segmented Work, Divided Workers. The Historical Transformation of Labor in the United States*. New York: Cambridge University Press, 1982.

Greider, William. *Secrets of the Temple. How the Federal Reserve Runs the Country*. New York: Simon and Schuster, 1987.

Harrison, Bennett and Barry Bluestone. *The Great U Turn: Corporate Re-structuring and the Polarization of America*. New York: Basic Books, 1988.

Havens, A. Eugene (ed.). *Studies in the Transformation of United States Agriculture*. Boulder (Col.) and London: Westview Press, 1986.

Hughes, Jonathon, R. T. *American Economic History*. Glenview (Ill.) and London: Scott, Foresman Co. Second edition, 1987.

Hughes, Jonathon, R. T. *The Governmental Habit: Economic Controls from Colonial Times to the Present*. New York: Basic Books, 1977.

Issel, William. *Social Change in the United States, 1945–1983*. London: Macmillan, 1985.

Julien, Claude. *America's Empire*. New York: Pantheon Books, 1971.

Kamer, Pearl M., *The U.S. Economy in Crisis: Adjusting to the New Realities*. New York: Praeger, 1988.

Koistinen, Paul A. C. *The Military-Industrial Complex: An Historical Perspective*. New York: Praeger, 1980.

Kurstman, Joel. *The Decline and Crash of the American Economy*. New York and London: W. W. Norton, 1988.

Leuchtenburg, William E. *Franklin D. Roosevelt and the New Deal 1932–1940*. New York: Harper & Row, 1963.

Levine, Rhonda, F. *Class Struggle and the New Deal*. Lawrence (Kansas): University Press of Kansas, 1988.

Lichtenstein, Nelson. *Labor's War at Home: the CIO in World War II*. New York: Cambridge University Press, 1982.

Lotta, Raymond. *America in Decline: an analysis of the development toward war and revolution in the U.S. and worldwide in the 1980s*. Chicago: Banner Press, 1984.

Magaziner, Ira C. and Robert B. Reich. *Minding America's Business: The Decline and Rise of the American Economy*. New York: Vintage Books, 1983.

Magdoff, Harry and Paul M. Sweezy. *The End of Prosperity: The American Economy in the 1970s*. New York: Monthly Review Press, 1977.

Magdoff, Harry and Paul M. Sweezy. *The Deepening Crisis of U.S. Capitalism*. New York: Monthly Review Press, 1981.

Magdoff, Harry and Paul M. Sweezy. *Stagnation and the Financial Explosion*. New York: Monthly Review Press, 1987.

Melloan, George and Joan Melloan. *The Carter Economy*. New York: John Wiley and Sons, 1978.

Montgomery, David. *Worker's Control in America*. Cambridge: Cambridge University Press, 1979.

Munkis, John R. *The Transformation of American Capitalism*. New York and London: M.E. Sharpe, 1985.

Nieni, Albert W. *United States Economic History*. Second edition. Chicago: Rand McNally, 1980.

North, Douglass C. *Growth and Welfare in the American Past*. Engelwood Cliffs (N.J.): Prentice-Hall, 1966.

Obey, David and Paul Sarbanes (eds). *The Changing American Economy*. New York and Oxford: Basil Blackwell, 1986.

O'Rourke, A. Desmond. *The Changing Dimensions of U.S. Agricultural Policy*. New York: Prentice-Hall, 1978.

Palmer, John L. and Isabel Sawhill (eds). *The Reagan Record: An Assessment of America's Changing Domestic Priorities*. Cambridge (Mass): Ballinger Publishing Co., 1984.

Peterson, William C. *Our Overloaded Economy: Inflation, Unemployment and the Crisis in American Capitalism*. New York: M.E. Sharpe, 1982.

Potter, Jim. *The American Economy Between the Wars*. Second Edition. London: Macmillan, 1985.

Primack, Martin L. and James F. Willis. *An Economic History of the United States*. Menlo Park (Cal.): The Benjamin-Cummings Publishing Co., 1980.

Purcell, Carroll W. *The Military-Industrial Complex*. New York: Harper & Row, 1972.

Puth, Robert C. *American Economic History*. Second Edition. Chicago and London: The Dryden Press, 1988.

Ransom, Roger L. *Coping With Capitalism: The Economic Transformation of the United States 1776–1980*. *Englewood* Cliffs (N.J.): Prentice-Hall, 1981.

Reich, Robert B. *The Next American Frontier: A Provocative Program for Economic Renewal*. Harmondsworth: Penguin Books, 1984.

Roberts, Paul Craig. *The Supply-Side Revolution*. Cambridge (Mass.) and London: Harvard University Press, 1984.

Rochester, Anna. *Why Farmers Are Poor*. New York; International Publishers, 1940.

Rosenoff, Theodore. *Dogma, Depression and the New Deal*. New York: Kenikat, 1975.

Rothbard, Murray N. *America's Greatest Depression*. New York: Van Nostrand, 1963.

Saint-Etienne, Christian. *The Great Depression 1929–1938: Lessons for the 1980s*. Stanford (Cal.): Hoover Institution Press, 1984.

Saloutos, Thedore. *The American Farmer and the New Deal*. Ames: Iowa State University Press, 1982.

Sharkansky, Ira. *The United States Revisited: A Study of a Still Developing Country*. New York and London: Longman 1982.

Steindl, Josef. *Maturity and Stagnation in American Capitalism*. New York: Monthly Review Press, 1952.

Stevens, Robert W. *Vain Hopes, Grim Realities: The Economic Consequences of the Vietnam War*. New York: New Viewpoints 1976.

Stubblebine, William Craig and Thomas D. Willett. *Reaganomics: A Mid-term Report*. San Francisco: ICS Press, 1983.

Sweezy, Paul and Harry Magdoff. *The Dynamics of American Capitalism*. New York: Monthly Review Press, 1972.

Temin, Peter, *Causal Factors in American Economic Growth in the Nineteenth Century*. London: Macmillan, 1975.

Temin, Peter. *Did Monetary Factors Cause the Great Depression?* New York: W.W. Norton, 1976.

Thurlow, Lester C. *The Zero-Sum Society: Distribution and the Possibilities of Economic Change*. Harmondsworth: Penguin Books, 1981.

Vatter, Harold G. *The U.S. Economy in the 1950s*. Chicago and London: University of Chicago, 1963.

Vogeler, Ingolf. *The Myth of the Family Farm; Agro-business Dominance of U.S. Agriculture*. Boulder (Col.): Westview Press, 1981.

Weintraub Sydney and Mann Goldstein, *Reaganomics in the Stagflation Economy*. Philadelphia: University of Pennsylvania Press, 1983.
Woodruff, William. *America's Impact on the World*. London: Macmillan, 1975.
Zinn, Howard. *Postwar America 1945–1971*. Indianopolis (Ill.): Bobs-Merrill Co., 1973.

Index